W9-BAR-124

E875 .C36 1984
A Campaign of ideas : the 1980 Ande
Kennedy Sch of Govt   AFH8606

3 2044 015 039 472

A CAMPAIGN
OF IDEAS

Recent Titles in
Contributions in American Studies
Series Editor: Robert H. Walker

A CAMPAIGN
OF IDEAS
The 1980 Anderson/Lucey Platform

Compiled by Clifford W. Brown, Jr.,
and Robert J. Walker

Contributions in American Studies, Number 76

Greenwood Press
Westport, Connecticut • London, England

E
875
.C36
1984

7167

RECEIVED

JAN 1 1 1985

KENNEDY SCHOOL OF
GOVERNMENT LIBRARY

Library of Congress Cataloging in Publication Data

Main entry under title:

A Campaign of ideas.

(Contributions in American studies, ISSN 0084-9227 ;
no. 76)
Includes index.
1. Presidents—United States—Election—1980—Sources.
2. Anderson, John Bayard, 1922-   3. Lucey,
Patrick J., 1918-   4. United States—Politics and
government—1977-1981—Sources.   I. Brown, Clifford W.
(Clifford Waters), 1942-   II. Walker, Robert J.,
1951-   III. Title.   IV. Series.
E875.C36   1984   324.973'0926   84-6564
ISBN 0-313-24535-5 (lib. bdg.)

Copyright © 1984 by Clifford W. Brown, Jr., and Robert J. Walker

All rights reserved. No portion of this book may be
reproduced, by any process or technique, without the
express written consent of the publisher.

Library of Congress Catalog Card Number: 84-6564
ISBN: 0-313-24535-5
ISSN: 0084-9227

First published in 1984

Greenwood Press
A division of Congressional Information Service, Inc.
88 Post Road West, Westport, Connecticut 06881

Printed in the United States of America

10 9 8 7 6 5 4 3 2 1

CONTENTS

SERIES FOREWORD

Did the Anderson-Lucey candidacy in 1980 provide an important moment in the history of presidential politics? It is surely too soon to tell. At least it offered the unusual spectacle of a new political movement fighting for a place in the center. It served to test the meaning of "major candidate" in terms of television coverage and federal financial support. It left some interesting documents.

In stressing the platform over the campaign, as this volume implicitly does, we are not dismissing the fight for election. We are proposing that, from the perspective of history, this platform will prove to be one of the durably significant long-term legacies of that political year. The platform has been praised for its ability to identify the major issues for the upcoming decade and to cast these issues in terms of policy statements. Even more impressive, in its way, is the budget impact statement which shows--more carefully and extensively than in any previous attempt--that it is possible to come to grips with the likely costs of recommended programs. In its detailed, extensive, and uncompromising confrontation with issues and costs, this platform becomes a standard against which others can be measured.

The historian is accustomed to thoughtful, idealistic platforms from the edge of the political spectrum. This one is aimed for the exact center. John Anderson was hoping to attract moderate Independents, Republicans who found Ronald Reagan too conservative, and Democrats whose viewpoint was closer to Woodrow Wilson than to James E. Carter. Thus this platform becomes a singularly valuable definition of the American political center for the 1980s.

It will take some time to answer all the questions raised in this volume. Now is the perfect time, as the parties gather in 1984 to bring forth their words and their leaders, to offer this remarkable reminder of the previous campaign, set in its proper context and illuminated with the informed gloss that only Clifford W. Brown and Robert J. Walker are equipped by knowledge and experience to provide.

Robert H. Walker

PREFACE

The Anderson-Lucey presidential campaign of 1980 produced three related platform documents: *The Program of the Anderson/Lucey National Unity Campaign,* the full platform; *Rebuilding a Society that Works: an Agenda for America,* a summary version of the platform; and the *Budget Impact Statement* which provided a concrete financial dimension to the platform. We offer these three documents here together in one volume for the first time. They are reproduced from the original typescript with no attempts at correction or alteration, even though the original did contain some typographical errors.

The introduction to these two documents is not impartial. As the presentation makes clear, we were both centrally involved in the campaign itself as well as in the preparation of these materials. At this writing, one of us (CWB) is still associated with Mr. Anderson. Although we have made an effort to locate these documents in their historical setting as well as in their 1980 political setting, we are offering what is essentially an insider's view. Detached observers and impartial scholars will have to assess the quality and political importance of these documents. Our principal task, as we have seen it, is to outline the way in which they were produced and to give some general background about the campaign effort which led to their creation. We have tried to identify and evaluate the important features of the campaign and the platform-writing process as they appeared to us from the inside, but we do not present a full history of the Anderson campaign itself.

We wish to thank the following for their encouragement and assistance: John Anderson, Howard Gillette, Jonathan Knight, George Lehner, Michael MacLeod, William McKenzie, and Robert H. Walker.

Clifford W. Brown, Jr.

Robert J. Walker

INTRODUCTION

Platform-making as a formal political exercise did not begin until 1840. The Democratic Party that year held a convention in Baltimore to nominate Martin Van Buren for reelection and adopt a "platform" advocating states' rights and rejecting calls for a national bank. While Van Buren failed in his reelection bid, platform making has become a time-honored tradition and an integral part of the electoral process.[1]

Beginning with the Liberty Party's anti-slavery platform of 1844, minor parties have also issued platforms. In fact few minor parties have failed to do so.

The 1980 Anderson/Lucey platform--or "program" as it was formally called--was the first platform to be written and published by presidential and vice-presidential candidates completely independent of a political party. As such, it was a unique document in American political history.[2] In its formulation, the traditional roles of candidates, platform chairs, platform committees, special interests, convention delegates, and party staffs were fundamentally altered or eliminated altogether. It was longer and more detailed than most other platforms. In an unprecedented step, it was accompanied by an appendix containing a full cost accounting of its various provisions. Still, the Anderson/Lucey program was designed to serve the same functions as its traditional counterparts; and, like many third or minor party platforms of the past, it offered new proposals which were later embraced by one or both of the major parties.

Politicians and political scientists have long debated the significance of platforms. As a rule, they have played to mixed reviews. One observer charged that:

The low esteem that most Americans hold for platform making is generally exceeded only by their ignorance of the contents of these party documents. Nor do the party platforms generate much enthusiasm among the party faithful. This disinterest mirrors the general view that party platforms have little relationship to subsequent governmental policy-making.[3]

The complaints vary, but most critics charge that platforms are too general, too dishonest, too ambiguous, too consensus-oriented, and that platforms are too often ignored by candidates. Wendell Willkie, himself a candidate in 1940, declared them to be "fusions of ambiguity."[4] Another critic, Lord Bryce, said they were designed "neither to define nor to convince, but rather to attract and confuse."[5] Barry Goldwater concluded, "At best, political platforms are a pack of misinformation and lies."[6]

Not everyone, however, shares these views. In 1948 President Truman said, "To me, party platforms are contracts with the people, and I always looked upon them as contracts to be carried out."[7] President Eisenhower apparently regarded the 1952 Republican platform with equal seriousness and, according to one study, implemented "two-thirds of this document."[8] An exhaustive study of major party platforms by Gerald Pomper concluded that platforms are highly significant[9] and that a remarkable percentage of platform pledges are actually acted upon (72 percent for the period 1944-66; 63 percent for the period 1968-78).[10]

Pomper also found that less than one-fifth of platform statements on the average were pure rhetoric[11] and that platforms were increasingly programmatic, with a growing percentage of platform statements dealing with future policy recommendations (about 40 percent for the period 1944-66; about 60 percent for the period 1968-76).[12] Furthermore, in characterizing platform pledges he found that over half were reasonably specific[13] and that half were "rational,"[14] by which he meant useful in making rational choices.   He concluded, "Although much in platforms is not helpful to the rational voter, there would appear to be sufficient material to help him or her to make an informed choice."[15]

Platforms over the years have grown enormously in size.   Early platforms averaged around 1,000 words, but by 1972 the Democratic Party Platform had expanded to 25,000 words and by 1976 the Republican Platform reached 20,000.   A new record was established in 1980 by the 40,000 word platform adopted by the Democratic Convention in New York.   In both major parties much of the increase has been programmatic.

As platforms have become more programmatic they have become increasingly unrealistic and decidedly less concerned with the fiscal consequences of their proposed programs.   This problem has afflicted both major parties, but particularly the "outs."   The Democratic Platform of 1976 promised a long shopping list, including national health insurance, federalized welfare, and a number of full employment programs.   It also promised a balanced federal budget.   Likewise, the Republican Platform of 1980 promised a 30 percent personal income tax cut, a major defense buildup, sharply lower taxes for business, *and*, of course, a balanced budget.[16]

There are several reasons for this trend towards internal inconsistency.   Platforms are written in a highly politicized atmosphere in which the attempt to please everyone creates a bidding war that produces inflated and unrealistic promises.   Also, the compartmentalized process of producing the different planks in subcommittees discourages a unified approach to policy making.   Furthermore, there are no built-in institutional mechanisms to

ensure consistency. Finally, the platform is seldom regarded by its writers as fully binding. As a consequence,
the need for coherence diminishes in the view of its authors. The result is a process even more chaotic than
the congressional budget-making procedures that existed
before the reforms of the mid-1970's forced Congress to
adopt a unified budget.

The only exceptions to this pattern of confusion are
platforms written when a sitting president has full control
of the nominating convention. Then the platform is expected to reflect administration positions, and this, in
turn, imposes some discipline on the process. Even in
these circumstances, however, presidents have used platforms to create consolation prizes for potentially unruly
or disgruntled factions of the party and have, as a consequence, permitted the documents to wander from
reality.[17]

In years past the platform-drafting process did not
begin formally until about a week before the convention
when the platform committees convened, held public
hearings, and then retired into executive session for actual drafting. The process, however, has been substantially
lengthened in recent years. The Republicans in 1980 began to hold regional public hearings on January 14, although committee members, including the chair and the
vice chairs, were not selected until later. The Democrats
that year scheduled their early platform committee
deliberations for June, well in advance of the August
convention. The trend towards lengthy field hearings,
however, received a setback in 1984 when the Republicans
canceled theirs, probably in response to administration
concerns about adverse publicity.

While the platform-drafting timetables have changed
in recent years, the basic process has remained the same.
In both major parties the final drafting responsibility rests

with a Committee on Resolutions consisting of delegates from each state and territory. This committee is appointed by a platform chair who has been previously selected by the party's national committee. The chair is usually a senior member of Congress. In 1980, for example, the Republicans chose Senator John Tower. If an incumbent president is in full control of the party machinery, then the platform chair selects the committee and subcommittee members after consulting closely with the White House staff. If the party has no clear leader, the process can become much more fractious when political and factional concerns create pressure on the chair and often influence the selection of committee members. This was the case, for example, in 1980 when the Carter and Kennedy partisans battled for control of the platform. As a rule, committee staffs are selected by the chair and subcommittee chairs. They can be drawn from academia, Capitol Hill, party staff, candidate staffs, or the White House staff if the party is in power.

Public hearings, which used to follow the selection of the committee, now often take place earlier. These hearings, according to most observers, have little or no impact upon the actual drafting of the platform. The candidates and other party dignitaries testify before the panels, seemingly more for the benefit of the cameras than for the benefit of committee deliberations. Representatives of special interest groups also make appearances at the hearings, but they wield their real influence in private talks with the staff and with committee members.

Special interests do make their mark on party platforms. Often they submit language that is later incorporated with little or no modification. At other times they persuade the committee to delete offensive sections. These moves are all part of the general give-and-take that characterizes the formation of major party platforms. While much of the bartering and drafting is done at the staff level, the committee membership clearly exercises decisive authority in more important matters.

The committee's task and that of its chair are relatively easy when the party's nomination is locked up by an incumbent president facing no serious party challenge or when there is a close race for the nomination. In the former situation, the platform will, in effect, usually be written by the White House;[18] in the latter, candidates typically avoid platform fights and focus on the nomination contest. In the distant past votes on a platform plank have been used as a "test vote" by candidates in close conventions to demonstrate delegate strength, but during the last fifty years test votes generally have come on credentials and rules fights, not on platform fights.[19] The views of the candidate(s), the demands of special interests, and the general election strategy are harmonized to the greatest extent possible when there is no major fight. The consensus language is carefully drafted and redrafted at the subcommittee and committee levels.

Major platform fights typically occur when a candidate clearly controls a convention but is unacceptable to an important party faction. In such cases those factions may use the vehicle of a platform fight to wrest concessions from the candidates or to inflict electoral harm on them if concessions are not forthcoming. In these circumstances fights generally occur at the committee level and spill over onto the convention floor. For example, in 1964, Republican moderates, facing defeat by Goldwater, forced a platform fight on the civil rights plank which demonstrated the "extremist" credentials of the Goldwater delegates. At the 1968 Democratic Convention in Chicago there was a bitter split over an amendment calling for a halt to the bombing in Vietnam and a negotiated withdrawal of troops; it lost by a vote of 1567 3/4 to 1041 1/2.[20] In the more distant past, the Democratic Convention of 1860 rejected a minority anti-slavery plank and called upon the Supreme Court to decide the issue of slavery in the territories. In each of these cases and in similar instances, the party nominee subsequently lost the election.

Faced with the prospect of party-dividing platform fights, potential winners often make concessions on the platform to soothe opposition feelings or even let the other faction write the platform. It has been said that Taft succeeded in writing the 1952 Republican Platform, although Eisenhower became the nominee.[21]   Gerald Ford in 1976 made many platform concessions to the conservatives. One of the most famous examples of a candidate seeking to accommodate the views of a party faction was Richard Nixon's secret visit to New York Governor Nelson Rockefeller on the Saturday before the convention of 1960. Rockefeller, who was holding out for strong civil rights and defense planks, reached an agreement with Nixon on a statement called the "Fourteen-point Compact of Fifth Avenue" by some, and the "Munich of the Republican Party" by others.[22]

Many people have questioned whether candidates are--or should be--bound by party platforms. In fact, Democratic Party rules require the nominees to disavow publicly those planks they cannot endorse. Many candidates have disavowed particular planks, especially when they go against a long-established party position. Other candidates have simply interpreted the planks broadly and redefined them.

As a rule, however, candidates give their platforms a large degree of faith and credit. In addition to Pomper's study[23] there is the finding of John Kessel that platforms may be more accurate indicators of future political behavior than campaign speeches.[24]   The importance attached to the platforms is well illustrated by the fact that even lame-duck presidents have attempted to influence the process. This was the case in 1960 with

Eisenhower, who thought Rockefeller's defense proposals reflected badly on his administration, and in 1968 with Lyndon Johnson, who fought hard for a plank backing administration policies in Vietnam.

Candidates have also taken an interest in platforms for strategic reasons. When a candidate is clearly in control of a convention, he or she may have enough influence with the delegates to force the drafting of planks that are designed specifically to be consistent with a November election strategy. Whether they like it or not, candidates have to run on their party's platform during the general election, and if they cannot control the drafting process, they can be pinned against the platform's provisions by the opposition candidates. In 1968 Hubert Humphrey found himself saddled with a strong Vietnam plank that he was forced to endorse at Johnson's insistence. Candidates may also seek to use the process to assemble a broad coalition of interests, as Carter did in 1976 but failed to do in 1980.

Platforms, despite their many faults, have come to play a major role in American politics.[25] The 1980 Republican Platform foreshadowed Reaganomics, repudiated the party's long-standing support of ERA, and signaled a major reversal of the party's historic commitment to civil rights. Other platforms have been the cause as well as the symbol of party schisms.[26] They have come to play a major role in electing and defeating candidates.[27] At times they have set the tone of political debate, occasionally serving as what Paul T. David called "national plans."[28] Indeed, for documents that are thought by many to be meaningless, they certainly absorb an enormous amount of political time and effort.[29] Given this larger context and the general importance of platforms, what contribution did the Anderson/Lucey program of 1980 make to the development of platforms?

THE ANDERSON DIFFERENCE

John Anderson began his quest for the presidency as a candidate for the Republican nomination. In his June 8, 1979, announcement speech, which he wrote himself, Anderson declared, "Others may boast of superior organization or financial resources. Still others speak in glittering generalities of their talent for leadership. I want to arouse an appeal to the conscience and reason of America, to speak of the America yet to be. To return to the spirit that made America great."

In launching his bid, Anderson readily conceded that he was "the darkest of dark horses." Although he had served in Congress for nineteen years, had earned wide respect among his colleagues, and had received considerable attention from the Washington press corps, he was virtually unknown outside the nation's capital. Early opinion polls showed that few Americans could identify him and fewer still supported his presidential bid. His rise to national fame and celebrity status during the 1980 campaign is one of the great sagas of American Presidential politics.

Born and raised in Rockford, Illinois, Anderson went to Congress in 1960. Prior to that, he had served in Europe during the Second World War, had been a foreign service officer in Berlin, and had been elected State's Attorney for Winnebago County. His election to Congress followed a primary victory in a crowded field of candidates in Illinois's Sixteenth Congressional District.

During his early years in Congress, Anderson reflected the moderately conservative views of his district. He opposed a number of Great Society programs but supported the Civil Rights Act of 1964 and the Voting Rights Act of 1965. He was deeply affected by the social upheavals of the late 1960s, and during this period he began to acquire a more liberal outlook on national issues. Increasingly concerned about racial and economic inequality, he cast the deciding Rules Committee vote that allowed the Open Housing Act of 1968 to go to the House floor for passage. He later supported Nixon's Family Assistance Plan, which came under fire from his Republican colleagues in the House. Anderson also became a strong supporter of environmental and job safety legislation, yet retained his reputation for fiscal conservatism.

In 1969 he was elected Chairman of the House Republican Conference, making him the third ranking Republican in the House leadership. He retained his seat on the Rules Committee and, despite his new-found prominence, continued to demonstrate an independence of mind that won him the admiration of moderates and liberals and the enmity of unforgiving conservatives. During the 1970s, he became known in Washington as one of the finest orators in the House and one of the most intelligent members of Congress. As a consequence, he became well liked by the Washington press corps, was widely sought as a speaker, and appeared frequently on national programs, such as "Meet the Press."

Anderson took an active role in reforming House Rules and in other political reform movements. He joined with Democrat Morris Udall in sponsoring campaign finance legislation. He was also the first Republican in the House to call for President Nixon's resignation. These actions, together with his increasingly liberal views on social policy, antagonized conservatives to such an extent that he was targeted for defeat by New Right forces in 1978. He was challenged that year in a Republican primary by Don Lyon, a fundamentalist minister who received strong financial and political support from the conservative movement nationally. Unlike Clifford Case, another target of the Right Wing that year, Anderson survived his first serious election challenge in eighteen years by a 58 to 42 percent margin in the primary. As a result, he became a rallying point for beleaguered party liberals and people in both parties who opposed the politics and tactics of the New Right. After his successful reelection, New Right Republican conservatives in the House mounted a challenge to his party leadership position. Again the effort failed, with Anderson receiving support from many Republican traditionalists as well as from moderates and liberals.

Angered by these events, by the conservatives' attacks on other moderates, and by their obvious success in moving the Republican Party still further to the right, Anderson began to take seriously suggestions that he should quit the Congress and run for the presidential nomination in 1980. In the late summer of 1978, he had already made known his interest in an interview with David Broder of the *Washington Post*.[30] In the months that followed his reelection, he carefully reviewed his prospects. It was already evident that the Republican field would be crowded in 1980 despite the strong support enjoyed by the front-runner Ronald Reagan. It was also clear that the party's conservative vote might be fractured enough by John Connally's candidacy to allow a liberal like Anderson to score some victories early in the season. He was aware that he had a claim upon a narrow but persistent band of Republican liberals who would support him and contribute money in very modest amounts to his candidacy. His friend and colleague Morris Udall had already shown in the previous election that members of the House could mount serious campaigns for president.

Still, the obstacles were awesome. Anderson had no existing organization. The state-by-state distribution of convention delegate slots heavily favored the conservatives. The party rank-and-file had increased its conservative profile during the 1970s. The old Eastern Establishment, with which he enjoyed good rapport as a member of the Council on Foreign Relations, had diminished even more in significance since the days when it unsuccessfully tried to nominate Scranton, Romney, and Rockefeller. Furthermore, moderate Republicans were notorious for being moderate contributors, and they were far less organized than the conservatives. With Baker, Bush, and Dole in the race, the moderates had even more major candidates than did the conservatives to divide a smaller vote in the primaries. In the end, however, Anderson decided to make the effort. He had already resolved to quit the House. He toyed with the tempting opportunity to run for the Senate seat vacated by Adlai Stevenson but did not relish the prospect of facing more Right Wing calumnies in Illinois.

The Anderson campaign, despite its "Doonesbury" reputation, did pay attention from the very beginning to strategic concerns. People associated with the campaign were aware from the start that in recent history successful candidates for the nomination in both major parties were either sitting presidents or individuals who could attract a devoted, although not necessarily large constituency. These candidates could outlast their "image-based" counterparts because the inevitable setbacks in the nominating process would not prove instantly fatal (as they had for Romney, Muskie, Bayh, and Lindsay, for example, and later would for Dole and Baker). Candidates with solid constituencies (like Kennedy with Catholic voters, Humphrey with labor, McGovern with the anti-war protesters, and Carter with born-again Christians, both black and white) had the edge because they could count on continuing financial and electoral support, no matter where they stood at a given moment in the campaign.

Anderson's first requirement was to create such a constituency within the party and to make it his exclusive domain. Moderate to liberal Republicans and

progressive Independents were an obvious target. Independent voters, many of them young professionals, were
another rich field for constituency building. Since
Republican moderates and other potential Anderson supporters were concentrated in only a few regions of the
country, their location heavily influenced the early
geographic strategy of the campaign. Early in the summer of 1979 the staff developed a four-state strategy:
(1) New Hampshire, because it held the first primary and
because, despite its conservative reputation, it contained
a small, but solid, liberal Republican constituency to build
on; (2) Massachusetts, because the state had a progressive Republican tradition and because it contained many
professionals whose large number overshadowed the state's
miniscule number of Republican Party adherents; (3) Illinois, because it was Anderson's home state; and (4)
Wisconsin, because it had a progressive tradition, large
pockets of liberal Republicans, and election laws that
permitted Democrats and Independents to vote in the
Republican primary.

In pursuit of this strategy, detailed staff plans were
made for the New Hampshire and Massachusetts
primaries. Using data from both presidential and state-
wide races, these plans identified the specific towns
where moderate Republicans had done well against conservatives in past primaries. The plans became the basis
for organizing, voter targeting, and scheduling strategies.
(In the actual event, the traditional voting patterns held
true, and the projections made in the summer of 1979
were strongly validated by the results in February and
March of 1980.) Similar plans were later developed for
Illinois and Wisconsin.

At the beginning of the campaign, Anderson shared
the moderate and progressive Republican constituencies
with Howard Baker and, to a lesser extent, with George
Bush and Robert Dole. Thus, it was necessary to do
more than pursue a geographic strategy. From the very

beginning both candidate and staff realized the need to create what was later to be called "The Anderson Difference" in order to set him apart from the rest of the moderate candidates. Since the relevant competition was clearly committed to image-oriented strategies, an issues-oriented approach seemed appropriate. Furthermore, it was recognized by the staff that such a campaign would be highly consistent with Anderson's own instincts and approach to politics. Issues and policy formulation are his life's passion, and it was inevitable that at some point the campaign would reflect this. Moreover, Anderson's experience on the Rules Committee, through which pass all major pieces of legislation, gave him an acquaintance with issues which was shared by few other people in Congress and by no other presidential candidate. (The possible exception was Howard Baker, whose position as minority leader made it extremely difficult for him to take specific and independent stands on issues during the campaign.) Therefore, from the very outset, Anderson was determined to conduct a "Campaign of Ideas."

Shortly after announcing his candidacy in June 1979, Anderson asked his principal legislative advisor, Robert Walker, to draft alternatives to the Carter gasoline rationing scheme that had been recently defeated in the House. While a standby gasoline tax of fifty cents a gallon had been proposed to him as one option, Anderson decided that the times required a permanent tax of this magnitude. The United States was importing nearly half of its oil, much of it from the troubled waters of the Persian Gulf. Oil analysts were concerned about the stocks of home heating fuel, and America's oil import bill was aproaching $60 billion.

When Walker later suggested that the revenues might be applied to help rescue the social security system, Anderson asked that a plan be drafted. In the meantime, he sought the advice of his political advisors,

many of whom were aghast at the possible political consequences.   At a July meeting in Boston with his principal Massachusetts supporters, he floated the tax proposal and received a nearly unanimous set of strangled
negative replies from the shocked assemblage.   The sole
exception was Josiah Spaulding, a major figure in Massachusetts Republican politics, who seemed intrigued by
the suggestion.   Despite the timidity of his political advisors, Anderson decided to proceed.

In August he submitted an article to the *New York
Times* outlining the proposal:

Perhaps now is the time to consider a higher
gasoline tax.   A 50-cent-a-gallon "energy-conservation
tax" on all motor fuels could reduce our gasoline
consumption by 5 to 10 percent, saving us 365,000 to
730,000 barrels of fuel per day. . . . Revenues from
an "energy conservation tax" could be earmarked for
the social security trust funds.   The proceeds of the
tax would then enable us to make major cutbacks in
the existing payroll tax. . . . Some safeguards,
however, would have to accompany any hike in the
gasoline tax . . . for business use of motor fuels . . .
the impact on the elderly . . . and relief for those
state and federal workers not currently contributing
to Social Security. . . .[31]

Initial public reaction to Anderson's proposal was not
favorable.   Most Americans were clearly not prepared to
accept such an idea, but the tax attracted surprising
editorial support in major newspapers across the nation.
Robert J. Samuelson, economist and columnist for the
National Journal, wrote:

If there were a handbook for candidates, one
chapter would surely begin, "Don't propose a gasoline
tax."   But Anderson's very obscurity and the lengthy

odds against his success give him some extra liberty to violate the rules, even, perhaps, to the point of saying something he believes.[32]

Another columnist, Michael Killian of the *Chicago Tribune,* said:

> . . . in proposing it, Anderson is candidly facing up to a serious unpleasant reality with an eminently workable, if admittedly painful solution, just as he'd have to do as President.
> No wonder so many political writers say he isn't a serious candidate.[33]

A *Washington Star* editorial lamented, "There seems to be a sort of inverse relationship between the 'seriousness' of a presidential candidacy--at least, as conventionally measured--and the seriousness of the candidate's ideas."[34] The plan received favorable editorial comments from over seventy newspapers throughout the country. Political cartoonists, like Herblock, gave it flattering coverage. Even conservative columnist William F. Buckley supported the idea.[35]   Rarely has such a new controversial proposal received as much editorial support.

In the fall of 1979 Anderson made a sustained effort to go beyond the gas tax idea and present other new proposals. He decried the lack of an American "Industrial Policy" at a time when the idea was "little more than a ripple on the pond of public opinion." He called for the creation of a multinational Agency for International Energy Development to assist Third World nations in developing their energy resources. He discussed the need for new job training initiatives to combat structural unemployment. He proposed new incentives to boost personal savings. He urged the creation of labor-management-government council meetings, modeled after Germany's "Konzirte-Aktion." He warned that sustained hostility

towards the Soviet Union could push it towards rap-
prochement with China. Summing up his campaign
philosophy in a speech before the National Press Club on
October 25, he warned:

It is an all too common tendency in democracies such as ours for political figures and national
leaders to follow the path of least political resistance, whether it be in the field of energy,
economics, or foreign policy. We now know where
the path of least political resistance leads. It leads
to gas lines. It leads to natural gas and home heating oil shortages. It leads to economic stagnation
and disruption. It leads to declining growth in real
incomes. It leads to a waning respect for our public
institutions, and ultimately it leads to the erosion of
our national character and inner resolve.

Despite his efforts to set himself apart from the
other candidates and present a new approach to political
campaigning, Anderson failed during the fall of 1979 to
gain much national recognition beyond the political pun-
dits and editorial writers. Many of them praised his suggestions, but all discounted his chances of capturing the
nomination. He was barely able to raise enough money
by the end of the year to meet the Federal Election
Commission's requirements for federal matching funds.
The fact that he did so, however, qualified him for an
invitation from the League of Women Voters to debate
with the other Republican candidates in Iowa.

It was the Iowa debate, which took place in early
January, that brought Anderson to national public attention. Some campaign staff members had argued against
his participation, noting that he had made no previous
effort in Iowa and that the debate appearance might vali-
date a negligible showing in the Iowa caucuses. Others
argued strenuously that credibility was his major problem

and that he should always appear at forums where the other candidates were present. The latter logic was consistent with Anderson's own instincts. He not only agreed to attend, but he also took the appearance very seriously, preparing carefully for it.

Extensive materials on the issue positions of other candidates were assembled by the staff and outside volunteers. Issue briefing papers were written. A closing statement was carefully prepared and reviewed by Anderson. The staff wrote a strategy memorandum and discussed it with the candidate in a brief meeting immediately before his departure. This memorandum stated in part:

It is equally fundamental that Mr. Anderson address himself to the national audience, not to the other candidates, nor to the questioner, the auditorium audience or to Iowa. It is my hope that the others, worried about Iowa, will "Iowa it" all night, while we speak to the country. . . . In short, he must remember that this is *not* a debate but a presentation of his views to the public.

Shortly before the debate, President Carter announced the imposition of a grain embargo against the Soviet Union in retaliation for the invasion of Afghanistan. Among the six Republican candidates present, only Anderson endorsed the president's action, stating:

. . . it seems to me that it is passing strange that those who are critical of our foreign policy as being deficient on the grounds that it is weak, when the first real test comes of responding to the kind of overt aggression that has just been taken by the Soviet Union against Afghanistan, are unwilling to accept any measure of sacrifice.

Attacked on his gasoline tax/social security package, he stoutly defended it, criticizing his opponents for their unwillingness to confront the perils of our energy dependence. These uncompromising stands and his precise responses to the other questions were very well received.

The Iowa debate was a significant turning point in the campaign. To the national media, it was a dramatic confirmation of their belief that Anderson was highly qualified to be president. To others, it was a confirmation of their judgment in supporting his candidacy. To the party hierarchy, it was a refreshing, and not yet threatening, performance. To the national audience of four million who saw the debate on public television, it was an introduction to Anderson's unique qualities. Looking back on the debate and the nomination campaign nearly four years later, one may speculate about what might have occurred had the national networks carried out their original intention of broadcasting it live on prime time to an audience of thirty to fifty million people.

Shortly after the Iowa debate the Republican candidates appeared before the Gun Owners Association of New Hampshire. Again Anderson separated himself from his rivals, this time by supporting tougher gun control laws. Once more the press and much of the public were delighted. Anderson was not only conducting a self-proclaimed campaign of ideas, but he was also doing it with courage and strong conviction in ways fully consistent with the "Anderson Difference" slogan adopted in the campaign's advertising. His first strategic objective had been accomplished: he was now successfully set apart from Bush, Dole, and Baker and had established a strong constituency base among moderate Republicans and independently minded professionals that would remain with him until the election in November.

A striking example of this new constituency's significance was its willingness to contribute money. For instance, the campaign took a full page advertisement in the *New York Times* just after the Iowa debate. Costing about $20,000, it netted about $100,000, excluding federal matching funds. Responses to direct mail appeals for money, which had received disappointing returns before Iowa, suddenly exploded. Much to its amazement, the campaign now had enough money to mount a credible, if belated, effort in the first two primary states.

After the Iowa debate the Anderson candidacy began to attract many celebrities. These served to create a celebrity status for the candidate himself. Appearances in "Doonesbury" and on "Saturday Night Live" added to his novelty and to his constituency by reinforcing his growing appeal to college students and young people. By the eve of the New Hampshire primary, Anderson was well positioned to make a mark on the nomination process.

Anderson's performance in New Hampshire was regarded by the staff as a disappointment. However, in retrospect, his 9.9 percent was a reasonable showing in a conservative state with the moderate vote split three ways. The constituency to which Anderson appealed was intrinsically small in New Hampshire, but its loyalty gave him enough support to make him one of the survivors when the primary narrowed the field to four--an accomplishment considered unattainable by the national press just a few weeks before.

The big news from New Hampshire was George Bush's crushing defeat coming on the heels of polling results that predicted a significant victory for him. This shattered his Iowa momentum, sent the moderates looking for alternatives, and set the stage for Massachusetts.

The Bay State had long been regarded by Anderson strategists as the perfect setting for a major ambush. Here the constituency to which Anderson appealed was intrinsically much larger than in New Hampshire and the number of Republicans was proportionally much smaller. Furthermore, liberal registration laws which enabled voters to switch parties until shortly before the primary-- and then to switch back immediately after the primary-- were regarded as an opportunity to attract a significant number of sympathetic voters who otherwise would not vote in a Republican primary. The importance of Massachusetts to the campaign was demonstrated by the fact that for a long time it had the only full-time paid field operative.

The Massachusetts near victory (Bush 31.0 percent, Anderson 30.7 percent, Reagan 28.8 percent) was the result of many factors: good organization; a well-prepared candidate schedule during the week between the New Hampshire and Massachusetts primaries; strong performances on the stump by Anderson throughout that week; the endorsement of the influential *Boston Globe* (based on Anderson's issue positions and demonstrated political courage); the collapse and confusion in the Bush camp (Bush, convinced that he would win in New Hampshire, had planned to campaign lightly in Massachusetts, feeling certain of victory in this, one of his four home states, and was therefore unprepared to put together a good schedule on short notice); and, above all, the ratio between the intrinsic Anderson constituency and the number of Republicans who vote in Massachusetts primaries.

The near win in the Massachusetts primary (Anderson's lead in the returns until very late in the evening led some morning papers to declare him the winner) and the accompanying near win in Vermont--where Reagan beat him by the razor-thin margin of 30.1 percent to 29.0 percent--had an enormous impact. No one in the press had expected this. Few in the campaign had either.

Since the surge had come in the last two or three days, the polls had not picked it up. It was the single biggest political surprise of the year. From that point on, few in the press could be certain that Anderson might not create another surprise. The shock value of Massachusetts and Vermont, the admiration of the press for Anderson's issues campaign, his new-found celebrity status, and the increasingly evident willingness of his constituency to contribute money established his credentials for the media as an important political force. He had finally achieved credibility. Although the campaign trail through November was to have many disappointments, some of which were soon to occur, Anderson never lost this credibility.

The near victories in Massachusetts and Vermont solved the credibility problem and momentarily eased the financial problem, but in the short run they could not help the organizational problem which existed throughout the country. The Anderson campaign was organizationally weak in Illinois, the next major primary state. Outside of the college towns, hardly any organization existed downstate, a situation that could not be repaired in two weeks. The Illinois campaign was also hurt when Anderson's Republican opponents launched a concerted attack on his party credentials, ignoring his years of party leadership in the House. In the Illinois debate, questions were also raised about Anderson's willingness to support Reagan should he become the party's nominee.

Despite these attacks, Anderson continued to wage his Campaign of Ideas. At one point in the Illinois campaign, he backed up his claim that the budget should be cut by $10 billion with a detailed list of areas to be cut--something unprecedented in a modern presidential campaign. At the same time he continued to hammer away at the need for a gas tax to cut energy dependence. These stands won him the endorsement of Chicago's two major newspapers, but Reagan's organizational strength and his own solid constituency were enough to produce a 48 percent to 37 percent victory over Anderson, with Bush trailing far behind.   Anderson's performance was still impressive, but inflated expectations that he would actually beat Reagan caused the press to interpret Illinois as a crushing Anderson defeat.   A week later he finished a respectable third in Connecticut.   The week after that he also finished third in Wisconsin and his chances for winning the Republican nomination dropped to almost nil.

Just before the March 18 Illinois primary, speculation began to mount in the press that Anderson was considering an independent bid.   This speculation was encouraged by his Republican opposition in Illinois and probably by some Anderson supporters who favored such a move.   Whatever its source, the public speculation did not help the Illinois effort.

The case for an independent candidacy was first made seriously to Anderson during the week after the New Hampshire primary by Tom Matthews, a partner in the direct mail firm that handled the campaign's fundraising.   Matthews, strongly impressed by the geometrical increase in nationwide responses to Anderson's mail appeals, made the case that Anderson had touched a strong political nerve that went far beyond his own candidacy for the Republican nomination.   Matthews argued that whatever the results might be in the Republican primaries the "Anderson Family," as he styled the campaign contributors, should not be permitted to dissipate.   An independent candidacy, he suggested, would keep them together.

Anderson listened carefully to this February presentation, but thoughts of an independent candidacy were temporarily eclipsed by the results in Massachusetts a week later.   After the Illinois defeat, however, serious and extended internal discussions began to take place.

There were many persuasive arguments set forth at the time in support of the independent candidacy. It was increasingly doubtful that Anderson could win the Republican nomination. Because of an organizational mix-up, he was not on the ballot in Pennsylvania. In most of the caucus states, there was hardly any organization in place to match Reagan's intensely motivated conservative campaign workers. The next major primary possibility beyond Pennsylvania was Indiana, where Reagan had defeated Ford in 1976, making it at best a doubtful proposition.

Moreover, there was strong staff support for the independent bid. People wanted to keep going. They had briefly tasted the euphoria of Massachusetts. They felt that they could make a go of it with enough time and money. They didn't want to see it all end so soon.

The strongest arguments for the independent candidacy, however, did not come from the staff. Norman Lear, Stanley Scheinbaum, Stewart Mott, and other major contributors added their support to Matthews' advocacy. Just before the Wisconsin Primary in early April, a meeting was held in Milwaukee at which Matthews eloquently presented the case for an independent candidacy to Anderson in the presence of Lear, Scheinbaum, Campaign Manager Michael MacLeod, David Garth, and some other staff members. He argued that the Republican nomination could not be won, that an independent bid just might be successful, and that the effort, win or lose, could become the beginning of something truly lasting in American politics.

The case against was presented by Clifford Brown. He argued that the Republican nomination might still be winnable (because Reagan had almost reached his expenditure limit and could not fully finance any subsequent primary campaigns) and that staying in the Republican Party might be best for Anderson's long-range future.

However, he also insisted that it was a decision of con-science and that Anderson should not decide on the basis of short-range, win-lose projections. At the meeting Anderson seemed inclined to make the run, but he made no formal commitments and said that he would postpone any final decisions until after the Wisconsin primary.

It was several weeks before Anderson decided to leave the Republican Party--the party to which he had devoted his career, to the leadership of which he had been elected, and for which he had sacrificed much time and energy to do the thousand things that party leaders are expected to do. He clearly understood that there would be no going back. As he later told a staff aide, "I have left the church."

It was an intensely personal decision, and it is dif-ficult to speculate about his actual motivations. Certain-ly he had a strong dislike of Ronald Reagan and his politics. Anderson had spent much of his long political career seeking to broaden the base of the Republican Party by urging the full participation of blacks, Hispanics, and women in party affairs. Reagan represented what Anderson regarded as a "country club mentality" that sought to maintain the party as a white male preserve. Moreover, Anderson took sharp issue with Reagan's views on the economy, defense spending, SALT, ERA, and social issues, such as abortion. Staying in the Republican Party would have meant embracing a party modeled in Ronald Reagan's image, and John Anderson was not about to take a loyalty oath to Ronald Reagan.

Beyond these concerns, Anderson was no doubt also responsive to the arguments set forth by Matthews, Garth, and others that his efforts had served to energize a lethargic electorate and an otherwise dull national pres-idential campaign. He felt that the seeming disillusion-ment with the Reagan-Carter choice was real, that his own standing in the national polls accurately reflected this, and that there was an outside chance of winning. Faced with an April 27 filing deadline in New Jersey, Anderson announced his decision on April 24 in a speech at the National Press Club. He would abandon the effort to obtain the nomination of the Republican Party and would "seek an independent course," although a formal announcement would be delayed until he had qualified for the ballot in enough states to make the effort feasible.

THE ANDERSON RESEARCH OPERATION

One of the first tasks of the new effort was to create a staff operation consistent with the candidate's "Campaign of Ideas." A research department responsible for formulating policy initiatives had existed as a small unit in the Republican phase of the Anderson effort. At the beginning it consisted entirely of Clifford Brown and his assistant William McKenzie, a recent graduate of the University of Texas at Austin. During the spring it grew with the addition of a few staffers, but it remained a small operation by the standards of most presidential campaigns.

Its efforts were strongly augmented by the after-hours volunteer help of Anderson congressional staff members, including Robert Walker, Forrest Frank, Alex West, Paula Scott, and Bruce Post; by outside volunteers, including Lee Auspitz (a former president of the Ripon Society), Howard Gillette (a professor at George Washington University and a past president of the Ripon Society, and John Topping (then current president of the Ripon Society); and Washington attorneys Michael Astrue, Donald Bliss, Martin Gerry, Wes Heppler, Fred Kellogg, Mary MacArthur, and Susan Philp.

When the campaign entered its independent phase, it was evident that the research effort could no longer rely primarily upon volunteer help. If Anderson was to retain his issues orientation, he needed a first-class operation to match the efforts of Reagan and Carter who had much larger resources upon which to draw. Shortly after the independent phase began, Brown sent a memorandum to Michael MacLeod, the campaign manager, requesting significant staff support. After several discussions between Brown, MacLeod, and David Garth, the request was granted and the creation of an issues staff was given enthusiastic support from the top.

Recruitment began in May. To save money, most of the staff members were "quasi-volunteers," people who received about $100 per week for a possible time commitment of sixty hours. Supervisory staff included Brown, as Research Director; Robert Walker, Domestic Policy Advisor, who left the congressional staff to join the campaign; and Alton Frye, Director of Policy Planning, who took a leave of absence from the Council on Foreign Relations for the duration of the effort.

The Research Department was organized along the following functional lines:

Political Research, including the analysis of past election data, the formulation of geographic and electoral college strategies, and the creation of a "block schedule" to allocate the candidates' time in conformity with the geographic strategy;

State and Local Research, to prepare materials to brief the candidate on local issues and local press commentaries;

Opposition Research, to prepare extensive briefing materials on the public records of Carter and Reagan;

Issues Research, to prepare in-depth policy recommendations to support the writing of speeches and articles, to write position papers for public release, and to draft platform planks;

Speech-writing, which became fully independent of the issues function during the fall;

Article Preparation, which included the drafting of nearly two hundred articles which were sent out in response to requests by publications;

Road liason and clearance, which served as a communications link between the department and the candidates and which also carefully reviewed and often reworked the materials submitted from the speechwriters and others.

At different times during the campaign, the research staff also had responsibility for answering public issues inquiries and responding to questionnaires.

The issues operation constituted the heart of the Research Department. Conceptually, there are two ways in which such an operation can be organized. The first is a staff model, the second, a task force model. The staff model operates basically the way a congressional office does, usually with a central supervisor to assign tasks and with staff members responsible for various policy areas. Each staff member serves in a research capacity, develops an expertise in his or her area of specialty, consults with outside authorities, and prepares briefing memoranda, speeches, or other materials. The task force model relies on panels of outside experts to develop policy positions which, after due deliberation, are submitted to the candidate and to a generally much smaller issues staff.

There are several advantages of the staff model over the task force model. With a single person responsible for the final product, deadlines are easier to meet. With staff members in constant communication with each other, policy output is likely to be more coherent. Quality control is easier. Staffs consisting of low-key professionals are less prone to personality clashes than task forces. Staffs can also more easily avoid the "least common denominator" problems associated with committees. Just as importantly, staffs can respond quickly to requests for materials which task forces often cannot.

Alternatively, the task force model has certain advantages over the staff model. Task forces have greater public visibility. They are able to attract "big names." They can sift through vast amounts of information. They may make possible a more in-depth approach to a subject area. Their membership provides the press with answers to the question "Who are the candidate's chief advisors"?

The Anderson campaign attempted to combine both models by creating an in-house staff and a series of advisory committees which could serve as functional equivalents of task forces. In this way genuine assistance was sought from outside, but the discipline of the staff model was maintained.

With the enormous demands made by Anderson upon the research operation, there was simply no alternative to having a large in-house staff. During the campaign Anderson exhibited a voracious appetite for information relating to public policy. He also wanted the staff to cast the net widely for new, yet practical, ideas. Furthermore, he requested a large variety of substantive speeches, specific in nature, touching on all major policy areas. Therefore the sheer quantity of materials developed by the Research Department was enormous, even by the standards of a presidential campaign. It included approximately eighty speeches, over sixty of which were on specific substantive topics, such as health care, industrial policy, or energy policy (See Appendix I, Table 4); a 317 page platform; some forty specialized position statements; approximately two dozen comprehensive issue briefing books; materials for countless articles; responses to scores of questionaires; and much other written matter. In addition to producing these, the staff had the responsibility of evaluating numerous proposals submitted to the campaign from the outside.

There was at least one issue coordinator for each of the following domestic policy areas: the economy, health, urban affairs, civil rights, women's rights, the environment, energy, labor, transportation, agriculture, welfare, science/technology/space, and education. There were four full-time issue coordinators for foreign and defense policy areas under the direction of a single head coordinator, Dr. Jonathan Knight, a specialist in international relations on leave from the American Association of University Professors. (See Appendix II.)

The speech-writing operation was closely integrated with the issues research operation. In contrast to many campaigns where the speechwriters travel with the "road show," the Anderson speechwriters primarily worked at the headquarters in the same room as the issue coordinators to maximize the interaction between them. This enabled the staff to maintain quality control over the speech drafts, to make sure that the proposals they contained were internally consistent, and to determine that they reflected accurately the candidate's issue positions, all very high priorities in an issues-oriented campaign. Dr. William Galston, a professor of political science at the University of Texas at Austin, was selected chief speechwriter and was supported by a small staff of other writers during the fall months.

The Research Department had its own representative with the candidate on the road at all times. George

Lehner, a Washington attorney with State Department experience, filled this difficult task. It was his responsibility to clear with the candidate all the materials produced by the staff and then to provide staff members with Anderson's feedback. In this way a constant flow of information was maintained to and from the road. If an organization is set up with staff and speechwriters located at the headquarters, then the liason must be a very special kind of person, sensitive to the candidate's desires and needs while in constant communication with the headquarters staff. Otherwise the system can easily break down. Lehner also served as a speechwriter in his own right and was responsible, at Anderson's direction, for making last minute changes in the speeches sent from Washington.

To ensure quality control, a simple but effective clearance system was instituted. All materials destined for the road or for the public which concerned domestic matters were cleared by the respective issue coordinator and by Walker and Brown. All materials dealing with foreign policy were cleared by the relevant issue coordinator and by Frye and Brown. All materials were then reviewed on the road by Lehner and finally by Anderson.

This fairly rigorous clearance process was mandated by Anderson's own demand for accuracy. Understandably, he never wanted to be put in a position of being inaccurate or untruthful. He demanded precision work and wanted to be thoroughly briefed on all aspects of new proposals so that he could handle the material with ease in press conferences and scheduled media interviews, of which he held a combined total of 349 during the independent phase of the campaign, not including numerous unscheduled interviews given on the plane during travel time. (See Appendix I, Table 2.)

It is easy to oversimplify the structure of the research operation; nothing is ever neat in campaigns, especially ones of this variety. The atmosphere in the research area of the headquarters often resembled that of a chaotic city room in a medium-sized metropolitan newspaper. For several months while the Washington headquarters was located behind Union Station, the department operated in ghastly physical surroundings with people crowded into small rooms or spread around the halls. The air-conditioning broke down in hundred degree Washington weather for about a week before the headquarters was moved to Georgetown. This led Galston to quip, "They riot in Calcutta over conditions better than these."

DRAFTING THE PLATFORM

From the very beginning of the independent campaign, it had been assumed that there would be a platform. Donald Bliss made a suggestion to this effect in April, just after the independent phase began. Others, both inside and outside the campaign, echoed his call. On several occasions in May Anderson made known to MacLeod his desire for a comprehensive platform that would contain his issue positions in a single document and that would emphasize the new policy directions he wanted to advocate. Preliminary work on platform issue positions began early in the season under the direction of William McKenzie, Deputy Director of Research, with each issue coordinator developing memoranda in his or her special area.

Furthermore, beginning in May as a prelude to the platform-writing process, the research staff scheduled a series of forums at which the candidate was briefed by national experts in a wide range of policy areas. Over forty such sessions were held during the summer months, including more than a dozen in advance of a trip to Europe in early July. (See Appendix I, Table 5.) These served as the functional equivalent of platform hearings, but they were generally off-the-record working sessions that permitted a candid exchange of views between Anderson and the participants. The latter included some of the most noted academic experts in their fields; senior members of the foreign policy establishment, the armed services, and the intelligence community; the chief executive officers of General Motors, Ford, U.S. Steel, Bethlehem Steel, and other representatives of industry; labor leaders; economists; energy experts; and civil rights leaders.[36] At most sessions, a staff member was present so that the ideas set forth could be correctly interpreted during the policy-making process. Some sessions were more successful than others, but the briefings taken as a whole proved quite useful both to the candidate and to the staff.

Just before Anderson departed on his European trip, he asked the research staff to work on a preliminary platform draft that would reflect his views on domestic and foreign issues and that would serve as a focal point for his fall campaign. He did not specify the length of the document, but he made it clear that it was to be given a high priority.

It was evident to the research staff that the platform ideally would have to meet several requirements. Given the sagging fortunes of the campaign during the summer months, it would have to make a significant impression on the press and public. It would have to enhance Anderson's credibility. It therefore would have to offer realistic appraisals of existing conditions and avoid political hyperbole.

Moreover, to maintain the "Anderson Difference" the platform would have to be more specific and more candid than its major party counterparts. Yet, to be defensible it would have to be both internally coherent and consistent with Anderson's past record and current speeches. It would have to feature the many outspoken stands already taken by Anderson. It was also felt by the staff that the platform would have to be specific enough to be seen as a "program" rather than as a traditional platform and that it would have to set forth a fiscally responsible policy mix. Finally, for stylistic purposes it would have to be comprehensive yet balanced, with no policy area receiving a disproportionate amount of attention.

At the outset there was an internal debate whether the platform should be terse and crisp or long and detailed. There were evidently many advantages to brevity, but a short platform simply could not meet the desired criterion of programmatic specificity upon which Brown and others insisted, especially since Anderson wanted a document that would provide a solid intellectual underpinning for the campaign. Thus it was decided that there would be two versions of the platform: a comprehensive edition to set forth Anderson's program in detail and a shorter version to serve as a concise summary of the principal arguments. Frye, who had a broad understanding of the issues and who was an accomplished stylist, accepted the task of preparing the concise version, while the issues coordinators under Brown, Walker, and Knight undertook the production of the longer version. It was agreed that the two efforts would proceed simultaneously with close consultation and coordination to keep the versions consistent.

Anderson had promised the press that he would release his platform before Labor Day, thereby establishing a deadline for the completion of both documents. August was a chaotic month for many reasons, but work proceeded steadily. The issue coordinators prepared draft planks for their respective areas of expertise. These drafts were sent on to the candidate and then returned to the staff for revision. Walker, who had been on Anderson's congressional staff for many years, reviewed the material to ensure its consistency with Anderson's past record and with his fiscal commitments.

Anderson's extensive legislative history and his traditional practice of taking very specific stands on issues had created a long public record which defined the substantive parameters of the platform. His willingness throughout the campaign to take tough stands created its political context. In drafting the planks the issue coordinators drew upon memoranda submitted by members of advisory councils, notes from the briefing sessions, previously delivered Anderson speeches,[37] issue briefs released during the spring and summer months, and the advice of experts solicited during the drafting phase.

For example, the defense plank was drafted by Knight in consultation with Frye and Robert Bowie, a former Director of the Center for International Affairs at Harvard. The draft was then circulated to other defense experts. Among these were Barry Blechman, Steven Canby, Forrest Frank, Richard Garwin, Franklin Lindsey, Barry Posen, Robert Pranger, Robert Schoetzel, Deborah Shapley, R. James Woolsey, and Peter Zimmerman, all of whom reviewed either parts of the document or the plank in its entirety.

Several of these people were present at a series of long sessions which carefully worked over the draft for comment and further revision before its submission to Anderson. Although some of the participants in the process were political supporters of Anderson, others, in their capacity as outside experts, simply agreed to review the materials out of courtesy.

As another example, the energy plank was prepared by two issue coordinators, both with experience in the energy field: Rosamond Katz had worked for Resources for the Future, and Brian De Boinville had worked for the Department of Energy. Again the coordinators consulted

with members of the advisory groups, such as Robert
Williams and Paul Craig. Other experts, including Daniel
Yergin and Robert Pindyk, played a significant role in
developing energy policy throughout the campaign, and
many of their suggestions were incorporated into the
platform.

The staff included several additional people with
much experience in specialized issue areas who could
draw upon their own knowledge and who had direct access
to a wide range of experts. For example, Catherine
East, who drafted the plank on women's rights, had served
in a senior staff capacity on all the presidential advisory
commissions on the status of women from 1962 until 1977
and had done extensive research on many women's issues,
including ERA, domestic relations law, abortion, employment, and education. Grace Pierce, who played a major
role in drafting the environmental plank,[38] had been a
field representative and a legislative researcher for the
Wilderness Society. Elissa Sanchez, who worked on the
civil rights plank, had extensive contacts throughout the
Hispanic community.

In contrast to the normal procedure in the major
parties, very little outside interest group pressure was
brought directly to bear on the drafting process. There
were no major party factions to accomodate, no ideological divisions to smooth over, no threats of minority
planks, no possibility of embarrassing floor fights. Nor
was the staff beset by a wide range of important lobbyists promising political support or threatening political
retaliation.

Many staff members surmised that organized lobbies
were so accustomed to operating within the structure of
the two party system that they found it difficult to deal
with Anderson's independent candidacy. Few of the major
special interest lobbies ever considered endorsing Anderson. Fearing that they might jeopardize existing relations

with one or both of the major parties, they either ignored his candidacy or actively opposed it. As a consequence, few actively lobbied the campaign for inclusion of their views in Anderson's platform.[39]

Despite the absense of direct ouside pressure, however, issue coordinators were not blind to the larger political implications of their recommendations. Potential public reaction to the platform was certainly a concern of all who participated in the drafting process. To anticipate this, the staff sought advice from a wide range of people, including lobbyists and representatives of interest groups, who were always willing to supply information when asked. The drafters sought to be fully aware of the views of many potential constituencies. They also sought to understand the precise nuances attached by groups to key words in specialized policy areas so that the platform would exhibit a professional sensitivity to issues which groups regarded as important.

Even though advice was sought from a variety of interest groups, the initiative lay with the Anderson staff itself, and there was very little give-and-take between serious lobbyists and the staff. For example, contrary to practices in the two major parties, draft platform planks were not submitted to representatives of interest groups for their prior approval. Nor were such groups given advance access to any part of the platform. In this vein neither the fund-raising nor political divisions of the campaign made significant contributions to the platform.

There has been much speculation about the role of campaign strategist and media advisor David Garth with respect to issues development.[40] Garth made important contributions to formulating Mideast policy. He made suggestions of emphasis that were adopted in the areas of defense policy and the role of labor in the American economy. His backing had helped make possible the creation of the research staff in the first place.

Garth, however, played no direct role in the plat-form-drafting process; the research staff dealt directly with Anderson himself and eventually with Patrick Lucey on matters of policy.   Garth's chief concern was to ar-range for the mechanics and publicity coverage of the platform's release, not its content.

The platform-drafting process was not without its disputes.   Issue coordinators put forth many attractive suggestions which simply could not be funded within the constraints of the Anderson budget proposals.   Also, the farm plank, Cambodia, nuclear power, electoral college reform, Third World assistance, the Middle East, and several other areas produced extensive or intensive de-bates among the staff at various times.   In the end dis-putes between issue coordinators or other policy advisors could either be resolved by the supervisory staff or, if sufficiently important, by Anderson himself.

On the Monday before the Friday release date, Pat-rick Lucey was announced as Anderson's running mate. The research staff immediately gave him a draft of the work completed to that date and sought his views. Taking his role very seriously, he read the entire docu-ment, presented the staff with his annotated suggestions, and submitted the draft to his own policy advisors.   They responded with many useful and important suggestions that were quickly incorporated into the document. Lucey's suggestions for the civil rights plank were espe-cially important.

Lucey himself was generally pleased with the Ander-son platform draft.   He was disappointed that it did not endorse wage and price controls or a national health in-surance program, but he gave way to Anderson's reasoning for purposes of the platform, reserving his right as an "independent" Vice President to hold independent views on these two issues.

As the Labor Day deadline neared, work took on a frenetic quality.   Several marathon sessions were held with both Anderson and Lucey to iron out last minute changes.   The economic plank was reviewed word for word by Anderson in a working session with staff members during a long afternoon in the headquarters' upstairs kitchen, which also doubled as a conference room.   Two other lengthy sessions dealing with the remaining issues took place in available rooms on Capitol Hill.

An executive summary of the long version was prepared by Galston and Lehner, who then worked closely with Frye to ensure that the long and short versions were consistent.   As the deadline neared, remaining policy disputes between staff members were resolved by Anderson and Lucey.   After the final changes had been made, the staff worked all Thursday night to meet the Friday distribution deadline.   Early Friday morning, staff members were called to Anderson's office to clarify a few remaining points and to make some last minute changes in the text.   The relevant pages were pulled from the collated copies, retyped, and reinserted.   The completed copies of both the short and long versions were then released to the press at a briefing session called for that purpose on Friday afternoon, August 29.

THE PLATFORM IN POLITICAL PERSPECTIVE

The full Anderson/Lucey program was nearly 80,000 words in length--twice the size of the record-breaking 1980 Democratic Platform issued just a few weeks before. It claimed to offer a "new public philosophy" and a clear alternative to the "outdated quarrel between the old liberalism and an even older conservatism."

Early in the campaign Anderson had used the slogan (suggested to him by Lee Auspitz) that his "heart was on the left and his wallet was on the right." In many respects this phrase epitomized the platform.

The Anderson/Lucey economic proposals were considerably more conservative--in the sense of being fiscally responsible--than those of either the Republicans or the Democrats. Written at a time of recession, high interest rates, burgeoning deficits, and rising prices, the platform retains much of its validity four years later. Unlike the Republican Platform, it did not call for a massive personal income tax cut, extensive business tax cuts, or large increases in military spending. Its tax cut proposals for both individuals and businesses were targeted to achieve specific policy aims and were modest in their impact on the budget. Indexing of the personal income tax was proposed, but the platform stated that it could responsibly take effect only after the deficit had been brought under control.

Unlike the Democratic Platform, the Anderson/Lucey program did not embrace a large increase in public service (CETA) jobs to combat unemployment nor did it call for an expensive national health insurance plan. Its proposed spending increases were primarily for urban redevelopment (where special taxes were envisioned to fund it) and for rebuilding the American scientific and technological plant, with a special emphasis on energy research and space. By holding spending proposals in line and by not proposing large tax cuts, the platform realistically envisioned a declining deficit leading to a realizable surplus in about three years. Neither major party could have honestly promised this had all the provisions of its platform been fully carried out.

With respect to human rights issues, the Anderson/Lucey ticket was decidedly liberal. In these areas it was designed to distance itself from the Republican Platform. Anderson, who had a very strong civil rights record in Congress, was particularly appalled by the Republican

Party's retreat from its historic support for civil rights. He was especially upset by the Republican Platform's failure to endorse ERA, by its anti-abortion planks, and by its pledge that the next Republican president would use a person's stand on abortion as a criterion for appointing judges. His invitation to Mary Crisp to be the Campaign Chairperson immediately after she had been forced out of her position as Republican Cochairman by the party's right wing symbolized Anderson's belief that there was no longer a place within the Republican Party for any serious person concerned with the rights of women. The strong and far-reaching women's rights plank in his own platform was in part a response to the actions of the Republicans in Detroit. Similarly, the Anderson platform contained strong civil rights planks of concern to blacks, Hispanics, Native Americans, and other minorities.

Other liberal positions which set the Anderson program apart from that of the Republicans were its strong and extensive environmental section and its support for measures such as occupational safety.

Traditionally liberal positions that would lead to large federal expenditures, however, were treated with circumspection, thus separating the Anderson/Lucey platform from that of the Democrats. Although specific suggestions were made to improve federal programs in the areas of health care, education, welfare, and support for senior citizens, these proposals did not envision extensive increases in federal funding. It was Anderson's position that the budget simply could not afford these. Unlike the Republicans, however, he did not envision major cutbacks either. Both the defense and civilian sectors of the economy were to bear the burden of fiscal restraint, but neither was to undergo massive liquidation.

The first section of the platform, "The Economy," represented about one-third of its total length, and thus was given the greatest emphasis. Not only did this plank call for fiscal restraint and budgetary caution, it also called for:

--immediate anti-recessionary measures including extended unemployment compensation benefits, countercyclical revenue sharing and mortgage interest rate subsidies;

--an inflation-fighting strategy that buttressed monetary and fiscal restraint with a tax-based wage and price incentives program;

--a revised approach to combatting structural unemployment that stressed less reliance upon public sector jobs and greater emphasis upon job retraining with private sector participation;

--personal savings incentives, including expanded Individual Retirement Accounts (IRAs), large interest and dividend income tax exclusions, and liberalized capital gains treatment;

--increased private and public sector investment through liberalized depreciation allowances, temporary refundability of the investment tax credit, and increased support for government-owned infrastructure;

--the promotion of research and development, particularly basic research, through R&D tax credits, patent reform, and an increased government contribution;

--steps to reduce sharply our energy dependence, including a fifty cent a gallon gasoline tax, conservation initiatives, and expanded use of coal, solar, and other nonrenewable energy sources;

--a nuclear energy policy linking the future of nuclear power to reactor safety standards and action on nuclear waste;

--an industrial policy centered around an Industrial
Development Council composed of labor, management, and
government representatives and an Industrial Development
Administration to help stagnant industries adopt and
develop new production technologies.[41]

Beyond these general economic prescriptions, the Ander-
son/Lucey program addressed several specific concerns:
advocating tax breaks for small businesses, deregulation of
transportation industries, a farm export program, a revitalized space program, the creation of a Coal Export
Administration, and the legalization of Export Trading
Companies.

The "Meeting Human Needs" section of the program
struck a middle ground between the Democratic and
Republican Platforms, rejecting the lavish promises of the
Democrats and repudiating the Republican philosophy of
"benign neglect" towards the cities, the elderly, the handicapped, and the unemployed.

Taking note of the deteriorating capital stock in our
urban areas, Anderson and Lucey called for the creation
of an "Urban Reinvestment Trust Fund" that would provide a dedicated source of funding for major capital improvements of the "infrastructural" variety at a time
when few others were calling for investments of this
type.   A second trust fund, the "Community Transportation Trust Fund," was designed to provide similar funding
for nonhighway transportation needs.

While rejecting Democratic appeals for national
health insurance, the Anderson/Lucey program, called for
greater emphasis on preventive health care, health care
cost controls, and gradual expansion of Medicaid eligibility.   It rejected Republican plans to make welfare a state
responsibility and urged a larger federal welfare role
aimed at establishing a national minimum benefit level
for Aid to Families with Dependent Children (AFDC)

recipients, raising the federal contribution level, and providing work incentives.

The platform also supported a variety of provisions aimed at strengthening families, including elimination of the "marriage tax," increased federal child care support, and reform of alimony enforcement machinery. Recognizing the very special needs of Vietnam veterans, it supported more counseling and outreach programs for the victims of Agent Orange poisoning.

In the area of education Anderson and Lucey rejected the tuition tax credits and program retrenchments embraced by the Republicans and supported instead a strengthening of student loan programs for the economically disadvantaged. They also proposed a Presidential Commission on Primary and Secondary Education to study the crisis in public education and to make recommendations.

The Anderson/Lucey program contained a lengthy and detailed environmental plank covering ocean and coastal areas, public lands, Alaska, forestry, wilderness lands, urban parks, air and water quality, wildlife, water projects, and toxic substances. In all these areas Anderson and Lucey took environmentally responsible positions, particularly on such things as the Clean Air Act and the Toxic Waste Superfund.

The third major section of the platform was entitled "Guaranteeing Rights and Promoting Justice." This contained the extensive women's rights plank which called for ratification of ERA, for reproductive freedom, and for extending the rights of the homemaker. The section also contained other proposals aimed at combating discrimination, promoting minority business development programs, toughening enforcement of federal fair housing laws, and repealing federal laws that discriminated on the basis of sexual orientation.

The rights and justice section also supported handgun controls, pay equity reform for women, privacy safeguards, prison reform, and federal school desegregation aid, while opposing constitutional amendments barring or restricting abortion.

The final section of the platform set forth the Anderson/Lucey "Security Policy."   It began by saying:

> The first priority . . . must be to put our own house in order. Our economy and our technological base have always been the principal sources of our strength. Their decline is now the principal source of our weakness. . . . The next priority . . . is to restore and nurture our historic alliances, which have been neglected in the pursuit of global power balances that play our potential adversaries against each other.

The program called for regular talks with our allies on economic, energy, and trade matters and for prior consultation on actions requiring allied cooperation or affecting their vital interests. With reference to the Soviet Union, Anderson and Lucey promised that an Anderson administration "will not hesitate to take serious measures to resist Soviet political and military thrusts, but we will exercise our power in a responsible manner."

Consistent with their long-time support of Israel, Anderson and Lucey backed the Camp David Accords and the ongoing peace process. While opposing the creation of a West Bank Palestinian State, they supported a Jordanian role in "resolving the Palestinian questions." They further counseled "restraint in approving arms transfers to those nations which oppose the peace process and do not cooperate with our diplomatic efforts."

The Anderson/Lucey program called for a much broader American effort in building the economies of the

underdeveloped areas of the world and for strong measures to halt the proliferation of nuclear weapons.

The platform also contained an extensive defense
plank. In response to the Soviet military buildup, it ad-
vocated further strengthening of America's strategic and
conventional forces. It also emphasized that "we must
apply the most exacting standards of efficiency and accountability to the way we spend defense dollars." Programs, such as the MX missile, which did not meet such
standards were opposed, thus separating Anderson and
Lucey from both Reagan and Carter. Better purchasing
practices for the armed services were outlined.

The defense plank also stressed preserving deterrence, thereby rejecting by implication the "nuclear war
fighting" strategy of the Carter administration contained
in its Presidential Directive 59 which surfaced during the
summer months when the platform was being written. In
contrast to the positions of both Carter and Reagan at
the time the platform appeared, the defense plank contained a strong commitment to the SALT process.

Taken in its entirety, the platform was an attempt
to present a blueprint which would be a guide for future
policy decisions. This was both its principal strength and
its principal weakness. Its policy orientation tended to
attract the admiration of the press and issue specialists,
but it was not a document that could ever enjoy wide
circulation. As Jeff Greenfield put it, the platform "was
widely praised and largely unexamined (Anderson himself
said it seemed to bore audiences), but [it] helped bolster
the sense that Anderson was, in fact, a candidate of
ideas."[42] One staff member commented, neither in jest
nor entirely with approbation, "politicians are governing as
if they were campaigning. We have been campaigning as
if we were governing."

Still, such behavior was highly consistent with Anderson's public image and his own long-standing "good government" principles. There is little question that for Anderson and Lucey the platform was indeed a detailed contract with the people. In their cover letter accompanying the platform, they declared, "Too often party platforms are ignored by the candidates, after the election and even during the campaign. There is no ambiguity about our commitment to our platform. It's ours, we mean every word of it, and we'll stand by it, during and after the national campaign."

THE PLATFORM'S RECEPTION

The Anderson/Lucey campaign was pleased with the way the program was received. For the most part, press reaction was highly favorable. While some observers felt that it did not go far enough in staking out new territory, most gave it positive reviews. David Broder, a widely respected political columnist, said:

Independent Presidential candidate John B. Anderson has some interesting ideas to offer in the election year. . . . The 317-page platform that Anderson and his running mate, former Wisconsin Governor Patrick J. Lucey, issued last week is studded with specific proposals that are eminently worth discussion . . . maybe the best collection of new ideas ever assembled for the 1980s. . . .[43]

The *New York Times* editorialized, "It offers some welcome new ideas. . . . Even more useful is Mr. Anderson's willingness to address the central issues of the campaign."[44] The *Congressional Quarterly* reported, "The 317-page document put forth specific proposals on a vast array of national issues. . . ."[45]

Political commentators accurately measured the program's attempt to present a centrist approach to national problems. The *New York Times* in its August 31 cover story said:

> While a comparison of the independents' platform with those of the major parties risks oversimplification, the Anderson/Lucey proposals appear to be somewhat more conservative than the Democratic equivalent on social programs--lower spending and less government involvement--and more liberal than the Republican version--firmer on civil rights, energy and the environment. . . .

The paper wrote later on its editorial page, "In drafting his platform, Mr. Anderson was unencumbered by party ... and free to shoot at obvious targets. He aimed neither too far right nor left, but centered on independent voters and ticket-splitting Democrats.[46]

A *Washington Post* article described the economic proposals in the program as striking "a middle ground between the fiscal pronouncements in the two major party platforms."[47]

Commentators generally concurred that the Anderson/Lucey program was more fiscally responsible than the major party platforms:

> He advocated no dramatic new spending programs, proposing instead to revive the economy by spurring greater employment and spending in the private sector. . . .[48]

On economic matters, the independents are considerably more conservative about cutting taxes and increasing spending than either the Democrats or the Republicans. . . .[49]

Anderson and Lucey said in their opening letter that the program could be accomplished without "any massive new expenditures." Indeed, the platform proposed relatively modest new spending, relying mostly upon tax incentives to achieve its many goals. . . .[50]

Moreover, political writers observed that the program was consistent with Anderson's earlier pronouncements. One report concluded, "Generally, the positions taken were fiscally conservative and socially liberal, remaining true to the philosophical bent demonstrated by Anderson's more recent votes in Congress."[51] Another noted, "A 50 cents a gallon tax on gasoline is Independent Presidential Candidate John B. Anderson's most famous campaign idea. Fittingly, then, the gasoline tax is reflected both in letter and spirit in the energy program of Anderson's 'National Unity Campaign Platform.'"[52]

Others observed that the Anderson/Lucey program shunned excessive optimism. One report said, ". . . while hopeful in tone, the platform's theme was not cheerful. It pictured the United States as a short-sighted nation that would have to pay the price to regain economic and national security."[53]

Beyond the substantive differences with the major party platforms, the Anderson/Lucey program was seen as politically unique:

The Anderson-Lucey program differs markedly from party platforms in that it represents a personal pledge by the candidates to work for its provisions. Controversial planks in the Democratic and Republican platforms are often ignored during the campaign and thereafter.

The independent platform was also the product of a different process: constituted by more than a dozen Anderson aides with a wide variety of outside authorities, followed by a draft personally reviewed by Mr. Anderson. . . .[54]

While unique, the program also served to marshall public support, raise the campaign's credibility, and enhance Anderson's image as a serious contender. A few weeks after its release, the *Congressional Quarterly* reported, "The candidate's late summer rise in the polls was partially related to the release August 30 of a campaign platform, titled, 'The Program of the Anderson/Lucey National Unity Campaign.'"[55]

At the same time, the platform's release bolstered the argument for including Anderson in any presidential debates.   The League of Women Voters announced in early September that Anderson would be included, although the decision was made primarily on the basis of Anderson's standing in the polls.

THE BUDGET IMPACT STATEMENT

When the Anderson/Lucey program was unveiled on August 30th, it was also announced that an appendix, outlining its budgetary and inflationary implications, would be subsequently released. The *New York Times* reported:

. . . Anderson policy advisors plan to supplement the platform with a detailed budget analysis, estimating costs of the new programs, savings and where revenues will come from to approximate a balanced budget.

Such an account will be a novelty for his campaign. Ordinarily platforms of both major parties run

heavily toward promises of more government services
and lower taxes with little or no attempt to indicate
how much income would be required to finance the
overall package. . . .[56]

The idea itself was wholly consistent with Anderson's
emphasis on honesty about issues and wholly at odds with
platform tradition.   In truth, it was unprecedented.   No
party--major or minor--had ever before sought to put a
price on the complete set of its platform promises.

A few decades earlier, when major party platforms
were reasonably consistent with the goal of a balanced
budget, such an exercise may not have been needed.
Within the past twenty years, however, platforms have
become increasingly divorced from fiscal reality, inevita-
bly giving homage to the goal of a balanced budget while
proposing tax cuts and new programs whose enactment
would make such a goal clearly unattainable.

At the outset the drafters of the Anderson/Lucey
program hoped that the appendix could be released at the
same time as the platform.   Work on the appendix,
however, had to be delayed when timely completion of
the platform became a higher priority.   When the platform was released at the end of August, as promised
early that summer by the candidate, reporters were told
that the appendix would be ready in three weeks, a self-
imposed deadline that later slipped by another three
weeks, largely because the demand for substantive
speeches rose dramatically after Labor Day (see Appendix
I) and because the staff was heavily involved with the
preparation for the Reagan debate.   Anderson repeated
the pledge to release a financial accounting during the
Baltimore debate in response to a question by Jane
Bryant Quinn.

The campaign's domestic policy advisor, Robert
Walker, assumed the principal responsibility for assembling

the project. With a background in economics and several years experience on Capitol Hill, he was best suited for the task. As a first step, all budget items in the platform were carefully cataloged and their costs or revenue impacts estimated according to official Congressional Budget Office cost estimates and revenue projections provided by the Joint Committee on Taxation. In those areas where no official estimates existed, in-house estimates were made after consulting with program or budget experts on the Hill.

To give real meaning to those numbers, however, a baseline budget had to be used for a basis of comparison. The budget for fiscal year 1981, as approved by the Senate Budget Committee in its report on the Second Concurrent Budget Resolution, was chosen for that purpose.[57] The economic assumptions used in formulating the committee's report were regarded as a fair consensus forecast, and its recommendations reflected what the next administration was likely to inherit in the way of a budget.

The next step was to draft a revised version of the Senate Budget Committee's budget report that would reflect accurately what an Anderson administration budget would be like for each of the fiscal years covered by the report (fiscal years 1981 through 1985). The Senate Committee's report broke the budget down into the thirteen functional budget categories that comprise a Congressional Budget Resolution and then further subdivided each function into several "missions" or subcategories, like "Strategic Forces" under the defense function or "Farm Income Stabilization" under the agriculture function.

In those areas where the Senate Budget Committee's recommendations cut deeper than the Anderson/Lucey program, appropriate upward adjustments were made. Likewise, downward adjustments were made when committee recommendations clearly exceeded Anderson/Lucey

plans. In each instance the appendix explained any differences in figures or totals. Finally, from these figures
aggregrate outlays and revenues were calculated along
with the resulting deficits and surpluses.

The final product, released October 13, showed the
Anderson/Lucey program leading to a balanced budget by
fiscal year 1983 if the underlying economic assumptions
held true. It showed a $26 billion surplus by fiscal year
1985. When the report was presented, however, the
transmittal letter warned:

> While the program analysis that follows projects
> a balanced budget for fiscal year 1983 . . . we make
> no such pledge. Nor do we promise a specified level
> of tax relief, even though the accompanying projec-
> tions show considerable room for tax relief, beginning
> in fiscal year 1983.
> We believe, however, that the accompanying
> budget analysis reveals the realistic nature of the
> Anderson/Lucey program. It does not rely upon "mir-
> rors." No attempt has been made to put forth
> spurious, self-serving claims regarding the ability of
> the next administration to root out fraud and abuse
> in federal programs. . . . Nor does it make claims of
> large "revenue feedbacks" from proposed tax reduc-
> tions. . . .

In releasing the report, Anderson and Lucey also
chided and challenged their opponents: "It is our hope
that the two major party candidates will present a full
and fair cost accounting of their respective party platforms. We are confident that any such objective would
reveal internal inconsistencies of a very fundamental
nature."

There were, of course, such fundamental inconsistencies.
Both major party platforms promised a balanced budget:

the Republicans pledged to, "balance the budget and reduce spending through legislative actions," and the Democrats vowed to, "live within the limits of our anticipated
revenues." Yet both prescribed policies that virtually
guaranteed ever increasing deficits.

Senator Orrin Hatch's office undertook a study of
the Democratic Platform and discovered, using Congressional Budget Office program estimates, that it "would
add $30 billion in outlays in fiscal year 1981 and $389
billion over the fiscal years 1981 to 1985."[58] Hatch's
study concluded that Democratic spending plans combined
with President Carter's proposed tax cut would push the
deficit to $106 billion by fiscal year 1982.

Republicans, if anything, were even more irresponsible. The Carter administration published an informal
study of Republican plans and concluded that their tax
cut proposals threatened to reduce fiscal year 1985 budget receipts by as much as $285 billion and would result
in a deficit of $212 billion unless spending was cut. This
prediction proved to be surprisingly accurate.

After releasing the Anderson/Lucey program appendix, the Anderson campaign presented its own evaluation
of the Republican and Democratic Platforms. It concluded that even under conservative budget assumptions
the major party platforms would lead to ever-widening
deficits, particularly the Republican Platform. Projections
for the latter showed federal deficits exceeding $100 bil-
lion even if the economy remained strong.

The experience of the Budget appendix, indeed the
whole experience of the platform-writing process, showed
the crucial role that can be played by an issues staff in
a modern campaign. If campaigns of the future are to
produce sophisticated and coherent platforms and policy
statements to which candidates can be held accountable,

then those campaigns will have to rely more upon good staff work to produce such documents.

There are enormous opportunities, both in the major parties and in the new smaller parties, for improvement in the platform writing process and in the production of quality campaign materials. Just as Congress found during the 1960s and 1970s that its legislative mission could not be adequately performed without a significant staff, so too may presidential candidates and political parties be forced to develop more extensive staffs in the future to produce credible issue proposals that will bear the scrutiny of ever more sophisticated political consumers in the press and among the public.

Given the experience of recent years, it should be the case that some audiences, at least, will demand stricter accountability from politicians with respect to the implementability of their platforms. It should not be surprising if the press and opinion leaders in the future demand credible assessments of a platform's impact upon such areas as the budget, the environment, minority employment, and inflation. If this occurs, then the importance of staff work will be increased, and the relationship between staff input and traditional political inputs may have to be redefined.

*   *   *

In the election of 1980 the Anderson/Lucey ticket received just under seven percent of the national vote cast for president. Even though Anderson lost, his candidacy, like earlier independent or third party bids, left a lasting political impact. Many issues raised by him received wider national attention as a result. Many of his ideas were adopted quietly by the major parties. More important, his willingness to tackle tough i openly and with intellectual honesty and vigor l a new level of expectations among the American public. It is hoped that major party platforms in the future will be more specific, programmatic, and realistic as a result of the 1980 Anderson effort and the model he presented to the public.

NOTES

1. For a compilation of platforms, dating from the Democratic Platform of 1840, see Donald Bruce Johnson, ed., *National Party Platforms 1840-1956*, and *Volume II, 1956-1976* (Urbana, Illinois, 1978).

2. In 1924 La Follette issued a short platform statement, but it was issued in connection with the Conference for Progressive Political Action. George Wallace's 1968 platform was issued under the authority of the American Independent Party that he formed.

3. James W. Davis, *National Conventions: Nominations Under the Big Top*, (Woodbury, New York, 1972), 41.

4. Malcom Moos and Stephen Hess, *Hats in the Ring: The Making of Presidential Candidates* (New York, 1960), 102.

5. Hugh A. Bone, *American Politics and the Party System* (New York, 1965), 326.

6. Ibid.

7. *National Democratic Platform 1976*, cover.

8. Edward W. Chester, *A Guide to Political Platforms* (Hamden, Connecticut, 1977), 43. See reference to Marvin Weisbord, "Again the Platform Builders Hammer Away," *New York Times Magazine*, 5 July 1964, 2B.

9. Gerald Pomper, *Elections in America: Control and Influence in Democratic Politics*, 2d ed. (New York, 1980), 128-77. See also, Pomper, "Controls and Influence

in American Elections," *American Behavioral Scientist*, vol. 13, November-December 1969, 223-28.

10. Pomper, *Elections in America*, 163.

11. Ibid., 134-35.

12. Ibid., 141.

13. Ibid.

14. Ibid., 150-51.

15. Ibid., 151.

16. These are not the only examples of major inconsistencies. For instance, the 1980 Republican Platform urged a strengthened dollar in the paragraph immediately preceding a call for dramatic increases in exports; it cited inflation as primarily a monetary problem (too many dollars chasing too few goods) but presented mostly fiscal remedies; and it deprecated the Democrats' "spending away" the Social Security Trust Fund monies while simultaneously pledging to maintain the level of social security support.

17. The 1976 Republican Platform, for instance, contained a number of concessions to the conservative wing of the party.

18. Although not always. The White House apparently lost a significant amount of its control over the process at the Republican Convention in 1976. See Martha Weinberg, "Writing the Republican Platform," *Political Science Quarterly*, Winter 1977-78. The concessions, however, may have been a conscious strategem to shore up conservative support.

19. See Richard C. Bain, *Convention Decisions and Voting Records* (Washington D.C., 1960).   In conventions since 1956 the pattern has not changed.   See also Paul T. David, "Party Platforms as National Plans," *Public Administration Review*, vol. 31, May-June 1971, 305.

20. See Congressional Quarterly, Inc., *National Party Conventions 1831-1976* (Washington, D.C., 1979).

21. See, Judith H. Parris, *The Convention Problem: Issues in the Reform of Presidential Nominating Procedures* (Washington, D.C., 1972), 120.

22. Bone, *American Politics*, 324.

23. Results less spectacular but still consistent with Pomper's were found on the state level (in Illinois and Wisconsin) by Richard C. Elling.   See "State Party Platforms and State Legislative Performance: A Comparative Analysis," *American Journal of Political Science,* May 1979, 383-405.

24. John Kessel, "The Seasons of Presidential Politics," *Social Science Quarterly,* December 1977, 433.

25. See Gerald Pomper, *Nominating the President* (Chicago, 1963), 75-82.

26. Prohibition is a good historic example; the 1964 Republican Platform is a more recent illustration.

27. Harry Truman began his successful climb from perceived political oblivion in 1948 by calling the Republican Congress back into session after the nominating conventions and asking it to enact the Republican Platform (which it wouldn't)--thereby calling Dewey's bluff and giving credence to the epithet "Do-nothing Congress."

28. Paul T. David, "Party Platforms,"   303-15.

29. Ibid., 303-04.

30. 30 August 1978.

31. 28 August 1979.

32. Robert J. Samuelson, "Politics and a Gas Tax," *National Journal*, 8 September 1979, 1493.

33. 17 October 1979.

34. 17 September 1979.

35. *Washington Star*, 21 December 1979.

36. For example, the briefing session on Soviet-American relations, which took place on 30 May 1980, in New York, included as participants: Cyril Black, director of the Center for International Studies at Princeton (Soviet history and culture); Joseph Berliner, Professor of Economics at Brandeis (Soviet economy); William Corey, president of B'nai B'rith (Soviet human rights policies); Erik Hoffmann, Professor of Political Science at the State University of New York at Albany (Soviet science and technology); Kenneth Maxwell, Columbia University (Soviet Third World relations); and Robin Laird, Visiting scholar, Woodrow Wilson Center (Soviet military strategy). The briefing session on France included: James Goldsborough, research associate, Carnegie Endowment; Nicholas Wahl, director of the Institute for French Studies, New York University; Andrew Pierre, Council on Foreign Relations, and Robin Laird, as above.

37. For example, the urban plank drew substantially upon speech drafts and position papers developed during the early summer by William Galston who, in turn, built upon earlier speech drafts written during the Republican phase by Howard Gillette and John Topping.

38. See the description of the writing of the environmental plank in the *Washington Post,* 31 August 1980, A6-A7.

39. One significant exception was AIPAC; Gay Rights organizations were another. Many smaller lobbies made their presence known. A prize for persistence should have been awarded to the "save the porpoises" lobby whose representative continually importuned the staff with eloquence on behalf of his cetaceous clients.

40. See Mark Bisnow, *The Diary of a Dark Horse* (Carbondale, Illinois), 1983.

41. Consideration was given to Felix Rohatyn's proposed multibillion dollar Reconstruction Finance Corporation to help ailing industries and cities, but it was rejected as being too ambitious and costly.

42. Jeff Greenfield, *The Real Campaign* (New York, 1982), 204.

43. *Washington Post,* 7 September 1980.

44. 3 September 1980.

45. Richard Whittle, "John Anderson Still Trying to Dump his 'Spoiler' Image," *Congressional Quarterly,* 27 September 1980, 2835.

46. 3 September 1980.

47. T. R. Reid, 5 September 1980.

48. Rhodes Cook, "Anderson Proposes Platform Reflecting 'Wallet on Right, Heart on Left' Philosophy," *Congressional Quarterly,* 6 September 1980.

49. *Washington Post,* 31 August 1980.

50. Whittle, "'Spoiler' Image."

51. Ibid.

52. T.R. Reid, *Washington Post*, 7 September 1980.

53. Whittle, "'Spoiler' Image."

54. *New York Times*, 31 August 1980.

55. Whittle, "'Spoiler' Image."

56. 31 August 1980.

57. Issued 27 August 1980.

58. *Congressional Record*, 23 September 1980, S13155.

THE PROGRAM
OF THE
ANDERSON/LUCEY
NATIONAL UNITY CAMPAIGN

JOHN B. ANDERSON
PATRICK J. LUCEY
THE NATIONAL UNITY CAMPAIGN

TABLE OF CONTENTS

3

Security Policy (continued)

Erratum: There is no page 257.

6

TO THE AMERICAN PEOPLE:

In the past few weeks, the traditional political parties have released their traditional platforms. Now we are releasing ours -- an untraditional program for America that responds to new challenges in new ways.

Our program is presented in two related documents. The first, "Rebuilding a Society that Works; An Agenda for America" highlights many of the major themes and proposals that our National Unity Campaign will offer to the nation. It is relatively short and deliberately selective. It states our goals and sketches in general terms how we intend to promote them. It is intended as a synthesis and an introduction to our program.

The second document, "The Program of the Anderson/Lucey National Unity Campaign," presents the details of our legislative and executive program in every major area of concern to this nation. It is divided into three sections. First, the Introduction sets forth the public philosophy that guides and unifies our program. The second, the body of the document, details our program in the general areas of economic policy, foreign and defense policy, social policy, and civil and human rights. The final section deals with the practical problems of governance. It substantiates our conviction that an Independent administration can effectively govern this nation.

7

It should be clear that we do not desire to implement every proposal in this program in the first year of an Anderson Administration. The full fiscal impacts of these intiatives are to be spread over the next four years. It would be fiscally irresponsible to do otherwise.

The program does not contain any massive new expenditures on the scale of a $60 billion land-based missile or a $25 billion-a-year comprehensive national health insurance scheme. Nor does the program call for large personal income tax cuts in advance of a balanced budget.

Moreover, we anticipate that the initiatives outlined in this program are small enough in their revenue impacts to be accommodated by the normal real dollar growth in revenues associated with an expanding economy. We will, within the next three weeks, issue a budgetary impact statement for our program.

How does our program differ from traditional party platforms?

First, it is specific. We have not been satisfied to express a vague commitment to abstract goals. We have spelled out our intentions; in many instances we have proposed specific legislation.

Second, it is directed toward problem-solving. We believe that government must be bold and active, but that it should not act for the sake of acting. We firmly believe in the old maxim, "If it isn't broken, don't fix it." In each section of our program, therefore, we begin by stating the real, pressing, unavoidable problems we face. And everything

iii

program, therefore, we begin by stating the real, pressing, unavoidable problems we face. And everything we propose is intended to advance this nation towards solving these problems.

Third, our program is <u>coherent</u>. We believe that government fails when it loses its sense of overall purpose and direction. We believe that the public interest is neglected when government disintegrates into a grab-bag of uncoordinated, contradictory efforts to serve special interests.

Our proposals are consistent with the public philosophy which guides our unity campaign. Its principles are both simple and profound. We believe America is in peril because our tradition of self-government has been eroded. We believe we must prepare for the future; that we must be cognizant of its limits, and aggresively pursue its opportunities. We believe we must rebuild America, and that the government must act as a catalyst to encourage every American to participate in the task of rebuilding. We believe that the rebuilding of America will not have succeeded unless we have persevered in our efforts to establish justice for all Americans.

Fourth, our program is <u>realistic</u>. We know that our resources are limited and that they must be applied to our most basic and pressing needs. We have not promised more than our federal budget and our national economy can bear. And we have not avoided the hard choices. As we constructed this program, we thought in terms of what our responsibilities would be if we were governing this nation. It is a strategy of governance, not a game plan for winning the election.

Fifth, our program is a personal <u>commitment</u>. Harry Truman was right when he said that a platform ought to be a contract with the American people. But too often party platforms are ignored by the candidates, after the election and even during the campaign. This year, for example, the Democratic National Convention repudiated much of the economic program of its own party's nominee, and he, in turn, rejected their decisions. Alternatively, the Republican Vice Presidential candidate ran virtually his whole primary campaign <u>against</u> proposals appearing in the platform upon which he is now running. There is no ambiguity about our commitment to our platform. It's <u>ours</u>, we mean every word of it, and we'll stand by it, during and after the national campaign.

Although our program is a personal commitment, it is not the work of our hands alone. We have consulted with business executives and assembly-line workers and farmers and with citizens concerned about our nation's future. We have analyzed and debated every proposal, and we have drafted and redrafted them until we were fully satisfied. We are proud of this program and we will fight hard for it.

We urge you to read and consider the program, and to compare it with those of the traditional parties. At this time of national testing, we must move beyond the politics of empty tactics and superficial images. We must face and debate the real issues. You may disagree with what we say, but we want you to know what we believe and what we will do if elected. You have a right to know what we stand for and what we will we will try to get enacted into legislation. The program will also help you identify the main issues we must debate and the problems we must solve. Our country needs the energy, the involvement, the concern of each one of you.

Sincerely,

John B. Anderson

Patrick J. Lucey

I. INTRODUCTION

Nearly thirty years ago, at the beginning of his campaign
for the Presidency, Adlai Stevenson declared:

> Let's talk sense to the American people. Let's
> tell them the truth, that there are no gains
> without pains.

This courageous warning is as necessary now as it was in 1952.
We cannot expect that the 1980s will be an easy decade. Our
nation faces its gravest challenge since the Second World War.
We cannot expect that our problems will solve themselves.
They are not going to go away like some bad dream. We must
make changes, and in the short run they will be painful.
We can rebuild our economy and regain control of our national
destiny, but we will have to pay a price for our recovery.

To cure our nation's ills, we must begin by understanding
them.

In the century after the Civil War, we Americans built
the greatest economy and society the world has ever seen. We
planned for the future, and we invested in it. We built
railroads and dams and factories and cities. We invented
the telephone and mass-produced automobiles at prices most
people could afford. We created an unsurpassed system of
public education and universities. We invested in systems of

security for the ill, the aged, and the unemployed. Our nation
worked, and other countries admired our efficient, undogmatic
common sense. When the world asked: What is the future?, the
answer always was: Look to America.

But in the past twenty years our political leaders and
political parties have failed the nation. We gradually abandoned
the practices that made us great. We stopped planning, we
stopped saving, and we stopped investing. We ignored the needs
of tomorrow. We failed to take care of what we had built. And
we lived beyond our means.

Nations, like families, cannot postpone their bills
indefinitely. And our nation's bills have now come due.

---Our economy is locked in a cycle of inflation, recession,
and high interest rates.

---Our factories are outdated and uncompetitive in world
markets.

---The foundations of our older cities--the bridges, the
streets, the water mains--are crumbling.

---Our system of public education is no longer teaching
many of our children the skills they need to get jobs and
survive in our society.

---We have neglected our military equipment and our
military personnel.

---Worst of all, we have lost control over our economy, our
foreign policy, indeed our very destiny, because we have lacked
the will to declare our independence from foreign oil.

4

A generation of political leaders has told us that we could run bigger and bigger budget deficits without raising inflation and interest rates. A generation of political leaders has told us that we could concentrate on the interests of particular groups in our society and that the general interest of the nation would somehow take care of itself. A generation of political leaders has told us that we could get something for nothing.

---We were told that we could fight a war without paying for it.

---We were told that we could clean up the environment without paying for it.

---We were told that we could increase pensions and social services without paying for them.

---We were told that we could increase our consumption of ever-costlier foreign oil, without paying for it.

It has been a time of deception and illusion. And it must end now. Let us never again be told that we can get something for nothing. And let us never again be told that we can govern ourselves without making hard choices.

Turning this country around won't be easy. Our political system is now dominated by a jumble of special interest groups locked in a heedless struggle for private gain, ignoring the greater good of a healthier and more just society. We are close to becoming a stalemated society, locked into a politics of paralysis, where each interest group blocks any policy, no matter how wise and how necessary, if its own interests are threatened.

But our difficulties go even deeper than political illusion
and political stalemate. We are also suffering from the manifest
exhaustion of our political ideas.

Nearly half a century ago, Franklin Roosevelt took office
amidst a national crisis and set in motion the policies that we
have come to call the New Deal. These policies were designed
to solve specific problems and to confront the devastation of the
Great Depression. They were appropriate to the times, and they
contributed to the relief of human misery and to the national
recovery.

The Democratic party still clings to the policies of the
New Deal. But today our circumstances are very different.
The policies that once battled deflation now spur inflation.
The policies that stimulated production now diminish productivity.
The policies that attacked unemployment now actually contribute
to it. The policies that once ministered to human misery now
perpetuate it.

The Republican party has responded to the exhaustion of
the New Deal approach in two contradictory, and equally
erroneous, ways: it has embraced New Deal economics while it
seeks to repeal New Deal social policy.

The Republicans tell us that we should cut personal income
taxes across the board, by one-third. If we follow this advice,
we will not save and invest more, we will spend and consume more.
We will have skyrocketing interest rates that will choke off
economic recovery, further stifle our automobile and housing
industries, and plunge us into an even deeper recession. We will

have record budget deficits and, to finance them, we will have an
explosive growth in the money supply that will produce a record
inflation. This is not a program for national recovery; it
is a formula for national bankruptcy.

At the same time, Republicans advocate massive cutbacks in
social programs. Their platform talks incessantly about freedom,
but hardly ever about justice. It talks of liberating individuals
from big government, but it would only liberate those least in
need of assistance from their responsibilities to the nation.

This outdated quarrel between the old liberalism and an
even older conservatism, which the two major parties are about
to resume, has ceased to illuminate our most pressing public problems.
Far away from the discord and rancour of party strife, the American
people have reflected on the experience of this century, and we
now agree on some basic truths.

We are all liberals, we are all conservatives. We all believe
that prosperity without justice is unacceptable, and that justice
without prosperity is unattainable. We all know that government
must be bold and purposeful, but that it cannot do for us what we
can only do for ourselves. We all believe that individuals are
responsible for their acts, but not for the conditions within
which they act. We all believe that life without liberty is
intolerable, but that liberty without order is self-defeating.
And we all know that this consensus must guide us as we
seek solutions to our problems.

The Anderson campaign is based on a new public philosophy
--one that neither repeats nor repeals the past, but rather builds
upon it. Its principles are clear and simple. America is in
peril because her foundations have been neglected in the past
generation. We must plan for the future, we must save for the
future, and we must invest in it. We must rebuild America.
For the most part, government cannot do this directly. Rather,
it must act boldly to create a new climate, and a new framework
of incentives, that encourage individuals and businesses to
get to work at the task of rebuilding. All Americans must
contribute to, and help pay for, our national recovery, but the
burdens must be allocated in proportion to the ability of
individuals and groups to bear them. The rebuilding of America
cannot succeed unless we move toward the future united; but we
cannot remain united unless we persevere in our efforts to
establish justice for all Americans.

To rebuild America, we must begin by restoring our economic
vitality. To do this, an Anderson Administration will move forward
on three fronts.

First, we will use the tax code to limit consumption, and
increase savings and capital formation.

Second, we will use fiscal policy to bring inflation under
control and to restore a stable, predictable environment for
long-term planning and investment. We cannot halt inflation
until we stop printing money faster than we produce goods and
services. But we can only slow the creation of money if we
restore the balance of our federal budget, not in every year

necessarily, but rather over the course of each business cycle.
This will require moderation, discipline, and the willingness
to make hard, explicit choices.

Third, an Anderson Administration will move aggressively
to keep American capital at home to be used for American purposes,
by sharply reducing our dependence on imported oil. We will tax
gasoline to reduce consumption, and we will set in motion
programs to save energy in transportation, in our homes, and
indeed in every aspect of our lives.

These measures will generate a substantial pool of investment
capital. An Anderson administration will use these funds to
put Americans back to work rebuilding America by creating new
arenas for their energy and inventiveness.

---We will put Americans back to work retooling our aging
factories. We will not allow the Detroits and the Youngstowns
of this nation to die. And as we retool our factories, we will
preserve the kinds of jobs American workers want and deserve
--permanent, productive jobs with prospects for advancement,
not temporary, make-work, dead-end jobs.

---We will assist the smaller businesses that have always
produced most of the new ideas and new jobs for America and will
do so again, if only we lift the burden of taxation and regulation
from their backs.

---We will stimulate technological innovation by providing
new tax incentives to industry for research and development, and
by increasing federal support for basic scientific research and
for our space program.

---We will put Americans back to work rebuilding the street
the bridges, and the water mains of our crumbling cities with a
$4 billion annual Urban Reinvestment Trust Fund. We will put
our unemployed construction workers back to work building
housing for America with cost-effective mortgage subsidies,
and tax-exempt mortgage savings accounts for young couples. And
we will use tax incentives and direct subsidies to neighborhood
organizations to put Americans to work renovating the dwellings
and rebuilding the economic base of the decaying neighborhoods
of our inner cities.

---We will put Americans back to work building public
transportation for the 1980s with a $4 billion annual Community
Transportation Trust Fund. At the same time, we will move toward
the transportation system our economy needs, by rebuilding the
railroads, the highways, and the ports of this country.

---We will rebuild our system of public education. We
will make public education an attractive career once again
for our ablest college graduates, and we will vigorously employ
the new Department of Education to promote quality basic educati
for all our children.

---We will keep Americans at work in our most basic industr
agriculture, by taking steps to preserve the family farm. We
will treat farmers as small businessmen, and give them tax break
for investment in machinery and buildings. We will change the
tax code to recognize the contribution of farm women and
to reduce obstacles to the transmission of family farms from
parents to children.

---An Anderson Administration will rebuild American
military strength. We will pay the men and women in our
volunteer armed forces what they need and richly deserve.
We will rehabilitate our military equipment, so that it
is really ready for use in emergencies. And we will restore
the military balance with efficient and reliable new weapons
systems, but not with costly boondoggles like the MX missile
that will not increase our security but will only take away
scarce resources from the weapons we really need.

As we move toward energy self-reliance, and as we rebuild
our economy and our military strength, we will once again be
able to deal consistently with friend and foe alike.

An Anderson administration will follow the prudent policy
of rebuilding America's alliances with the nations that most
closely share our interests and our values, by treating them
as equal partners. We will never act in matters of joint concern
without consulting them, and we will never expect them to
follow us blindly.

To our adversaries, an Anderson Administration will always
offer opportunities for negotiation, for the reduction of arms,
and for the easing of tensions. We will press for the
ratification of SALT II and for the next stage in arms control
negotiations--a real reduction, not just limitation, of
strategic weapons. At the same time, we will allow no one to
mistake moderation for weakness. We will make it clear to
our adversaries that we will resist to the utmost any attempt
at subversion and conquest. And we will never fear to aid

those who are truly fighting for freedom.

As we rebuild America, at home and abroad, we will hold fast to our vision of a just America.

---An Anderson Administration will work for the even-handed application of our statutes to all citizens, and we will strongly support the efforts of the United States Commission on Civil Rights to impose reasonable, uniform standards on police use of deadly force.

---An Anderson Administration will work for fair housing laws with teeth in them.

---An Anderson Administration will carefully review the report of the Select Commission on Immigration, with the goal of devising a truly color-blind immigration policy.

---An Anderson Administration will use its resources of persuasion to obtain enactment of the Equal Rights Amendment and to block adoption of statutory and Constitutional restrictions on every woman's freedom of choice in matters of reproduction.

---An Anderson Administration will strive to promote economic justice. We will work for a more equitable system of taxation, and we will resist tax cuts, such as the Reagan-Kemp-Roth proposal, that give a bonanza to the rich, crumbs to the middle class, and nothing at all to the poor. As we reduce unemployment, we will seek to reduce disparities in the rate of unemployment among different groups in our population. We will not continue to tolerate unemployment

rates above 40% in our inner cities. And we will not use
unemployment as a weapon in the fight against inflation.

These measures are all part of a larger whole--the
American vision of a society in which all enjoy genuinely
equal opportunity to develop their gift and to go as far as
their talents and energies will allow. This is the justice
the Preamble of our Constitution requires us to establish.

The struggle to rebuild America and to establish justice
will be long and arduous. But we can do the job. The American
people do not suffer from any mysterious malaise. They are
weary of bad government, to be sure. But they are bursting with
ideas, with energy, and with the desire for a better future.
They are willing to sacrifice to gain that future. All
they want is a government that presents them with a clear,
believable program for the future, that enables them to save
and to plan with confidence, that encourages innovation and
risk-taking, that reduces regulation and liberates their energies.
This is the kind of government an Anderson administration will
give them.

With sensible policies, we cannot fail to surmount our
current problems. We are rich in natural resources, and in
human skill and energy. We have stable and flexible political
institutions. We hold fast to a vision of human freedom that
brings streams of refugees to our shores each year.

13

So let us take heart as we recall our strengths. We must
make sacrifices, to be sure. We must allocate them openly and
honestly. We must protect those who cannot easily bear additional
burdens. Those of us who have prospered in America must
contribute generously to the task of rebuilding the nation. And
we must move toward the future resolutely united, as <u>one</u>
nation, <u>indivisible</u>. For, as Theodore Roosevelt once reminded
us,

> The fundamental rule in our national life--
> the rule which underlies all others--is that
> in the long run, we shall go up or down together.

II. THE ECONOMY

Introduction

Something has gone wrong. A nation whose productive
capacity made it the arsenal of democracy and the envy of
the world today finds itself plagued by a shrinking capacity to produce and a growing inability to compete in the
world marketplace.

Once the world's leading producer of steel, we now
find our output surpassed by both the Soviet Union and
Japan. A year ago, the United States was the leading
manufacturer of automobiles. Today, we are second. Even
in high technology markets, once the near-exclusive reserve
of American business, we find ourselves increasingly unable
to compete.

Something indeed is wrong.

The nation's productive capacity has suffered from a
decade of neglect. The "guns and butter" policies of the
late 1960's led to a level of public and private consumption

that ignored the critical investment needs of the economy. During the course of the past decade, the rate of personal savings has declined sharply, and government borrowing has dramatically increased. As a result, our rate of capital investment, which long ago fell behind the efforts of our chief foreign competitors, has declined further still. Our continuing failure to save and invest imperils our economic vitality and mortgages our hopes for a better and more prosperous tomorrow.

We can no longer afford to live off our past labors, manufacturing in obsolete plants with outmoded technology. There is an urgent need to rebuild our productive capacity to create jobs for the unemployed and to lessen inflationary pressures. The continuing failure of the Carter administration to take necessary actions threatens to generate yet another decade of economic stagnation with a resulting loss of purchasing power and employment opportunities.

Our tax laws penalize thrift. A penny saved is no longer a penny earned. Although inflation erodes the value of personal savings, the federal government still taxes the nominal interest received. As a consequence, the personal savings rate has declined steadily in recent years. In

January of this year, the personal savings rate fell to a
29-year low.

Our tax laws have discouraged investment in capital
plant and equipment. Between 1962 and 1968, real business
investment expanded at an annual rate of 7 percent. During
the past six years, however, real business investment has
expanded at an annual average of only 2 percent.

A nation, once famed for its entrepreneurial spirit,
is in danger of losing its competitive vitality. Small businesses, burdened by excessive taxation and regulation and
saddled by high interest rates, have failed in recent years
to generate the necessary jobs and technology. Large businesses, hampered by inadequate depreciation allowances, have
failed to undertake the necessary retooling--resulting in an
erosion of our industrial base.

Throughout most of the 1950's and 1960's, productivity grew
at an annual rate of nearly 3 percent. Growth slowed to less
than 2 percent in the 1970's. And in the first half of 1980,
after 18 months of near constant decline, productivity has
fallen to 1977 levels.

As individuals, as businesses, and as a nation, we have
lost our ability to plan for the future. We have become a
society that lives for today and ignores the needs of tomorrow.

The job of restoring our economic vitality requires a broad-based attack on the root causes of our economic decline. Nothing less than a comprehensive approach will suffice.

Our task is the rebuilding of America.

Immediate Problems

The 1980 Recession

The disastrous rise in interest rates to record peaks in the first half of 1980 precipitated one of the worst, if not the worst, recession in the post-war era. Auto sales in May fell 42 percent below the previous year's level. Housing starts declined from an annual rate of 1.8 million earlier in the year to less than 1.0 million new starts in May.

Today, over 250,000 auto workers are on indefinite lay-offs with 50,000 more on temporary layoffs. Over 2 million Americans have been added to the unemployment rolls in the past four months. While there are preliminary indications that the housing and auto sectors of the economy are begin-ning to recover, unemployment is expected to rise still higher in the months ahead.

We cannot remain indifferent to the hardship of those who have lost their jobs, nor to the threat of future lay-offs. We must expand the eligibility for extended unemploy-ment compensation and adopt a countercyclical revenue sharing

program providing $500 million in relief for hard-pressed
communities in fiscal year 1981 and $1 billion for fiscal
year 1982. We must ensure adequate funding of summer youth
jobs programs and other youth employment initiatives. We
must also seek effective implementation of the Brooke-Cranston
program to revive the housing market if present conditions pers

Most important, however, we must resist appeals for
either large-scale spending increases or massive tax cuts
that would serve to further exacerbate the $30 billion def-
icit anticipated for fiscal year 1981. A larger deficit
at this juncture would mean increased government borrowing
and higher interest rates. The resulting credit squeeze
would further retard the recovery of the interest-sensitive
sectors of the economy, including the auto, housing, and the
capital goods industries. This danger requires a very cautious
and selective approach to all fiscal policy choices.

Inflation

Although inflation, as measured by the consumer price
index, has receded from the 18 percent rate recorded in the
first quarter of 1980, the underlying inflation rate remains

at historically high levels. A central focus of national
economic policy must be a progressive, year-by-year reduction in the inflation rate until reasonable price stability
is achieved.

While fiscal and monetary restraint is essential to the
achievement of price stability, we must also endeavor to
reach a broader national accord on appropriate wage and price
increases. Upon taking office, we will construct a Wage-Price
Incentives Program. An Anderson Administration will seek to
call labor and management leaders together to agree upon fair
and realistic wage and price guidelines and to determine an
appropriate means of encouraging compliance with those
standards through tax-based incentives.

In the absence of sharp and prolonged increases in the
rate of inflation, the Anderson Administration will oppose
any mandatory wage and price standards. Experience has
demonstrated that such controls are difficult to administer
and result in a misallocation of economic resources.

Full Employment

A sound economic policy must incorporate a commitment to
full employment. We reaffirm the goals of the Humphrey-Hawkins

Act and condemn the President for his failure to consult
with Congress this past January before altering the timetables set forth in that Act. The establishment and attainment of national economic objectives is the joint responsibility of the President and Congress.

While the central focus of America's full employment
policy must be on the creation and preservation of productive,
private sector jobs, there will be a continuing need for creative and complementary federal employment programs to reach
areas of unmet needs.

Existing federal employment programs--administered under
the Comprehensive Employment and Training Act (CETA)--place
an undue reliance on public service employment and other jobs
programs that do not significantly upgrade the labor skills
or the employment prospects of program participants. While
recent program initiatives, such as Title VII of CETA, have
sought to expand the role of the private sector, such efforts
have been underfunded and underutilized. We propose to expand
the role and funding of the Private Industry Councils under
Title VII and to otherwise enlarge the role of private employers in federally sponsored job training efforts.

State unemployment compensation programs, for the most
part, are not linked to the retraining needs of displaced
workers. As a result, those who exhaust their unemployment
benefits frequently lack the necessary skills for gainful
employment. We propose establishing federally funded pilot
projects integrating State unemployment benefits with retraining benefits for those with long records of unemployment.

The Congress, in 1977 and again in 1978, approved an
employment tax credit of 50 percent of the first $6,000 in
wages of qualified new employees hired by small businesses.
Many small businesses, however, have not taken advantage of
the tax credit because they have no tax liability against
which to apply the credit. An Anderson Administration will
initiate an inter-department study on the advisability of
making the tax credit refundable on a one-year trial basis.

Special attention must be devoted to the problem of
youth unemployment, particularly minority youth unemployment.
Nationwide, the unemployment rate for black and other minority
youth is nearly 40 percent, and in many urban areas it
exceeds 50 percent! To deal with this critical social
problem an Anderson Administration will propose a number
of youth employment initiatives:

• enactment of the proposed Youth Act of 1980 that
will provide over $2 billion a year for job train-
ing and state and local educational programs designed to improve the employability of disadvantaged
and out-of-school youth;

• increased funding for youth career intern programs;

• a youth opportunity wage incentive that would exempt
eligible youths and their employers from social security taxes during the first six months of employment; and

• a Youth Energy Projects Act that would provide up
to $1 billion a year (by fiscal year 1983) for mul-
tiyear, large-scale energy and energy conservation
projects--including mass transit--offering career
opportunities for economically disadvantaged youth
between the ages of 18 and 24.

Structural Initiatives

If we are to rebuild the American economy, we cannot be
content with short-term measures employed first to stimulate
and then to dampen the swings of the business cycle. We must
address the basic long-term problems of job creation, inflation, productivity, economic growth, and the quality of life.

To solve these long-term problems, we must avoid stop-
and-go economic measures. We cannot fight higher prices with
higher unemployment and we cannot combat the decline of purchasing power with inflationary, across-the-board, consumption-
oriented tax cuts like the Reagan Kemp-Roth proposal.

We believe that America needs a coherent program for
long-term economic recovery and growth. This program must
be designed to stimulate investment and to hold back consumption in a fair and equitable way so that we can rebuild and
renew our capital plant--industrial, commercial, and public.

We believe that basic industry must be given the opportunity to rebuild and to restore its competitive edge by
creating a new climate for investment and entrepreneurship.
It is not our intention to use protection or direct subsidies
to achieve this end. Nor is it our intention to imitate the

the Japanese experience by putting the government into the business of picking the winners and losers of industrial competition. Such policies may be relevant to the requirements of those nations, but they are not relevant to a country that expects to be at the cutting edge of economic innovation and growth. Instead, we will create the conditions within which enterprises can flourish, provided they are well-managed by forward-looking entrepreneurs.

Although we will make every effort to facilitate the growth of major industry, and although we hope that major industry will expand strongly during the next decade, we believe that the major engine for American economic growth during the 1980's will come from small- and medium-sized businesses as they grow into large businesses. Therefore, we will also seek to encourage their formation and expansion in recognition of their role as the principal providers of new jobs and technologies in our economy.

To create a climate for economic recovery, rebuilding, and growth for businesses of all sizes, we will seek to enact five major structural initiatives:

First: We will use a prudent, restrained fiscal and monetary policy to dampen inflation, lower interest rates, and

foster a stable economic environment for long-range planning
by investors and government alike.

Second: We will use the tax code to encourage greater
personal savings and capital formation.

Third: We will use tax incentives and direct federal
assistance to stimulate research and development and to spur
productivity.

Fourth: We will use legislation and executive authority
to review and to prune regulations that waste capital and do
not adequately promote valid regulatory objectives.

Fifth: We will use a tough, conservation-oriented energy
program to curtail the rapid flow of American capital overseas
to pay for imported oil.

Without these measures, we cannot hope to offset our
economic decline. With them, we can produce a climate within
which investment will be possible and attractive. It will
then be the task of our managers and entrepreneurs to make
use of the opportunities our policies will create. If they
do--and we believe they will--our economy will once again
generate a wealth of new jobs and rising real incomes.

Monetary and Fiscal Stability

We need to create a stable economic climate conducive to industrial development and the .ull employment of our human resources. Efforts in recent years to 'fine tune' the economy have served to accentuate, rather than moderate, cyclical economic swings. The resulting economic dislocation has damaged our productive capacity. The record jump in interest rates experienced this past spring brought the corporate bond market near collapse, forced thousands of small businesses into bankruptcy and pushed the consumer price index to a post-war high.

An Anderson administration will seek to avoid "stop and go" economic policies and will work to achieve a better balancing of monetary and fiscal policies: we should not rely upon a monetary tourniquet to stop the hemorrhage of inflation.

In ordinary times, federal expenditures should not exceed revenues. Thus, while declining tax revenues and increasing transfer payments can be expected to unbalance the budget during times of economic difficulty, the budget should be in balance, or in surplus, during times of economic expansion.

It should be understood that fiscal stringency requires
an element of sacrifice on the part of all Americans. Fairness dictates, however, that no segment of our society should
be asked to bear a disproportionate share of the burden. Moreover, all federal expenditures--whether for defense or non-
defense related purposes--should be rigorously examined to
determine whether they are cost-effective means of achieving
national objectives.

Once balance in the federal budget has been achieved, the
Anderson administration will propose legislation "indexing"
the personal income tax brackets to prevent taxpayer incomes
from being pushed into higher tax brackets by inflation. To
the extent that further economies are made in federal spending,
we will propose tax cuts that go beyond the tax relief afforded
by indexing.

The Anderson adminstration, however, will not propose
tax cuts that run counter to the goal of balancing federal
revenues and expenditures. Proposals to cut personal income
tax rates by one-third are fiscally irresponsible. A tax cut
of that size would widen the deficit, increase government borrowing, hike interest rates, and accelerate inflationary expectations and underlying inflationary pressures. Rather

than spurring new investments and savings, the plan would
choke off recovery of the capital goods sector and lower
the personal savings rate.

The goal of fiscal and monetary stability taken in
the context of a fight against inflation will provide a climate of greater economic certainty in which investment deci-
sions--large and small--can be made more rationally. Without
such a climate of realizable expectations an investment oriented rational recovery program will be extremely difficult
to implement.

The independence of the Federal Reserve, which has
come under increasing attack in recent years, must be protected. While it is critically important for the Federal
Reserve Board to observe its responsibility to report to the
Congress and the President on the growth targets for the monetary aggregates, it is equally important that the Federal
Reserve be free from undue political pressures. An Anderson
Administration will respect the traditional independence of
the Federal Reserve.

While mindful of the need for fiscal discipline and
economic predictability, an Anderson Administration will
oppose any new Constitutional limitation on the spending

and taxing powers of Congress. Necessary budget reforms,
including the tying of government spending to an appropriate
percentage of GNP, should be enacted in the form of amendments
to the Congressional Budget Act in a manner that will reserve
to Congress and the President the power to adapt fiscal
policies to changing circumstances.

America's Capital Needs

Sustained economic recovery requires an adequate pool
of savings and capital. As individuals and as a nation, we
need to save and invest more. Current Federal tax laws--and
in some instances regulations--have served to foster debt
and penalize thrift.

An Anderson Administration will commit itself to working with Congress toward the formulation of a comprehensive
program designed to meet America's capital needs in the decade
ahead.

The personal savings rate should be increased. Individuals need to save, not only for retirement purposes, but
also to guard against unforeseen financial troubles. Personal
savings are also an important component of economic growth,
providing the resources with which to finance new housing
and capital expansion.

We must make it both possible and desirable for the
average American to save again. Lowering the inflation rate
will be a powerful stimulus to savings. The phasing out of
interest rate restrictions on savings accounts, recently
approved by Congress, will also be an important stimulant.
More remains to be done, however, to remove the disincentives
to savings and investment currently in our tax code. We propose the following initiatives:

●   expanding the existing interest and dividend income
     exclusion (now $200 for individuals and $400 for
     married couples filing jointly) to $750 for indi-
     viduals, $1500 for married couples filing jointly,
     by 1986;

●   liberalizing the eligibility and income requirements
     for Individual Retirement Accounts, particularly for
     homemakers; and

●   instituting a further review of capital gains tax
     treatment.

Our existing capital cost recovery system operates as
a strong deterrent to capital expansion of plant and equipment. The historic cost method of calculating depreciation
allowances vastly understates actual depreciation, effectively
boosting business tax liabilities and discouraging the purchase of the capital equipment needed to improve worker productivity. Capital cost recovery problems are particularly

34

acute for small businesses that do not take advantage of the

liberalized depreciation allowances afforded by the asset

depreciation range because of the complexity of the schedules.

We propose a comprehensive reform of the capital cost

recovery system that would:

- establish a Simplified Cost Recovery System (SCR) for
investments in capital equipment and machinery. Equipment should be assigned to one of four recovery accounts
with recovery periods of 2, 4, 7 or 10 years depending
upon its nature and normal useful life. Equipment and
machinery can be depreciated an average of 40 percent
faster than under existing law, and depreciation deductions should be computed by use of the "open-ended
account" system currently in use in Canada.

- reduce the current useful life depreciation of structures to a standard twenty-year straight line depreciation with Section 1250 recapture provisions. The new
depreciation guidelines would apply to all industrial
and commercial structures and qualified low-income
rental housing.

- provide a special 25 percent investment tax credit (in
lieu of the existing 10 percent investment tax credit)
for the rehabilitation of commercial and industrial
structures.

- allow small businesses to expense (write-off in one
year) the first $50,000 in annual expenditures for
equipment and machinery.

The current state of the economy and of our most basic

industries, including the auto and steel industries, requires

the adoption of added capital cost recovery measures designed

to insure that troubled companies and industries will not

suffer from a competitive tax disadvantage in undertaking
the necessary capital expansion and improvements in the forthcoming economic recovery.

The 10 percent investment tax credit, now permanent,
allows businesses to offset the credit against 80 percent
of tax liabilities in 1981 and 90 percent in 1982. Any part
of the credit which cannot be applied against current tax
year tax liability may be carried back three years and forward seven years. Restricting the credit to offsets against
federal tax liabilities effectively denies the full benefit
of the credit to businesses not currently showing a profit
(and hence having no tax liabilities). This inequity can be
resolved by making the investment tax credit refundable.
While Congress has been understandably reluctant to approve
the refundability of tax credits, the current state of many
of our most basic industries and businesses requires a re-
evaluation of this policy as it relates to the investment
tax credit.

To encourage unprofitable companies to modernize their
plants and equipment, an Anderson Administration will propose amendments to the existing investment tax credit provisions to accelerate the time for applying the 90 percent

limit based on tax liability and to provide for the prospective refundability of currently earned investment tax credits after the close of the year in which they are earned. To insure that Congress will have adequate opportunity to review and reconsider this measure, we propose to "sunset" the refundability provision three years after its enactment.

We believe that these measures will provide a strong stimulus to re-investment in America. An Anderson administration will, however, be prepared to go even further in the direction of investment-oriented incentives should that be necessary to complete the job of retooling our basic industries and to create a climate of rapid replacement for capital equipment so that our threatened firms can become internationally competitive once again.

Research and Development

Thirty years ago, three American scientists working for Bell Laboratories invented the transistor. As a technological breakthrough, it transformed communications, computing, education, entertainment and weaponry. In the early 1960's, scientists at Hughes Aircraft invented the laser, a

breakthrough for which the full potential is still to be realized. Between 1950 and 1970, American scientists constructed the great accelerators which opened up vast new areas
of human knowledge and technology.

These fundamental advances were the products of a
nation that recognized the importance of scientific achievements and the role that science plays in our everyday lives.
Total U.S. research and development spending as a percent
of the gross national product, however, has fallen by nearly
50 percent in the past 15 years. We are in danger of losing
our technological edge.

Declining technological growth has real consequences
for all Americans. Technological improvements account for
40 to 70 percent of productivity growth. We all benefit
from rising productivity in the form of increased purchasing
power and higher real incomes. It is more than coincidence
that our declining rate of productivity growth was preceded
by an equally serious decline in our research and development effort.

To revive our flagging R&D effort, we propose a number of new initiatives and program improvements. An Anderson
Administration will seek to:

- reverse the decline in the real dollar level of federal funding for research and development;

- provide a 10 percent investment tax credit for qualifying research and development expenditures;

- establish a federal program to re-equip the laboratories of our universities, our non-profit research centers, and our government facilities;

- redefine the working relationship between government and universities so as to avoid the substitution of paperwork for genuine creativity;

- provide fixed objectives and more predictable project funding for scientists and engineers on the cutting edge of technology;

- establish regional technology centers under the aegis of the National Science Foundation and NASA to lower the costs of selling and licensing new technologies to private business;

- establish a more uniform patent policy for all federal agencies;

- require federal agencies to determine in an expeditious manner whether they will retain the patent on inventions developed by private contractors with federal monies;

- reorganize and increase the funding of the Patent and Trademark Office to improve its operations and handling of patent requests;

- explore the possibility of creating a separate patent court to reduce the time needed to establish the validity of a patent.

Regulation

Federal regulations are required to protect workers
and consumers in such vital areas as health, safety, the
environment, and maintenance of competition. Attempts to
reform the regulatory process must recognize the contribution that appropriate regulations can make to a safer and
more prosperous economy.

The pledge of the Carter Administration notwith-
standing, the vast bulk of the federal regulatory machinery
has not been properly streamlined and scrutinized.
If we are to realize the widely-shared objective of reducing
the estimated $100 billion in regulatory compliance costs,
we must establish a comprehensive timetable for the review
of the entire regulatory framework, instead of relying upon
piecemeal review.

We will seek the passage of legislation that would:

- set forth an eight year timetable for thorough Congressional review of regulatory agencies;

- require the President by May 1st of the first session
  of each new Congress to submit a regulatory reform
  plan for each of the regulatory agencies scheduled
  for review in that Congress;

●   require Congress to act on the regulatory reform plan by August 1st of the second session;

●   provide "action-forcing" means of assuring Congressional action, including denying the affected agency the power to promulgate new rules and regulations until Congress has acted.

An Anderson Administration will be firmly committed to the growth and maintenance of competition in our modern economy. We support recent efforts toward deregulation of the transportation industry, and we will support thorough review of other federal laws affecting competition including our antitrust laws.

Energy

The availability and cost of energy have been among the
most important structural factors in the American economy during
the decade of the 1970's. Our increased dependence upon overseas
oil has been responsible for a massive capital outflow. The
rise in OPEC prices has fueled our inflation and precipitated
two major recessions. Ownership of American industry, land,
and structures is being transferred overseas to pay for our oil
bill. It is not an overstatement to say that our ability to
rebuild America will depend in large part upon our ability to
reduce our dependence on foreign oil.

Six years have passed since the Arab oil embargo made
energy a major issue in U.S. domestic and foreign policy.
Despite his proclamation characterizing the energy problem as
the "moral equivalent of war", President Carter has not succeeded in producing an effective comprehensive energy policy
for the nation. The present situation is dangerous not only
for the U.S. but also for world stability. It is time for us to
forward with consistent short-term and long-term policies
designed to protect our economic vitality, security, and
environmental health. This requires a new context for
energy --a new way of viewing the energy opportunities before
us, backed up by a set of policies to take advantage of those
opportunities.

A healthy economy and a high standard of living for all
citizens are not dependent on a given quantity of energy
consumed but on maximizing the services or benefits derived
from consumption. The goal of the Anderson energy program
is to design policies aimed at providing individual and
industrial consumers with all the heat, light, and mechanical
power they require at the least cost. Our policies must encourage
competition among various fuels and numerous technologies for
using energy more efficiently.

To create an economic environment which enhances
competition, energy supplies must be priced to reflect their
real economic value. The incentive provided by correct energy
pricing will hasten the transition away from scarce and expensive
energy sources to economical renewable resources and more
efficient ways of using finite supplies. Because these
technologies have been at a competitive disadvantage in the
past (due to price controls on oil and gas) they lack the
capital investment needed to exploit their full potential.
The Anderson energy program encourages economic investments
in conservation technologies, new sources of oil and gas
supplies, coal consumption technologies, and solar
applications. In addition, policies are required to reduce
our vulnerability to oil import disruptions and, for the
longer term, to explore new technologies not now economical
or fully developed.

While conservation is often thought of as simply doing
without, conservation policies included in this program
emphasize increasing the energy efficiency of housing, transportation, and industrial equipment that is needed to sustain
our economy. Since the goods and services required by society
can be produced by using various combinations of energy, capital,
and labor, a least-cost strategy can be followed by encouraging
technologies which require less energy to supply the same level
of services. Application of economic conservation technologies
to improve energy productivity now costs less than developing
new energy supplies and so reduces the total cost of providing
energy services to consumers.

These concerns are addressed by the programs covered in
the following sections.

Conservation Policy

Energy conservation deserves the highest priority in
U.S. energy planning because it is the least expensive way
to provide energy services for homes, transportation, and
industry. Conservation must be viewed as an additional option
for providing energy benefits in the same way oil, gas, coal,
and other technologies do. The energy services provided by
conservation have distinct advantages over those provided by
conventional fuels: they are cleaner, they are safe, they
do not rely on foreign sources, and most important they are

less costly. A recent study by the National Academy of
Sciences concluded that "throughout the economy, it is now a
better investment to save a BTU than to produce an additional
one". Conservation can be the most important method of providing
the energy benefits we need over the next decade. The problem is
that investments of major proportions are needed in conservation.
Several studies indicate that $400-500 billion in capital could
be invested in retrofitting homes, improving auto efficiency,

and increasing energy productivity in industry with economically
attractive returns. Unfortunately, those sectors of the economy
most in need of improved energy efficiency are also those least
able to generate the necessary capital. We need to shift
capital into energy-efficiency improvements, remove institutional
barriers to such investments, and provide technical assistance
and educational programs to motivate consumers to adopt energy-
savings measures. To realize these goals, we should:

Pricing Reform

●   Firmly support continued decontrol of domestic oil
and gas prices. Letting prices rise is the most
efficient way to exploit our conservation potential.
When consumers face the full economic value of the
energy they use (prices which reflect more expensive
domestic production costs, the insecurity of import
dependence, and environmental risks) they will respond
by substituting conservation technology to provide
the energy services required.

●   Urge further reform of utility pricing to better
reflect the varying costs of providing electricity
service, thereby giving accurate cost signals to
consumers. Since generating costs are higher during
peak demand periods, consumption will shift to off-
peak hours when power will be supplied by more
efficient baseload equipment. The federal government
should support local experiments around the country
to demonstrate the cost effectiveness of this pricing
strategy.

Residential/Commercial Buildings

●   Encourage utility companies to experiment with new
ways to deliver and finance building retrofits. For
example, interest-free loans could be offered to
consumers for weatherproofing or solar water heating
investments, with the costs of the program added into
the rate base rate of the utility. The federal
government should fund short-term demonstration programs
to help utilities start up such programs and then
disseminate the results to public utility commissions.

- Develop a residential energy performance rating system
  to reflect the relative energy efficiency of a dwelling
  for a given geographic location and size. FHA and VA
  appraisers should include such an evaluation in their
  housing assessments. Preferential treatment for
  conservation investments should be built into federal
  lending practices by requiring lower down payments for
  mortgage loans on homes with high energy performance
  ratings.

- Use local community action groups to educate consumers
  on energy conservation opportunities and their costs
  and benefits. Since effective conservation is the
  result of many individual decisions, we must establish
  informational and technical assistance programs directed
  to the individual consumer. Community block grant
  programs should expand funding for home audits, direct
  retrofit assistance, promotion of "life cycle" costing
  and other measures to help consumers make more economical
  choices and reduce their energy consumption.

- Promote a strategy for retrofitting existing
  buildings to reduce energy costs and provide new
  employment. Financing is generally a more difficult
  problem for retrofits than for new construction,
  especially for inner-city multi-family rental
  dwellings. To remove such barriers, the federal
  government should substantially increase the
  investment tax credit for building rehabilitation.
  (See the program section on America's capital needs.)

Conservation in Transportation

- Substantially increase the federal tax on motor
  fuels and use the proceeds to lower payroll taxes
  and increase social security benefits. A 50 cent per
  gallon tax would achieve a reduction in gas consumption
  of as much as 700,000 barrels per day in the short-run
  and over one million barrels per day in the longer term.
  It would also generate over $50 billion per year in net
  revenues to be returned to consumers through offsetting
  tax relief.

- Seek Congressional approval of an auto fuel economy
  standard of 40 miles per gallon by 1995. Enhanced fuel
  economy would save one million barrels per day over the
  level of consumption anticipated if the 1985 standard
  of 27.5 mpg is not raised. In addition, a special
  fuel economy minimum should be established for light
  trucks weighing 3 to 5 tons (a rapidly increasing
  share of the personal transportation market). By
  exempting these trucks from such standards, much of
  the conservation benefit of higher auto efficiency levels
  is being negated.

●   Enforce strict adherence to the 55-mile per hour speed
limit on all major highways. It has been estimated by
the Department of Transportation that this restriction
on excessive speed cuts U.S. gasoline consumption by
3.4 billion gallons annually. Even more convincing,
however, is that since its introduction in 1974, this
law has saved 37,500 lives and prevented untold numbers
of accidents on our roads.

●   Improve and expand mass transit to supplement the use
of private vehicles. Short-haul public transportation
designed to meet local commuter needs will reduce street
congestion and air pollution as well as energy consumption
A much greater federal investment in a variety of public
modes is required. (See the Community Transportation
Program.)

Conservation in Industry

●   Promote industrial cogeneration by increasing DOE funding
for demonstration projects and by providing technical
assistance to industries and utilities. Because cogeneration
is a highly efficient use of oil and gas, cogenerators
should not be restricted in the use of these fuels by
the Fuel Use Act and Windfall Profits Tax Act. Removal
of these barriers would stimulate the operation of
economic, decentralized systems to provide energy
services.

●   Provide incentives to investment in energy productivity
improvements including new conservation technologies.
Adoption of accelerated depreciation allowances would
stimulate general productivity increases as well as
promote the purchase of energy-saving equipment.
Also, consideration should be given to increasing the
tax credits for industrial conservation measures,
after careful evaluation of the response to existing
incentives.

Conservation in Government

●   Set high energy efficiency standards in federal, state,
and local government activities. Emphasizing conservation
in the acquisition and operation of buildings and motor
vehicle fleets demonstrates both the seriousness of
our energy problems and the cost -effectiveness of our solutions.

●   Provide a market for energy-saving technology. The
government should act as a proving   ground for new
conservation ideas directly through its procurement
practices and should widely publicize those that are
most successful.

Low-Income Energy Assistance

●   Continue federal financial aid to help pay residential
energy costs incurred by the poor. Higher prices which
result from oil and gas price decontrol will most
adversely affect low-income families because they are
most limited in what they can do to reduce their home
heating bills and electricity demand.

●   Continue federally funded weatherization services to
low income families, those least able to invest in
energy-saving measures. The recent changes in the
Weatherization Assistance Program to expand the labor
component and improve the selection of qualified local
agencies should help insure a more timely and efficient
program.

Petroleum Policy

Federal petroleum policy must address two major
problems. The first is the inability of the
domestic resource base to supply the huge volumes of oil and
gas required by the economy. Proved domestic reserves of
these fuels declined by about 30 percent in the last decade
because production levels far exceeded new discoveries. With
each increase in demand, the balance of the nation's oil
requirements was met by foreign imports. The second problem is the
vulnerability created by a dependence on imports. Aside from
the continuing problems of inflation and balance of payments
deficits, the U.S. could suffer enormous economic damage if a
sudden and severe disruption in supplies were to occur. Our
oil dependence, particularly during periods of economic growth,
contributes to instability in the world market by gradually reducing the market's flexibility which in turn leads to further large
OPEC price increases. Both components of the problem have been

aggravated by past policies that restricted the full development of domestic resources and subsidized greater imports.

The rate of decline in domestic reserves needs to be
reduced by policies that encourage enhanced recovery from
existing sources, increase -- subject to environmental
priorities -- the amount of federal land and off-shore tracts
available for exploration, and make greater use of previously
marginal resources of oil shales, heavy oil deposits, gas
trapped in tight sand formations, and similar unconventional
deposits. Since these sources will not be adequate in themselves, it is also necessary to produce synthetic oil and gas
using abundant coal reserves. Regulatory and pricing policies
must be changed to discourage imports and promote competition
among all sectors of the energy industry.

Problems caused by the extent of our dependence on foreign
oil cannot be solved immediately, but our vulnerability can be
reduced by the storage of a greater volume of emergency
supplies and effective advance preparation to handle the
effects of supply disruptions. It should also be recognized
that major price increases might be reduced in the future by
implementing supply and demand management programs well before
world market conditions become dangerously strained. To make
larger and more secure petroleum supplies available in the
future, we should:

Developing New Supplies

●   Continue federal support for research and development
     programs on enhanced oil recovery from existing reserves,
     production from oil shale, and heavy oil deposits.

- Expand the off-shore tracts and federal lands made available for petroleum exploration provided the best available and safest technology is used, cost effectiveness is demonstrated and environmental impacts are acceptable.

- Diversify the sources of foreign supply by establishing a supply development function -- an Agency for International Energy Development -- within the International Energy Agency, by providing additional financial assistance to existing World Bank and Agency for International Development programs, and by increasing technical assistance to developing countries that are not currently net oil exporters.

- Continue start-up funding for projects to develop synthetic gas and oil supplies using coal feedstocks. Support for production beyond present targets will depend on whether environmental problems are solved, whether technical feasibility is clearly demonstrated, and, most important, whether synthetics are more eco- nomic than other energy sources.

- Increase federal support for efforts to define the availability and characteristics of new gas resources from geopressurized methane, devonian shales, and tight sand formations.

- Restrict federal approval for new LNG projects until safety, siting, and security of supply issues have been resolved. This policy would not affect imports of gas by pipeline from either Mexico or Canada.

Contingency Planning

- Complete and fill the Strategic Petroleum Reserve. At least one billion barrels should be in storage in order to provide significant protection from possible supply disruptions. A regional reserve for the Northeast, an area particularly dependent on imported oil, should be constructed.

- Modify the current policy regarding use of oil in storage to permit withdrawal whenever world market conditions become overly rigid. In the past, accelerating demand for world oil supplies in the latter stages of the recovery cycle has strained the market to the point where a small disruption of supply causes disproportionately large increases in the world price. Use of the Strategic Petroleum Reserve to alleviate these conditions should require simultaneous economic measures to reduce overall demand.

● Cooperate with other members of the International
   Energy Agency to arrange for mandatory restrictions
   on unusually large purchases in periods of tight
   supply. Often in the past, petroleum companies,
   anticipating a major OPEC price increase, have
   contributed to its magnitude by increasing inventories
   for short-term benefits.

● Prepare several stand-by emergency conservation plans
   to promote fuel switching, electric power transfers,
   and reduced gasoline consumption in the event of an oil
   embargo.

● Revise the present emergency rationing plan to reduce
   the length of time needed to put it into operation.
   A plan that takes longer than three months to be
   implemented has limited usefulness.

Pricing and Regulatory Policy

● Continue the phasing out of price controls on oil and
   gas under the schedules provided in current legislation.
   The Windfall Profits Tax is necessary to meet national
   standards of equity.

● Since the elimination of well head price controls will
   give all refiners comparable costs, end the Entitlement
   Program. Emergency allocation authorities should be
   retained for use in a major supply disruption.

● Have the Energy Information Administration monitor
   transfer pricing practices by integrated petroleum
   companies to determine whether independent refiners
   are placed at an unfair competitive disadvantage by
   subsidies to the refining segment of integrated firms.
   Similarly, competitive conditions in the coal industry
   will be monitored to determine whether the use of
   profits from oil and gas operations give an excessive
   competitive advantage to the coal mining subsidies of
   oil companies in relation to independent coal companies.

Coal

This nation has the resources for coal to assume a much
larger share of our energy supply mix. In conjunction with
conservation, it offers an important alternative supply to
reduce our dependence on imported oil. Coal also can
serve to improve substantially our balance of payments through
exports to other industrialized countries. Despite these opportunities, the demand for this fuel has not kept pace with the
capability of coal industry miners and operators to produce it.
Greater coal production and use will depend on resolving
environmental and health problems and on rectifying constraints
in coal transportation.

The combustion of coal is a major source of several
air pollutants. There is evidence that large quantities of
sulfur oxides and nitrogen oxides emitted into the atmosphere
from midwest power plants are contributing significantly to
acid rainfall in New England and Canada. Such precipitation
is believed to account for declines in certain species of fish
and to have adversely affected crops and forests. In addition,
there is growing speculation that large increases of carbon
dioxide in the atmosphere will produce significant adverse
changes in climate around the world. While carbon dioxide
presents no direct threat to health or welfare at present
levels, scientists are concerned that greater coal use will
create a "greenhouse" effect, trapping heat that normally
radiates away from the earth, thereby raising global temperatures.

Another environmental problem associated with coal is
land degradation. Much of the expansion in output over the
next few decades will require strip mining, a method of production
which causes extensive land disruption and water problems if
not properly controlled. Standards must be maintained to
assure that land is returned to its original contour.

The expansion of coal output for both domestic and foreign
markets is hindered by bottlenecks in our transportation system.
Increased coal shipments, especially from Western states, would
strain rail and port facilities. The ability of railroads to
move coal on a timely and efficient basis requires increasing
mainline trackage and supplying rolling stock. At East
Coast ports, the capacity for storing and handling coal is
inadequate , causing high demurrage charges.

To improve the competitiveness of coal while limiting
adverse environmental impacts, we should:

Increase the Demand for Coal

- Expedite the conversion of oil-fired electric power
  plants to coal beginning with the 80 plants targeted
  in the Senate oil backout bill. The government should
  provide financial assistance in the form of grants or
  loans to be repaid out of the fuel savings subsequently
  realized. All conversions must meet current air quality
  standards.

- Encourage industrial use of coal by offering tax incentives
  to firms that convert from oil. The government has yet
  to implement regulations for the investment tax credit
  for coal-fired industrial boilers authorized in 1978.

54

Mitigate Environmental Impacts

• Reduce acid rainfall by requiring electric power pools
  to use available plant capacity on a least emissions
  rather than least cost basis. Mandatory pre-combustion
  coal "washing" may also be a cost-effective way of
  curbing area-wide sulfur dioxide emissions.

• Accelerate research and development of fluidized bed
  combustion and direct limestone injection processes to
  reduce air pollution. Adapting these technologies for
  new power plants offers a promising alternative to
  current expensive scrubber systems.

• Increase funding to established independent agencies for
  research on the possible climatic effects of carbon
  dioxide emissions. Since the problem is a global
  one, parallel efforts need to be undertaken on an
  international level.

• Support existing legislation to insure that states
  adequately regulate mining practices. Surface mining
  should not be allowed where land cannot be restored to
  the level of productive use which existed before
  strip mining.

Improve Coal Transportation

• Facilitate the movement of coal to domestic markets by
  reducing railroad regulation while providing protection
  for "captive" coal shippers. Rates set by the ICC must
  compensate railroad companies for building, maintaining,
  and equipping an adequate transportation system.

• Propose the establishment of a Coal Export Authority to
  review the need for expanded port facilities to accommodate
  coal for export and coastal movements. Where appropriate,
  this authority should undertake to aid in the funding of
  new coal terminals on both the East and West coasts. (See
  the Transportation Program.)

Reform the Regulatory Process

• Improve the stability and predictability of environmental
  regulations and occupational health and safety standards.
  All rule-making should be conducted openly and policies
  should be consistent over time. It is possible to
  eliminate costly and unnecessary delays in the regulatory
  process while maintaining strict operating standards.

● Resume the leasing of public land for coal production.
  Federal leasing policy should be designed to make low-
  cost coal available in efficient mining blocks, at a
  fair return to the public treasury, while insuring
  sound environmental practices.

56

Nuclear Power

Escalating problems with the cost and safety of
nuclear power have raised serious questions regarding
its role in America's energy future. The expansion of
nuclear power, which presently accounts for 10 percent
of the nation's electrical generating capacity,
must be linked to the resolution of the nuclear waste and
reactor safety problems, along with a reassessment of both
the full costs of nuclear power and the anticipated demand for
electrical generating capacity in the 1980's and 1990's. If
the safety and nuclear waste questions cannot be satisfactorily
resolved, we must halt the further expansion of nuclear power
and phase out existing plants. If those questions can be
satisfactorily answered, the future of nuclear power will be
contingent on competitive cost factors, as well as the need
for additional electrical generating capacity.

The Kemeny and Rogovin reports found major deficiencies
in the management and practices of the Nuclear Regulatory
Commission (NRC) and the industry itself. Both studies
recommended substantial changes affecting the organization of
the NRC, the operation and design of nuclear plants, evacuation
plans, and the training of plant operating personnel. Prudence
requires that we respond fully to their recommendations.
The NRC should be barred from issuing new operating licenses unless
the Commission certifies that the stringent safeguards adopted since

57

Three Mile Island have been incorporated into the plant's design, operating procedures and emergency plans, and that all other safety issues pertinent to the plant and its design have been resolved.

We propose a moratorium on new construction permits, beyond those now being processed, until work has commenced on a permanent geologic disposal site. We have postponed the nuclear waste question for too long. If no suitable means of permanent disposal is available or technically feasible, then it would be irresponsible to put more nuclear power plants on the drawing board. If, on the other hand, a suitably safe means exists, we should begin a demonstration project at the earliest appropriate time.

While safe, permanent disposal of all high level radioactive and transuranic waste must be the principal responsibility of the federal government, all levels of government -- including state, local, and tribal -- must be allowed to participate in the entire decision-making process.

While every state must be responsible for the management and disposal of all civilian low-level nuclear wastes generated within its boundaries, disposal should proceed on an acceptable regional basis. Regionalization is favored by cost, transportation

risk, geologic and other circumstances which make some states
unsuitable as sites. We endorse the Task Force Report on Low
Level Radioactive Waste Disposal of the National Governors'
Association, which recommends that Congress authorize states
to enter into compacts to select disposal sites.

Our commitment to nuclear power must be no greater than
our commitment to the safety of nuclear reactors and the safe
disposal of nuclear wastes. For twenty years now we have allowed
our thirst for a cheap and reliable source of energy to outstrip
the safeguards and other steps that should have accompanied
the development of nuclear power.

It is important to remember that what happened at Three
Mile Island was not merely a "loss of coolant"; there was also
a "loss-of-confidence": public confidence. Just as a "loss-of-
coolant" can lead to the shutdown of a nuclear reactor, so too
can a "loss-of-confidence" lead to a shutdown of the entire
nuclear industry. We must restore public confidence in nuclear
power; but we must restore it by the force of our actions,
rather than by the volume of our rhetoric.

In the meantime, we must begin in earnest to reduce our
demand for electricity through conservation and enhanced
energy efficiency, and to speed the development of renewable
energy sources, and other alternatives to nuclear power.

Direct Solar Energy

Harnessing the sun's energy in active and passive solar applications should be one of our most important energy sources. However, the breakthrough required to have the potential offered by the various solar technologies realized has yet to occur in practice.   In part, this has been due to the competitive advantage traditional fuels have enjoyed because of controlled prices and and also because the federal program in solar energy has failed to offer sustained and adequate support for the most promising technologies.   In the future, higher oil, gas, and electricity prices will sharply increase demand for the already cost-effective technologies and will provide necessary impetus for photovoltaic systems.   The federal government, however, should undertake a much larger effort to promote research and development, improve consumer confidence in solar technologies, remove institutional barriers, and make a substantial commitment in solar energy for its own use.   To attain the goal of meeting 20 percent of our energy needs from renewable resources by the year 2000, we should:

- Develop uniform performance standards for active solar systems.   This would significantly reduce consumer uncertainty about the prospective performance of solar devices by using standard performance criteria to facilitate comparisons between competing systems.

- Encourage public utilities to establish special lending arrangements to help finance the purchase or lease of economical solar devices.   Utility customers could then be supplied with a number of energy services at least cost.

● Reduce the cost of photovoltaic systems by authorizing
a larger federal procurement program. Significant federal
purchases of these systems would encourage mass production
by assuring manufacturers of an adequate intermediate
market, lower unit production costs, and generate useful
performance data. In addition, this program would
serve as a training ground for building trades workers
and increase consumer confidence in solar energy.

● Focus federal research and development programs on
identifying the basic reasons for the present high
capital or operating costs of solar systems and on
ways to reduce them. New construction materials and
methods and energy storage devices should be explored
seriously so that many options for using solar energy
will be available.

● Monitor the activities of the Solar Energy and Energy
Conservation Bank to determine whether the $525 million
authorized by Congress to subsidize solar energy for the
next three years will be sufficient to maximize the
long-term effectiveness of the program.

61

Other Energy Sources

In addition to the renewable and non-renewable energy
resources discussed so far, significant contributions to
meeting our energy needs can come from alternative energy
sources. It is in our nation's best interests to make substantial
investments in a wide range of promising technologies to
determine which can provide energy services at least cost.
Because our financial resources are limited, we must distinguish
between those options which will deliver within the next
twenty years and those which offer promise on a 30- to 50-
year horizon. In the near term, there are several
technologies, including wind and biomass energy systems, which
require no major technical breakthroughs for their introduction.
In the longer run, large quantities of energy from ocean
power, geothermal resources, and nuclear fusion may be
forthcoming,,provided technical and economic hurdles can be
overcome.

While greater reliance on these alternatives will
occur eventually, critical decisions should be made now to
speed the timing and reduce the costs of this transition.
New incentives are needed to encourage more rapid implementation
of these technologies beyond the demonstration stage. While
current federal programs provide some experience in establishing
financial incentives, development of a comprehensive and balanced
approach to alternative energy commercialization remains a
crucial problem.

Although many of the institutional and technical barriers
to development have been resolved, incentives to invest in
"new" energy sources have been limited in comparison with
conventional sources of supply. This has been due, in part,
to domestic price controls which maintain market prices
below true replacement costs. By giving investors a false
sense of the value of alternative sources, the market has
biased decisions away from more energy efficient,
economical, and environmentally benign systems. A second
barrier to full commercialization of alternative technologies
is the high cost and limited availability of capital. Projects
which are cost effective still have difficulty competing for
financing in a tight capital market with high interest rates.
Another difficulty is that private investors have been reluctant
to commit funds to innovative projects where the returns are
perceived to be uncertain. This has resulted in a cautious,
wait-and-see attitude on the part of many potential users.

Recent federal actions to deal with some of these
problems have included the passage of the Crude Oil Windfall
Profits Tax Act and the Energy Security Act. To further
stimulate the timely development and commercialization of
alternative energy sources, we will:

● Expand DOE funding for nonhardware activities. For
  small-scale decentralized systems, greater attention
  should be paid to increasing user awareness and acceptability,
  reducing utility interface problems, and developing
  competitive systems' manufacturing capability.

- Direct DOE to demonstrate the reliability of wind energy equipment. Operating experience with power production and maintenance will instill consumer confidence by providing valuable information on machine designs and economics.

- Emphasize smaller scale biomass conversion facilities to maximize its potential at least cost. Also, near term technologies, such as the production of methanol from wood, should be included in programs to commercialize biomass energy systems.

- Prepare a comprehensive plan for the development of ocean thermal energy conversion (OTEC) in order to estimate its total cost and the federal involvement required to bring it to commercialization. DOE should complete a detailed resource assessment of the potential for OTEC to determine where it is likely to be the least-cost alternative.

- Support accelerated funding of fusion energy research, contingent upon continued progress toward the demonstration of technical feasibility.

64

Targeted Measures

As we create a new climate that promotes economic stability, long-range planning, capital formation, investment, innovation, and risk-taking, we will lay a foundation for a resumption of steady growth, rising productivity, lowered inflation, and high employment.

In addition, however, we need specific initiatives to enable the various sectors of our economy to build on this foundation.

- We need an industrial policy sensitive to the special problems of our basic industries.

- We need to restore small business to its traditional role as a generator of new ideas and new jobs.

- We need to ensure that our transportation system can meet the demands of an economy changing in light of changing energy usage practices.

- We need to seek new solutions to the traditional problems of the farm economy.

- We need to revitalize our space program, another important source of innovation.

- We need to remove existing barriers to exports and to work aggressively to increase them.

- We need to protect our trade and our currency through increased international economic cooperation.

- Finally, we must preserve and extend the gains our working men and women have achieved in nearly a century of organization and struggle.

Industrial Policy

Once the Colossus of international trade and industry,
America is now losing its ability to compete in the world
marketplace. In 1968, U.S. manufacturing exports accounted
for 24 percent of work exports. Last, year, however, America's
share of world manufactured exports was only 17 percent.

Our inability to compete in the world marketplace not
only aggravates the balance of trade, it also erodes confidence
in the dollar overseas, and leads to a loss of jobs and
purchasing power here at home.

If we are to avoid yet another decade of economic
stagnation, we must rebuild our declining industrial base.
The rebuilding process must begin with a new industrial
policy. By industrial policy, we mean the sum of government
policies affecting industrial growth. Nothing less than a
comprehensive review of those policies will do.

Industrial policy, however, should not be a subterfuge
for the selective bailout of troubled companies or the
artificial propping up of failing industries. Rather, our
task is to promote a climate conducive to the recovery of

troubled industries, the advancement of growing industries, and the creation of new ones.

Neither should industrial policy be used as a vehicle for the elimination of necessary environmental and safety and health regulation. While regulatory objectives can sometimes be achieved by less burdensome and costly means of compliance, our environmental, safety, and health laws serve real public needs.

The principal focus of industrial policy must be on the five structural initiatives discussed above which we believe will spur industrial growth and innovation. Other important program initiatives include transportation and trade initiatives discussed below. There are, however, a number of other tasks that must be undertaken which are peculiar to the requirements of industry.

A decade of lagging research and development has led to a dangerous erosion of the competitiveness of some of our most basic industries, including the auto and steel industries. Many of those companies now lack the ability to attract the capital needed to finance the development of cost-saving innovations.

To assist in the recovery of established, but troubled,
industries, an Industrial Development Administration should be
established in the Department of Commerce. Like the existing
Economic Development Administration (also in the Commerce
Department), the Industrial Development Administration (IDA) shoul
be authorized to give loan guarantees for selected projects.
Unlike EDA, however, the new agency should be directed to assist
in the financing of projects involving the development of new
technologies and cost-saving techniques for industries as a
whole.

IDA's assistance should be targeted at troubled industries;
the agency should not be authorized to support projects in new
or expanding industries.

It should encompass a cooperative government-industry
program of directed basic research in automobile and steel
technologies. IDA's support in this and other areas, however,
should be limited to basic research and cost-saving production techniques.

Since IDA's limited objective is to assist in the
remodernization of America's basic industries in the difficult
decade ahead, authority to issue loan guarantees should expire
December 31, 1989. On that date, IDA's financial obligations

and responsibilities should be assumed by the Economic

Development Administration or a related Commerce Department

authority.

A commitment to the revitalization of American industry

requires a White House staff structure that ensures proper

attention to matters affecting the health of vital industries

and the wellbeing of the American worker. To achieve this

end, we propose to create, through legislative initiative,

an Industrial Development Council modeled in part on the

National Security Council.

The Council should be chaired by the President and have

as members relevant Cabinet officers, other executive branch

officials, and selected business and labor leaders. The

Council should also have an adequate staff, headed by a

Presidential advisor for Industrial Development to be

appointed by the President, subject to Senate confirmation.

The Council should be charged with the responsibility

of coordinating and reviewing those government policies which

touch on industrial matters, fostering closer relations between

leaders of management and labor, and encouraging American

industry to adapt to the rapidly changing developments in

international economics, technology, and consumer preferences.

Of particular importance is the need to open a closer
dialogue between management, labor, and government leaders.
When industries of major significance are in trouble, business,
labor, and government all have a common interest in a remedy.
The success of earlier labor-management committee experiments
in the United States suggests these cooperative efforts should
be conducted on a broader and more formal scale. The formation
of a limited number of national, industry-wide labor-management
committees could serve as useful adjuncts to the work of the
proposed Industrial Development Council by providing a vehicle
for direct input from the private sector.

The Auto Industry. The domestic auto industry is in trouble.
Foreign imports in May of this year accounted for 28 percent
of auto sales in this country. Domestic sales for May were
42 percent below last year's level, resulting in the lowest
sales rate since the early 1960's. This summer, 250,000 auto
workers have been on indefinite layoff and thousands more on
temporary layoff.

While there has been a summer rebound, auto sales remain
sluggish and the outlook clouded. Short-term prospects for
the industry will be determined by the availability of consumer
credit and the competitiveness and attractiveness of the
newer, more fuel efficient models due to be marketed this
fall and next spring. The longer term future of the industry

will be determined by the resourcefulness of management, the
cooperation of labor, the availability of capital and consumer
credit, the level of import competition,aand the tax and
regulatory policies of the federal government.

The policies of an Anderson Administration will serve to
assist the automotive industry's recovery:

● Lower interest rates will enable more people to finance
the purchase of automobiles.

● The liberalized depreciation allowances will be
specifically applicable to the special capital needs
of the auto industry.

● The refundability of the investment tax credit will
serve to lower the effective costs of capital expansion
and will be of special relevance to companies operating
at a loss, as the auto industry now is.

● The 10 percent investment tax credit for qualifying
research and development will help spur innovation
in an industry where demands for more fuel-efficient
products are great and where product redesign is
fundamental.

● The Industrial Development Administration will help, through
loan guarantees and other assistance, to establish
a cooperative government-industry program of directed
basic research in automotive technology.

● The Industrial Development Council, through its
industry-wide labor management committees, will provide
a vehicle for cooperation between industry, labor, and
government to coordinate a concerted attack on industry
problems.

Finally, an Anderson Administration will consult with
foreign automotive producers in an effort to avoid arbitrary
trade restrictions by persuading them to observe voluntary
restraint during times of sharply slumping domestic sales.

The Steel Industry. Once the world's leading producer
of steel, U.S. steel production recently fell into third
place, behind both the Soviet Union and Japan. Steel shipments for 1980 are estimated at 80-88 million tons, compared
to 100 million tons in 1979.

While U.S. steel shipments can be expected to rebound
as the economy recovers from the 1980 recession, the steel
industry faces serious long-term difficulties. A recent
Office of Technology Assessment report concluded that "continued low profitability and some Federal Government policies,
such as long depreciation time for new facilities, will cause
the domestic steel industry to contract substantially."

From the standpoint of jobs and national security we
must make every reasonable effort to revive the steel industry.
OTA's report concluded that the "U.S. steel industry can be
revitalized through increased investment in research and
development (R&D) and the adoption of new technology." It
is anticipated, however, that steelmakers will have to expand
their capital spending by 50 percent (to approximately $3
billion per year) in order to make the necessary moderniza-
tions in plant and equipment.

The policies of the Anderson Administration will help
rescue the steel industry as long as that industry is willing to make a commitment to its own future. The structural
initiatives set forth above will be important factors in the
steel industry's recovery--especially the liberalized depreciation allowances, the refundability of the investment tax
credit, and the R&D investment tax credit. The institutional
initiatives of the IDA and the IDC will also play important
roles. Efforts to revive the auto industry will, quite
rationally, also assist the steel industry. Furthermore,
the heavy emphasis on capital expenditures for industry,
as set forth above, and for basic urban and transportation
needs, as set forth below, will provide a strong and predictable domestic market for steel manufacturers during the
decade.

As with autos, an Anderson Administration will consult
with foreign steel producers in an effort to avoid arbitrary
trade restrictions by persuading them to observe voluntary
restraint during times of sharply slumping domestic sales.

73

Small Business

The strength and vitality of the American economy is dependent on the health and competitiveness of small businesses. Twelve million small businesses today account for nearly one-half of the gross national product and employ more than one-half of the work force.

Small businesses make up the cutting edge of our economy. They are responsible for a majority of the nation's technological innovations and create over 80 percent of all new jobs.

Despite their economic importance, shortsighted government policies have over-regulated and over-taxed small businesses. Between 1960 and 1976, the share of total corporate after-tax profits earned by small and medium-sized companies fell from 41 percent to 27 percent.

To reduce the excessive taxation of small business enterprises, we propose to:

●   allow small businesses to elect to write-off in the the first year the first $50,000 in investments in equipment and machinery each year, as described above.

●   provide simplified and liberalized depreciation allowances for capital equipment and structures.

74

- provide an investment tax credit for qualifying research and development expenditures;

- defer capital gains tax on the sale of a small business if the proceeds are reinvested in another qualified small business within six months;

- expand the eligibility for Subchapter S status by
  expanding the maximum number of allowable investors;

- initiate a further review of capital gains treatment;
  and

- reduce corporate tax rates by two percentage points
  across-the-board by 1986.

The regulatory problems affecting small business

deserve special consideration. Small businesses are often

less suited or equipped to deal with federal regulatory re-

quirements. Legislation should be enacted that would require

federal regulatory agencies to consider the feasibility of

enacting less burdensome regulatory requirements for small

businesses, providing the new regulations do not jeopardize

important safety and health objectives.

Transportation Policy

In a national program to rebuild our industrial base,
save energy, and meet special requirements such as the
export of coal and wheat, the quality of our transportation
network assumes a fundamental importance.

Much of America's transportation infrastructure was
designed at a time of declining fuel prices. That infrastructure must now be adapted to meet the nation's needs
during a time of growing energy scarcity and rising prices.
In transportation, as in other areas of the economy, there
are unmet capital needs. Many of the nation's railbeds are
in a state of serious disrepair. Highway maintenance costs
are escalating. Our port facilities must be upgraded to
meet rising and changing demands. Our traffic control systems
need to be updated. We ignore these problems at our peril.

Rail Policy. For ninety years, the railroad industry
has taken signals from government rather than from a free
market. The government has used the railroad industry to
promote economic and social goals, often forcing shippers on
profitable, heavily travelled routes to cross-subsidize
shippers on less renumerative lines. Competition from

other modes superimposed on this regulatory regime has fashioned a financially troubled industry. Not only has the railroad industry been unable to provide shippers with quality service at reasonable rates, it has also failed to exploit the fuel efficiency advantages it enjoys over the trucking industry.

We must revitalize our nation's rail system. Railroads must be freed from the anachronistic regulation which now encumbers many aspects of the industry. Government must shift its focus from preserving unprofitable portions of the system to preservation of the system itself. An Anderson Administration will:

- give railroads more flexibility to determine their pricing and operating policies. In many parts of the country, however, shippers of bulk commodities over long distances remain captive to rail carriage. For reasons of both equity, and in the case of coal, national security, an Anderson Administration will guarantee rate protection to such shippers.

- abolish procedures that allow railroads collectively to set general rates. We applaud the recent ICC decision to withdraw antitrust immunity from rate bureaus setting general rates.

- continue those provisions of the 4-R Act that provide matching funds to States for the purchase of abandoned lines to ease the impact of abandonments on State and local economies.

- make the investment tax credit refundable to provide additional investment incentives, particularly for railbed investment. This proposal will be helpful

to the weaker, marginally profitable and unprofitable
roads in their efforts to maintain and modernize.

● encourage the future formation of several long-haul
rail lines to maximize the efficiency of uninterrupted
rail movement.

● support Conrail at least until the United States Rail
Association, Conrail's oversight body, completes its
study and makes its recommendations to Congress this
coming December.

● continue financial support for Amtrak. Amtrak should
be provided with the funds necessary to meet its operating costs and to aid in roadbed improvements. Emphasis
must be placed on rapid line corridor service through
such programs as the Northeast Corridor Improvement
Program.

Port Policy. In the 1980's America must stop export-

ing its dollars and start exporting its industrial produce.

Our ports handle more than 95% of the tonnage moving in U.S.

overseas foreign trade. Foreign trade currently accounts

for 20 percent of our nation's GNP. That figure will grow through-

out the decade, and with it will grow the demands placed upon our po

We must take action to ensure that our ports will be able to

bear the responsibilities placed upon them.

Oil price increases have opened up prospects for dra-

matic increases in U.S. coal exports. These exports could

engineer a major turnaround in this nation's balance of pay-

ments. Yet a number of obstacles could delay or prevent

the growth of this valuable trade. Harbor channels must be
dredged to accommodate the deep-drafted vessels necessary
to transport coal shipments economically. Processing time
for dredging permits must be shortened and delays by environmental agencies and the Army Corps of Engineers minimized.
The environmental problems raised by port expansion must be
solved, including the development of an adequate method for
the disposal of contaminated spoil.

An Anderson Administration will establish a Coal
Export Authority within the Department of Commerce to accelerate the revitalization of our nation's ports. The Authority
will:

- explore the need for expanded and improved port facilities to accommodate coal for export and coastal movements.

- aid, where appropriate, in the funding of coal terminals
  on both the East and West coasts.

- reduce processing time for dredging permits. Specific
  criteria would be established for approving time ex-
  tensions, highlighting the Corps' and the federal agencies' performance in meeting time frames through periodic
  reports, and more clearly delineating specific areas of
  review for each agency.

- urgently work toward solving the problem of disposal
  of contaminated spoil from dredging operations. This
  will also reduce delays caused by the three environ-
  ental agencies.

Highway Rehabilitation.   In 1956, President Eisenhower launched the most successful transportation program in the nation's history--the Interstate Highway Program.   Today, however, the highways are deteriorating at an alarming rate.

The Highway Trust Fund was established by Congress to provide a stable source of revenue to finance construction of the Interstate system.   It provides the funds necessary for much of the rehabilitation work on both Interstate and non-Interstate roads as well as for the costs of new construction. But over the past two years expenditures have exceeded revenues. Revenues coming into the Trust Fund have declined while the costs of completion of the Interstate system and rehabilita- tion of federal-aid highways have skyrocketed.   If conditions remain unchanged, the current Trust Fund balance of $12.6 billion could be depleted in a matter of years.

We must make a strong commitment to maintain our na- tion's highways.   An Anderson Administration will:

● complete the few segments of our Interstate system which are deemed necessary in an energy-conscious and environ- mental conscious era.

● rehabilitate those federal highways which have deteri- orated to the point of eroding their serviceability.

● make a strong commitment to increasing revenues for the Highway Trust Fund, recognizing that the fund

may face lower revenues as fuel costs rise. We will
review the federal highway program's revenue policy in
order to develop additional sources adequate to meet
the nation's highway needs. This will probably mean
increased taxes no later than the mid 1980's.

Aviation Safety. Throughout its history the aviation

industry has maintained a commendable safety record. But

that record could be jeopardized without the implementation

of major improvements. Outdated air traffic control equip-

ment, and a steady increase in the number of flights,

has endangered scores of passengers in recent months.

An Anderson Administration will recognize the need to

revamp existing procedures and equipment to permit safe air

travel by our nation's air commuters. Our proposals are not

large budget items but will contribute significantly to avia-

tion safety. Specifically, an Anderson Administration will

recommend:

● replacement or upgrading of outdated traffic control
  equipment.

● installation of effective new control systems at airports of all sizes. New systems at small airports will
  allow small aircraft to land in bad weather, reducing
  congestion at the larger airports handling commercial
  aircraft.

● improvements, where necessary, in the certification,
  inspection and maintenance procedures utilized by the
  Federal Aviation Administration.

- study of the feasibility of improving the post-crash
  safety of planes. Prevention of the fires and noxious
  fumes which cause the majority of air crash fatalities
  would be addressed.

- redesign of regulations to improve the safety and licensing requirements of commuter airlines and private
  planes. Most aviation fatalities occur as a result
  of accidents involving these types of aircraft.

AGRICULTURE

Agriculture is America's most basic industry. The
American farmer, however, is in trouble. Net farm income
in the second quarter of this year fell by an estimated
40 percent over the prior year's level. Squeezed by low
grain and livestock prices, high interest rates, and
escalating farm production costs, net farm income for all
of 1980 is projected to fall an estimated 29 percent below
last year's level.

For farmers in many parts of this country, the news
has turned from bad to worse. A severe drought has crip-
pled farm production in several important agricultural
states, resulting in both higher prices for consumers and
financial hardship or ruin for many farmers.

Agricultural policy in the 1980's must restore the
fundamental strength of American agriculture. To achieve
that goal, we must expand farm exports, assure adequate
farm prices, restrain rising farm production costs, strengthen the
family farm, provide ample farm credit, preserve agricultural
land, and stabilize farm incomes.

Farm Exports

Agricultural products are the mainstay of U.S. exports.
Farm exports this year will total an estimated $40 billion.

World trade in farm commodities is heavily encumbered
by import restrictions and other barriers to fair competition.

An Anderson Administration will work to liberalize
world trade and expand U.S. exports. We propose to:

● negotiate agressively to reduce protectionist
  barriers overseas and to increase farm exports;

● provide for the maintenance of realistic inventories of basic farm commodities, principally in
  farmer-held reserves, sufficient to insure adequate
  and secure supplies at reasonably stable prices in
  the event of production shortfalls;

● expand export markets for American food products
  through continued support of economic development
  programs in the developing countries and to develop
  longer-range patterns of bilateral trade with those
  nations; and

● provide generous relief programs for the emergency
  feeding of refugees and the victims of famine or
  natural disaster.

Farm Prices

The collapse of farm incomes this year points to a
continuing need to maintain adequate farm prices. Neither
consumers nor producers are well served by the boom and
bust cycle of farm prices. It is in the best interests
of both parties to maintain full and ample farm production
at fair and stable prices.

Many government actions have powerful effects upon
the prices American farmers receive, some actions by
limiting commodity price decreases and others by restricting price increases contrary to actual supply and demand

conditions. Such actions have been taken during recent years without any recognized test of whether the resulting prices are fair. Both the recent Republican and Democratic Administrations have repudiated the parity formula established by law for that purpose. Government action which interferes with market forces in the establishment of commodity prices should be reduced to a minimum, but when it becomes necessary, the government should insure that the price consequences of its action will be fair. The current restriction on sales of grain to the Soviet Union is a case in point.

The Anderson Administration will re-examine the parity formula and other proposals for measuring the equitability of farm commodity prices. Such a review should call for the views of both farmers and consumers in an effort to determine fair and equitable returns for farmers.

We propose also to improve and administer farm price supports and other commodity programs so as to make them less cumbersome and their effects more predictable and stable.

Recent drought conditions have dramatized the continuing need to expand the eligibility of coverage of federal crop insurance programs to better protect farmers from the financial devastation of drought and other natural disasters, while also providing adequate emergency farm credit.

We also reaffirm our support for the Capper-Volstead Act,

the basic charter under which agricultural producers are empowered to organize for group action in pricing and marketing their products.

Farm Costs

Net farm incomes in recent years have been sharply affected by the rising costs of fuel, petroleum-based fertilizers and pesticides, transportation, and farm equipment. Restraining those costs and lowering interest rates can further boost America's already high agricultural productivity and raise net farm incomes.

We propose to:

- reduce the cost of energy for farmers by encouraging efficient programs to convert farm and forestry products into alcohol and other forms of energy and promoting and facilitating increased use of solar, wind, and water energy resources;

- continue efforts to free farmers from excessive federal regulation by requiring federal regulators to assess the special impacts of their rule-making on small businesses;

- assure consideration in rail deregulation legislation of the needs of captive rail shippers for access to their markets and distribution systems at reasonable costs;

- insure priority allocation of fuel for agricultural use in the event of supply shortages;

- insure farmers fair and adequate access to farm credit; and

- reduce farm costs overall by instituting sound federal fiscal policies designed to reduce government borrowing, lower interest rates, and curb inflation.

The Family Farm

The real strength of American agriculture is the
family farm. If we are to preserve this institution, however, we must adopt new measures designed to insure the
continuity of family farm ownership and eliminate those
aspects of current law that discriminate against the
family farmer.

An Anderson administration will:

● support further reform of estate and inheritance tax
  policies to permit opportunities for successor generations to assume ownership and management of farm enterprises without incurring crippling tax burdens;

● insure smaller farmers fair and equal access to federal
  credit programs;

● expand current, long-term low-equity financing programs
  to better enable young farm families to begin full-time
  farming enterprises while guarding against abuse of the
  program by speculators;

● recognize the vital role of women in the farm enterprise and work to repeal the application of the estate
  tax to the transfer of family farms between spouses --
  the so-called "widows tax"; and

● reform the tax laws to discourage the purchase of farm
  land for tax loss farming purposes.

Farm and Rural Women

The Anderson administration will strive to gain legal
recognition for the role of farm and rural women as full
partners with their husbands or brothers, sons or daughters.
Farm women contribute their time, their labor and in many
instances their money to the farming enterprise. They work

in the fields and barns, they keep farm accounts and they
participate in making farm business decisions.

Yet, today, because of high inflation and declining
farm income, many farm and rural women find they cannot
participate as they choose. Low farm returns force many to
seek additional employment and another income off their
farms, frequently to the detriment of their health and
emotional well being. We will support programs that assure
recognition of their contributions to the farming enterprise
and a sound economic policy that will allow farmers to
maintain a decent standard of living for their families.

Agricultural Lands

The U.S. loses an estimated 20,000 acres of its best
farmland each week to other uses. Much of it is irretrievably
lost due to the enormous costs of reclamation. Preliminary
statistics compiled by the National Agricultural Lands Study,
now being conducted by the U.S. Department of Agriculture
and the Council on Environmental Quality, suggests that the
nation may lose as much as 22.4 million acres (7 percent)
of its prime farmland by the year 2000. An Anderson administration will encourage state and local units of government
to develop programs to protect vital agricultural lands and
seek to bring federal actions into better conformity with
state and local plans for agricultural land use.

Soil and Water Conservation

Conservation of our increasingly valuable soil and
water resources is vital to America's future and to its
future generations. America grew up on its farms. However,
the pressures of rising population, economic growth and world
food requirements have subjected these resources to steadily
intensified competition and conflict among potential users.

Almost one-third of our total harvested acreage -- 109
million acres of cropland -- is being subjected to erosion
each year at a rate the USDA deems to be over "permissable
erosion rates." If this continues, it would eventually
destroy these lands' utility as cropland.

We must institute a closer, on-going review of soil and
water depletion rates, while seeking to increase the delivery
of technical and educational services. At the same time,
however, we must recognize the very difficult decisions
that will have to be made in these areas.

There are no easy solutions to the growing erosion,
salinization and water scarcity problems. The Anderson
administration will seek to frame these choices in the
frankest manner possible and strive for an equitable resolution of conflicting needs and claims.

Agricultural Policy and Consumers

Although the food distribution process begins on the
farm, food often goes through a complex chain of distributors

before it reaches the consumer. This process adds two-
thirds or more to the consumer's food bill. It is in the
processing, distribution and advertising costs of food that
the greatest potential for economies exist.

An Anderson administration will shift the federal
government's research efforts on food processing and marketing
toward reducing non-farm-added costs of food. Review should
include new food forms and more efficient marketing practices
and systems.

We also pledge to support and strengthen the food assistance programs, including the food stamp and school lunch
programs, to better meet the nutritional needs of the truly
needy.

The U.S. Space Program

Since its inception over twenty years ago, the U.S.
space program has yielded an impressive array of technological and economic benefits. But after achieving the Kennedy
Administration's goal of putting a man on the moon by 1970,
America's space effort has faltered. While the U.S. has
made impressive strides with the development of the space
shuttle, the overall level of dollar commitment has declined
in real terms.

We believe an invigorated space program can play an
important role in raising productivity and revitalizing our
economy since the space program funds basic research in a
wide range of fields such as photography, communications,
metallurgy, life-support systems, and many other areas of science
and engineering.

An expanded space program based generally on NASA's
current five-year plan should be established. The objectives
of that plan should be:

●	to fill the transportation and orbital needs of space
	missions in an economical and effective manner.

●	to improve our ability to apply space technology in
	areas that promise immediate or potential benefits

to humanity, including remote sensing, communication
and materials processing;

● to improve our ability to acquire, transmit, and process data;

● to increase our knowledge about the history of the
cosmos and expand our understanding of the evolutionary process involved; and

● to advance our fundamental knowledge of how energy
is transported from the sun and through the inter-
galactic medium and what effects that energy has
on Earth's environment.

NASA's current five-year plan does not include funding

for several vital programs needed for the development of

space science, technology, and industrialization. Many of

these programs, included in earlier plans and cut from the

current proposal by the Carter Administration, should be

reinstated. They include:

● an intensified effort to achieve routine operational
use of the Space Shuttle, with improvements in lift
and on-board power capabilities, that will enable it
to realize its full potential.

● establishment of an operational Landsat-type system
for Earth resources surveys, as repeatedly urged on
a bipartisan basis in Congress, in lieu of the hesi-
tant, half-hearted motions of the Carter Administration in this direction.

● proper support of a long-term program to explore the
solar system with unmanned space probes, avoiding the
costly starts and stops we have experienced under the
Carter Administration. The Galileo mission to Jupiter,
the Venus Orbiting Imaging Radar and Halley's Comet
Flyby missions are important steps in this program.

- full support for scientific study of the universe
  through completion and operation of the large optical
  space telescope and other specialized scientific satellites.

- eventual establishment of a permanent U.S. presence
  in space through planning and design of a general purpose orbiting space station to work with and be ser-
  viced by the space shuttle, thereby regaining the
  economically important lead in space research which
  the Soviet Union now enjoys as a result of its ongoing space operations.

- continuation and amplification of satellite power
  system evaluation (including the possible manufacture from nonterrestrial materials) in order to
  determine the practical desirability of collecting
  solar energy in space and safely transmitting it to
  Earth.

- active research on large space structures, expanded
  space power generation, and the other technological
  advances needed to form a sound basis for developing
  a substantial national space industrialization capability within the foreseeable future.

93

Export Promotion

A nation once famed for its "Yankee traders" now finds itself out-traded and out-manuevered in the world market place. If America is to prosper domestically, it must compete more effectively.

A nation, such as ours, which pays nearly $100 billion a year for foreign oil must export aggressively if it is to survive the decade ahead with its economy and currency intact. Viewed in that light, our export policy must be immediately invigorated. The policy of "benign neglect" that has characterized export administration in recent years cannot continue.

We propose a revitalized export promotion program, including the following new initiatives:

- expanded, competitive U.S. Export-Import Bank financing of U.S. exports;

- reduced taxation of American nationals living abroad and engaging in export activities;

- provision for duty-free entry of machinery and materials for use in export manufacture in foreign trade zones;

- amendments to the Webb-Pomerene law to permit business associations engaged in export activities to obtain pre-clearance anti-trust immunity for certified activities;

- measures designed to encourage the formation of export trading companies to assist small and medium sized firms in entering export markets;

- amendments to the Commodity Credit Corporation Charter Act creating an Agricultural Export Credit Revolving Fund to assure adequate financing of agricultural exports; and

- renewed efforts at obtaining international agreement on foreign business practices.

International Economic Relations

The present weakness of the U.S. economy reflects not only our own lack of capital investment and productivity improvements in recent years but also the larger fragility of the international economy due to the massive shifts of wealth from the oil-consuming nations to the oil-producing nations. It is anticipated that the current accounts surplus of the OPEC nations will reach $131 billion this year--a 15-fold increase over the 1978 surplus of $8.8 billion. By year's end, it is also expected that the industrialized countries will show an aggregate current account deficit of $49 billion, as compared to a 1978 surplus of $131 billion.

As severe as the oil-price pressures are to the industrialized West, they are even more severe for the non-oil exporting developing countries. Their deficit in 1980 is expected to reach nearly $70 billion, as compared to a $37.5 billion deficit in 1978. The combined debts of these countries has increased from $70 billion at the end of 1970 to approximately $300 billion by the end of 1979.

The continuing imbalance in world trade will put an enormous strain on world financial markets and test the limits

of our international monetary system. Now more than ever,
there is a need for closer international consultation and
cooperation on international trade and monetary affairs.
We cannot permit our shared problems to rupture either
international trade or the international monetary order.

To meet the recurring challenges to international
economic stability, we pledge:

● continued cooperation with our allies in attempting
to achieve the energy conservation and production
targets set forth in the recent Venice Summit Agreement;

● closer cooperation among our trading partners in an
effort to reduce through common agreement the frictions which, if left unattended, could lead to arbitrary trade restrictions and a resulting trade war;

● more effective and timely coordination of economic
and financial policy among the leading industrialized
nations, including the full use of facilities provided
by the International Monetary Fund (IMF) and the Organization for Economic Cooperation and Development
(OECD);

● continued efforts to enhance the effectiveness of
IMF exchange rate surveillance;

● expanded financial and technical assistance to non-
OPEC developing countries in their efforts to explore
and market new energy sources; and

● renewed efforts to establish a new stable monetary
order through further refinement and extension of
the Special Drawing Rights, rather than reverting
to an anachronistic and rigid gold standard as proposed by the Reagan platform.

97

Working Men and Women

An Anderson Administration will strive to improve the purchasing power of American workers, safeguard their working conditions, and protect their bargaining rights. In working toward these goals, we pledge to consult on a regular basis with the interested party -- the working man and woman of America.

Within the last year, the purchasing power of the average urban worker has declined by over 7 percent. This is the record by which the Carter Administration's labor policy must be judged; and, by any reasoned interpretation, it must be adjudged a failure.

The policies of the past four years have not served to reduce unemployment at the expense of purchasing power. They have served to aggravate both joblessness and inflation. Unemployment today is higher than when President Carter took office. The average American worker today is neither more secure in his job nor richer in his pay than when the President took office.

The collective bargaining rights of the American worker
must be protected. We find unacceptable the willingness of certain
employers to bear the cost of defying sanctions for unfair
labor practices. The administration and enforcement of
our labor laws must be strengthened through selective improvements
in the National Labor Relations Act.

An Anderson Administration will support measures designed
to expedite the National Labor Relations Board hearing process,
adequately compensate those who are illegally dismissed by
their employer for union-organizing activities, and give the
Secretary of Labor discretionary authority to withhold federal
contracts from employers guilty of flagrant or repeated labor
law violations.

We reaffirm our support for a fair and equitable federal
minimum wage. The minimum wage should bear a consistent
and reasonable relation to the average manufacturing wage.
Congress should exercise proper oversight of the federal
minimum wage laws by periodically reviewing both the level and
scope of minimum wage protection.

Upon proper review and evaluation, an Anderson Administration
will submit legislation in the first session of the 97th Congress
to ensure a fair and adequate minimum wage for 1982 and beyond.

We will oppose, however, efforts to "index" the minimum wage
to an arbitrary wage or price formula. The minimum wage
should be subject to normal and periodic review by Congress.

The health and safety of working men and women deserve
the highest measure of protection. We reaffirm our long-
standing support for the full and effective enforcement
of the Occupational Safety and Health Act of 1970. The
right of every American to a safe and healthful workplace
should be safeguarded by a fully funded Occupational Safety
and Health Administration (OSHA).

We pledge to oppose legislation, currently before the
Congress, which would effectively exempt 90 percent of all
workplaces from safety inspections, including inspections
triggered by employee complaints of hazardous working conditions.
The proposed legislation would put undue reliance upon "voluntary
compliance", jeopardizing the lives of thousands of American
workers. The proper role of OSHA is accident prevention,
not after-the-fact accident investigation.

In addition to fair wages and improved working conditions,
our working men and women want meaningful work. They have

unique knowledge of what lowers the quality and raises
the cost of what they make, and they have important views
on how the workplace can be organized more sensibly and
humanely. Workers in many of the world's healthiest
economies have won the right to cooperate with their companies
to help determine the structure of production. An Anderson
Administration will seek to encourage this development in the
United States in a prudent manner consistent with our own
traditions.

Workers on indefinite layoffs in distressed industries
such as the automobile, steel, and shipbuilding industries
require special assistance. We support an extension of
job-retraining and relocation assistance for displaced
workers and Economic Development Administration assistance
to distressed communities. We support on a pilot-project
basis the adoption of work-sharing programs designed to
minimize plant-layoffs through voluntary work-sharing
agreements supported by modified unemployment compensation
benefits for those working shortened hours.

We shall oppose efforts to repeal the Davis-Bacon Act
of 1931. Workers on federal projects should be paid the
prevailing wage of the community in which the construction

takes place. We reserve judgment, however, on the advisability
of extending prevailing wage protections into new areas.

III. MEETING HUMAN NEEDS

Introduction

A dynamic and growing economy is the necessary condition
of social progress, of domestic harmony and equity, and of
military strength and national security. And only such an
economy can allow all its citizens the basic freedom to
choose and to pursue their own occupations. But economic
health is not an end in itself. The worth of every society
is determined by what its members do--as individuals and as
citizens--with the wealth they create.

We believe that a modern society must accept its
responsibility to provide for basic human needs, in three ways.

First, it must act to furnish all its citizens with those
public goods that cannot be attained through individual effort,
but only through cooperative endeavors. It must, therefore, care
for its cities, its transportation, and its community environment.

Second, a modern society must accept responsibility for
those who cannot support themselves. It must provide sustenance
for those who are unable to work, income for those who have
reached the age of retirement from the workforce, and medical
care and other services for those who cannot afford them without
assistance.

Third, a modern society must create an environment
within which human beings can strive to fulfill their own
needs. It must encourage, not discourage, family life
through tax policies and child care. It must enable its

citizens to develop their abilities through systems of
education and training, and through a wide variety of cultural experiences. And it must enable them to apply their
abilities to their own betterment and that of their community, in productive and satisfying occupations. And it
must protect the larger environment in which we all must
live.

An Anderson Administration will accept these three
responsibilities. It will not seek to return this nation
to the 1920's, as the Republicans dream of doing, but neither
will it simply repeat the programs and ideas of the past,
as the Democrats do. Rather, it will propose new means to
attain the ends on which the overwhelming majority of
Americans are in agreement: means that are as efficient,
as equitable, and as humane as our ingenuity can devise.

THE FUTURE OF AMERICA'S CITIES

General Background

In the century after the Civil War, the United States underwent an economic expansion without precedent in world history. In the course of this great transformation, the United States, predominantly rural in 1865, became an urban nation. Once primarily service and trade centers, our cities became manufacturing centers as well. Massive urban capital investments were made -- not only in factories but also in housing, roads, bridges, public transportation, sewers, and water systems. Population steadily shifted from farms to cities as urban employment opportunities expanded and the efficiency of the agricultural sector increased. This human tide was swollen by European immigrants and by Southern blacks.

After the Second World War, many older cities -- particularly in the Northeast and Midwest -- entered a period of economic decline. The proliferation of the automobile, coupled with the construction of our highway system, made it possible for members of the middle class to leave the central city for the suburbs. This trend was encouraged by the FHA, which directed capital toward single-family suburban housing construction. The newly burgeoning economies of the South and Southwest began to attract capital, skilled workers, corporate headquarters, and government contracts. Simultaneously, older cities received large numbers of new residents, from the South and from abroad, with below-average income, skill, and education but above-average requirements for

public services. The net outflow of population these cities
experienced slowed the growth of property values and promoted
blight and crime in many neighborhoods.

These developments have had a marked effect on the
composition of the inner cities. Between 1970 and 1977, the
population of major American cities dropped by 4.6 percent,
compared with a growth in suburban population of 12.0 percent
and 10.7 percent in nonmetropolitan areas. The change has been
even more pronounced in the cities of the northeast and midwest
as population has shifted from those regions to the south and
west.

Of the total population below the government's poverty
level, 38 percent were living in the major cities by 1977,
compared with 34 percent in 1970. In contrast, the proportion
of the poor living outside the metropolitan areas fell during
the same period from 44 percent to 39 percent.

Racial and ethnic population statistics are equally dramatic
and disturbing. Fifty-five percent of the nation's black
population now live in the large cities, compared to 25 percent
of white Americans. Growing proportions of urban residents
today belong to Hispanic or female-headed households. These
three groups --Blacks , Hispanics, female-headed households --
suffer from severe deprivation in housing, jobs, and income.

A recently released major study demonstrates that despite
the massive government assistance cities have received in the

past two decades, the older, distressed cities of our nation are
in <u>worse</u> shape than they were in 1960. Clearly the old policy of
putting cities on welfare has not dealt successfully with their
real problems.

We must do better. But we must not fall into the trap of
seeking a new grand design or of attempting to devise a new
set of policies while ignoring what we now have. The Carter
Administration has tried to do this, and it has only made
matters worse.

We should not fear to innovate. But we must also be
concerned with the sound administration of existing programs.
Regulations must be simplified, and better linkages established
among related programs. Programs that work must be identified
and expanded, while those that do not should be terminated or
reoriented.

Federal urban policy should be guided by appropriate
general principles.

● We should strive for a suitable balance between federal
  and local initiatives, recognizing that neither
  centralization nor decentralization will succeed in all
  circumstances. Tasks, the equitable and efficient performance
  of which require national coordination should be handled
  at the federal level, while others are the proper function
  of states and localities.

- We must recognize that there is no major urban problem that the federal government can solve solely through its own efforts. Federal initiatives should seek to mobilize local resources and to involve the private sector. Federal policy should try to substitute incentives for regulations and prohibitions whenever possible. The federal government should aim to create a climate within which individual initiative is encouraged and rewarded.

- Some problems are best dealt with through sharply focused categorical programs. In general, however, the federal government should employ block grants to consolidate related programs, reduce burdensome regulations, and increase flexibility and access on the state and local level. We thus strongly support the general revenue sharing program.

- To advance truly national interests, the federal government should minimize the use of discretionary programs that vest excessive decision-making authority in the bureaucrac In general, formula-based allocation stemming from explicit, public legislative decision-making is sound public policy.

- The federal government must seek to identify the most urgent needs of our urban centers and to concentrate its efforts upon them. We propose that the federal involvement in urban problems be increased because of the unmet human needs in many of our nation's cities, not because cities as such deserve special attention.

- The federal government should distinguish between a short-term support function and a long-term investment function in its urban policies. While we meet today's needs, we should search for ways of rebuilding the economic capacity of our cities so that they can move toward eventual revenue independence and fiscal self-sufficiency.

The Urban Reinvestment Trust Fund

Most urban experts agree that the deterioration of our
massive investment in urban capital stock -- housing, roads,
bridges, public transportation, sewers, water systems -- is
the most serious problem now confronting the nation's cities.
Caught between declining tax bases and escalating costs, many
cities   particularly the older cities of the Northeast and
Midwest   have been forced to defer essential maintenance to
meet immediate operating needs. A recent comprehensive survey
of twenty-eight major cities concluded that:

- Deterioration in the capital stock of older cities has
  accelerated in the past five years as a consequence of
  fiscal stress and aging.

- As repair needs mount, maintenance workforces are being
  cut.

- In many cases, cities facing severe budgetary pressures
  have curtailed maintenance spending more sharply than
  spending for other current operations.

- Similarly, capital spending has been squeezed.

- Older cities, predominantly those located in the Northeast
  and Midwest, face investment backlogs and lack the financial
  capabilities to meet their needs from local resources.

To address this massive and urgent problem, an Anderson
Administration will propose an Urban Reinvestment Trust Fund
(URTF) to assist distressed cities in rehabilitating and replacing
their capital stock.

Funding. The URTF would be funded through 45 percent
of the federal alcohol and tobacco excise taxes, to be phased
in over a three-year period. When fully funded, it would
receive and disburse approximately $3.8 billion annually (in
1980 constant dollars).

Allocation. The URTF would be allocated to cities
and metropolitan areas on the basis of a three-factor formula:
pre-1939 housing stock (weighted 50 percent); population in
poverty (weighted 30 percent); population loss (weighted 20
percent). This formula is the best indicator of the two most
relevant dimensions of community need: degree of decay of
capital stock, and ability to raise and use tax revenues for
maintenance.

Disposition of funds. The funds made available
through the URTF would be used for:

● the upgrading and repair of existing capital plant and
equipment: streets, bridges, sidewalks, street lighting,
water mains, sewers, waste processing and sanitary facilities,
pollution control facilities and equipment, and related items;

● the replacement or installation of such plant and equipment
when current facilities are either beyond repair or altogether
lacking.

Local authorities would be free to determine their own
priorities and allocation procedures, subject to three constraint
Legislation would require:

● that equity prevail in the use of funds within cities,
with immediate emphasis on upgrading facilities in the most
severely decayed areas;

111

- that neighborhood organizations be adequately consulted in the process of determining community-wide priorities;

- that URTF funds supplement, not replace, local funds currently employed for capital stock maintenance and rehabilitation.

Because the revenues from the federal excise taxes on alcohol and tobacco have been rising more slowly than the rate of inflation, at the end of the phase-in period we will consider raising current excise tax rates to meet the urgent national needs to which our Trust Fund is addressed.

Housing

The quality of life in our cities, and throughout our
nation, is crucially affected by the availability of decent,
affordable housing for all citizens. But the Carter policy
of fighting inflation with tight money and high interest rates
has had a devastating effect on this sector of the economy.
Housing starts have declined to an annual rate of one million,
the lowest since World War Two and one million units lower than
predicted last year. This level of activity will result in:

-- the loss of 1.6 million jobs;

-- the loss of $27.6 billion in wages;

-- the loss of over $3.5 billion in federal tax
revenues and $7.5 billion in combined federal, state, and
local revenues. Moreover, this lost production will produce
an even more rapid inflation in housing costs as the economy
recovers from the Carter recession.

The underlying demand for housing is very strong and
will grow substantially through the 1980's. During this
decade, 41 million Americans will reach the prime homebuying
age, compared with 31 million in the previous decade, and
the rate of new household formation will be 25 percent higher.
This demand cannot be satisfied even by levels of production
considered high in the past. Unfortunately, the crisis in
rental housing means that new rentals will not be able to meet

113

any substantial portion of the existing demand. Recent
statistics show that in the past three years, there has
been an annual net <u>loss</u> of rental units of nearly 2 percent.
High interest rates, increased operating costs, and burdensome
regulations have nearly shut down the private construction of
rental housing. As a result, the nationwide multi-family
vacancy rate has fallen to the lowest level since this statistic
was first compiled twenty years ago. In many cities there is
virtually no vacant rental housing.

In the early part of the 1970's, the federal government
stepped into the breach by subsidizing the construction of
new rental housing. This assistance reached its peak in 1976.
Since then, because of soaring unit costs and fiscal constraints,
the amount of subsidized new construction has declined sharply.

If we do not undertake effective new initiatives, housing
will become a major source of social conflict in the 1980's,
as new families struggle with dwindling supplies and escalating
costs. In the past year, the percentage of families able to
afford the monthly payments on their first house has declined
sharply at the same time that rental housing has become
scarcer and less affordable. We run the risk of being split
into two nations: those who were fortunate enough to buy
while housing costs were a reasonable fraction of personal
incomes, and those who were unfortunate enough to arrive
on the scene too late.

To deal with our housing problems, we propose the following steps:

● We must begin to attack the housing problem in this
  nation by stabilizing our economy. Reckless spending and
  huge deficits lead to inflation which in turn escalates
  long-term interest rates, the key determinant of housing
  costs. In addition, inflation produces a flight from
  savings and paper money into real property, reducing
  funds available for mortgages and further hiking housing
  prices. The housing industry cannot function properly
  until we restore sound economic climate for planning and
  investment. This we pledge to do, as our first order
  of business.

● We must work to dampen the inefficient and damaging
  housing cycle. We support the reactivation of a program
  such as that proposed by Republican Senator Edward Brooke
  and Democratic Senator Alan Cranston, a countercyclical
  mortgage-subsidy program that would be automatically
  triggered whenever housing starts fall below a designated
  level for a significant length of time. This is not a
  permanent subsidy, but rather a low-cost, temporary,
  recoverable government investment that works effectively
  to place a floor under housing starts.

● We must embark on a comprehensive review of federal, state,
  and local regulations affecting housing construction and
  renovation, which have been estimated to add up to 20
  percent to the cost of each new unit. Where possible, we
  must simplify or eliminate this burdensome system of regulation

● We support the reauthorization of tax-exempt revenue bonds
  to support single and multi-family housing construction,
  subject to reasonable restrictions.

● We support new initiatives to stimulate the private
  construction and operation of multi-family housing,
  including:
        -- increased shallow interest rate subsidies
        -- increased tax incentives, particularly accelerated
           depreciation, for multi-family buildings.

● We support an urgent effort to increase the supply of
  urban housing stock to usable condition. All remaining
  federal restrictions on the use of HUD funds for renovation
  of existing housing should be eliminated. Programs, such

115

as urban homesteading, that mobilize local renovation
efforts should be encouraged. We especially support an
increased partnership between the federal government and
community organizations to put the people of our
neighborhoods to work rebuilding their own homes.

- We should explore policies that would increase the supply
of urban housing by encouraging the conversion of abandoned
buildings from other uses to housing. Such policies include
providing technical assistance, identifying and donating
surplus government buildings, and providing accelerated
depreciation.

- We support the extension of current programs that encourage
low and moderate income urban residents to develop a stake
in their community through ownership of their own residences.
The federal government should assist apartment dwellers to
form cooperative organizations to purchase and renovate their
buildings.

- To increase the supply of mortgage funds, and to assist
prospective homeowners, we support the gradual expansion
of the existing interest income exclusion ($200 for
individuals, $400 for married couples) to $750 for
individuals and $1,500 for married couples as stated
elsewhere in the platform.

Neighborhoods

A healthy city is a place of ethnic and economic diversity, neither a playground for the rich, nor a dumping ground for the poor. It is an association of stable, vigorous neighborhoods, secure in their differences, linked by common interests and purposes. A liveable physical environment is only a first step.

For too long, federal policy has discouraged or neglected neighborhoods. In the past, "urban renewal" obliterated existing neighborhoods, replacing them with public housing projects, highways, and office buildings. Today, although the federal government no longer levels whole neighborhoods, it continues to sponsor initiatives that damage neighborhood interests while neglecting and underfunding programs that directly benefit neighborhoods.

The following steps are essential to remedy this situation:

● The next administration must appoint a new, high-level executive task force to review and, where appropriate, to implement the recommendations of the National Commission on Neighborhoods. The Commission's report was released nearly eighteen months ago, after extensive research and numerous public hearings, but the Carter Administration has almost completely ignored its findings;

● We must promote the formation and activities of neighborhood associations, through such means as:
---a neighborhood improvement tax credit, providing an 80 percent credit on the first 50 dollars of each taxpayer's contribution to a neighborhood group;
---the provision of federal matching money to local neighborhood improvement groups in designated distressed areas;
---increased support for such ventures as the Neighborhood Housing Service, operating under the aegis of the Neighborhoc Reinvestment Corporation, which seeks to form partnerships among neighborhood associations, financial institutions, and local governments to increase the supply of affordable housir

---adequate funding for HUD's Office of Neighborhood Development which, in spite of significant accomplishments, has been neglected by the Carter Administration.

● We must promote economic development in neighborhoods through:
     ---directing the Small Business Administration to comply
with its authorizing legislation, which mandates that SBA
programs be made accessible to Community Development Corporations;
     ---reauthorizing the SBA's 502 direct loan program, which
is on the verge of termination in spite of its proven record of
stimulating small business in declining neighborhoods;
     ---insuring that the Urban Development Action Grant program
sponsors projects that distribute federal funds more equitably
within cities and more directly benefit neighborhoods;
     ---offering increased tax incentives to the private
sector to enter into partnerships with community development
corporations and other neighborhood-based economic
development groups.

● We must recognize that although the increased flow of
suburban dwellers back to our central cities has favorable
consequences for urban tax bases and housing stock, it
also generates a significant problem of dislocation,
particularly among the poor and elderly. In the past,
dislocation has meant declining housing quality, persistent
overcrowding, increased costs, and severe psychological
and social disruption for those forced to move.

Federal policy must be more responsive to the needs and

legitimate claims of those presently residing in neighborhoods

undergoing these changes. If some dislocation is unavoidable,

the federal government must accept its fair share of the responsibility

to assist displacees.

Enterprise Zones

Within our distressed older cities, there are neighborhoods

that can only be called zones of devastation. Dwellings are

boarded up and abandoned, or inhabited by derelicts. Businesses

are failing and fleeing. Arson is rife. Gangs fight for control

of the streets while ordinary citizens live in constant fear.

All who are able to escape do so, leaving behind those without

alternatives or hope. In the South Bronx, for example, 96 percent of the residents are now Black or Hispanic, compared to 66 percent in 1970. One-quarter of the residents live in households with annual incomes under $3,000. One-third of the population is entirely dependent on welfare.

Some have suggested what amounts to urban triage-- that we declare that certain areas are unsalvageable and leave them to their fate. We completely reject this proposal. It makes no economic sense to abandon our enormous investment in housing, factories, and capital stock, much of which is still usable or capable of being renovated. And it is inhumane to abandon viable neighborhoods where families have lived and worked for generations, and which still provide continuity and identity for many residents. Clearly, however, the traditional tools of federal urban and social policy have not worked, and cannot reasonably be expected to work, in these areas.

In an effort to give these devastated zones a chance to recover and thrive, Republican Congressman Jack Kemp and Democratic Congressman Robert Garcia have recently introduced a bill that would permit the designation of "enterprise zones".

The enterprise zone approach seeks to improve conditions in the most run-down urban areas by encouraging local governments to participate with the federal government in creating a climate favorable to the establishment and success of small business, by lowering existing corporate, capital gains, payroll, and property taxes and by furnishing new tax incentives. Two-thirds of all new jobs are in companies employing fewer than 20 people. Such companies are more able to develop new, profitable ideas and to utilize existing facilities. In

addition, entrepreneurs with marketable skills and ideas but little
capital are often willing to devote long hours in poor working
conditions to build up their businesses. Moreover, although
small business entrepreneurs often have little knowledge of
business skills when they begin, as their businesses grow they
gain management competence and are able to utilize increasing
amounts of local labor. In short, the enterprise zone concept
seeks to use federal legislation to mobilize already existing
local resources -- structurally sound buildings, surplus labor,
entrepreneurial spitit -- to help people in need to help themselves
and to work toward pride and independence.

The Kemp-Garcia bill is still in a relatively early stage
of legislative development and needs considerable refinement.
Specifically, we propose that:

● To be eligible to participate, local governments be
  required to lower sales taxes within the zones;

● A residency requirement be added to ensure that a significant
  percentage of those hired under the payroll tax reduction
  provision actually live in the zones; and

● Local lending institutions receive tax incentives
  to direct capital towards new ventures in the zones.

We believe that, appropriately amended, the enterprise
zone bill will give new hope to urban areas that presently have
no hope. Although it is an experiment, it will be undertaken only
in areas that have little if anything to lose. We therefore support
the passage and rapid implementation of well crafted enterprise
zone legislation.

COMMUNITY TRANSIT

Through years of planning negligence, profligate consumption, and lack of federal leadership, the United States
has slid into a state of dependence on foreign oil that
threatens our economic viability and national security.
Transportation consumes half the petroleum used in this
country, and the single-passenger automobile is the largest
consumer. While the automobile provides -- and will continue
to offer -- freedom of mobility and flexibility of response,
its technical performance must be improved and its efficient
use encouraged. Additionally, as a Nation, we must commit
ourselves fully to the development of a broad range of
transportation alternatives. Increasing transportation
choices requires strong federal support for public mass transit
and incentives to encourage the private sector provision of
energy-efficient and consumer-responsive transportation
service options. It further requires a dedicated and predictable federal funding source. Such a federal policy will
bring enormous fuel savings as well as increased and more
fuel-secure personal mobility.

An Anderson Administration will propose a plan to provide
a continuing and predictable federal commitment to:

● provide long-term financial support for the capital and
  operating costs of mass transit systems;

● finance effective auto management plans for urban areas;

• stimulate the innovative involvement of the private
  sector in offering options to the solo use of the
  automobile; and

• respond to the increasing need of rural populations
  for transportation alternatives.

A major part of this commitment will be met by the
establishment of a new Community Transportation Trust Fund
to fund capital and maintenance costs of metropolitan and
local transit systems. Operating costs and other assistance
programs would continue to be funded out of general revenues.

The CTTF would be funded through 45% of the federal
alcohol and tobacco excise taxes. Over the next five years,
15 billion dollars would be expended, $2.5 billion in fiscal
year 1981 alone. The surplus -- as much as an additional
$1.5 billion -- would be reserved as a hedge against inflation.
The reserve fund would be used to provide federal loan guarantees for automobile and other manufacturing companies that
produce transit vehicles. The companies could use their
federally guaranteed loans for research and development into
the design, safety, and energy-efficiency of transit vehicles
and for capital and tooling costs in manufacturing vehicles
that respond to local procurement requests.

The CTTF will provide for the maintenance and modernization of rail, light rail, and bus systems for metropolitan
areas, and for the building of new cost-efficient surface
light rail systems that contribute to rational land use

planning and development objectives in accordance with the
following priorities:

● assurance that long-term federal commitments to new
energy-efficient rapid transit lines are consistent
with sound urban planning objectives;

● more flexible funding to modernize, upgrade, and extend
older fixed-rail and light rail systems and stations;

● rigorous review of the cost- and energy-effectiveness
of any new fixed guideway transit systems proposals;

● investment in new light rail systems using existing
railroad right-of-ways highway medians, or urban
streets;

● production or rehabilitation and deployment of 10,000
buses annually for the next ten years;

● employment of "track-sharing" systems where feasible,
by which both commuters and freight-haulers make use of
the same urban railbeds.

An Anderson Administration will also use funds from
the CTTF to stimulate the revitalization of the cities. Urban
areas would be encouraged to bring together civic leaders
in making commitments to include: providing new jobs and
training; establishing strong affirmative action goals;
bringing new businesses and industries to the area; and
designing new private facilities that enhance the environment.

The beneficial impact of transportation investment on
urban economic development necessitates the coordination of
transportation policies with other public decisions. The
federal tax code, water and sewer grants, and highway programs
tend to encourage scattered suburban development. An Anderson

Administration will propose to realize the full economic
revitalization potential of transportation by supporting
transportation policy with other federal programs that
influence urban development patterns. Housing, environmental, and overall urban policy will be coordinated to
achieve this objective.

An Anderson Administration will prepare a twenty-year
community transportation financing plan with state and community participation, to be enacted by Congress. The plan
would provide both long-term funding predictability and
greater local decision-making flexibility, enabling local
transit agencies to plan more effectively and to allocate
their resources in response to overall community needs. The
long-term community transportation financing plan will have
the following objectives:

● establishment of a national goal of a ten percent annual
  growth rate in transit ridership and private ridesharing;

● establishment of a comprehensive bus or rail system for
  every urban area with a population of 200,000 or more
  by the end of the decade;

● establishment of effective ridesharing programs in all
  fifty states to provide alternatives to the automobile
  for urban and rural workers and others who are dependent
  on the automobile; and

● development of a nationwide, coordinated approach to providing transportation choices for all rural Americans.

Efficient use of federal funds to provide transportation
choices requires that communities also undertake comprehensive
programs to ensure the responsible use of the automobile. An

Anderson Administration will use federal funding, tax incentives, and technical assistance to encourage shared ridership
and effective traffic management planning. Funds should also
be administered to encourage all types of public and private
operators to offer specialized collective transportation
services.

   The dynamics of private competition must be reintroduced
into collective transportation. An Anderson Administration
will create opportunities for specialized profit-making
transit services. These opportunities include removing legal
barriers, providing tax credits, and amending the tax laws
to encourage the use of alternatives to the automobile.

   An Anderson Administration will encourage local alternatives to reverse the serious decline in transportation
services to rural Americans. Car pooling, block grants for
collective transportation, and technical assistance are vital
federal options which will be utilized.

   Federal support for local mass transit systems must be
placed on a predictable long-term basis, enabling communities
to respond to their transportation needs in the most effective manner. A creative Anderson Administration will achieve
this goal by establishment of the CTTF and the twenty-year
financing plan coupled with a flexible and realistic approach
to transportation planning.

HEALTH CARE

The underlying strength of the health care system in the United States lies in the quality, ingenuity, and diversity that is a hallmark of a free and diverse society. Federal health care policy must build on these strengths.

We cannot afford comprehensive, nationalized health care at this time. Nor can we afford a laissez faire attitude that simply blames our problems on federal regulation. The fundamental federal objective must be to contribute toward the overall health of our society while providing for those who cannot adequately take care of their own health care needs. We need an innovative, practical federal health policy which closes the gaps in our health care system, and complements and sustains the inherent strengths of a private-based system.

Federal health care policy must address the serious problems and weakness in our system, which include:

● rampant inflation in health care costs;

● gaps in health care coverage, including the limited access of the urban and rural poor to health care;

● the lack of a comprehensive, long-term care policy for the elderly; and

● the disproportionate emphasis of federal programs on the treatment of disease and the under-emphasis on preventive medicine and keeping people well.

Of these problems, the most severe is rampant inflation
in health care costs. The health care industry accounts
for 9% of GNP, nearly doubling since 1960. The average
cost of a day in a hospital has increased from $15 in 1950
to $225 in 1978, seven times the general rate of inflation.
Some of these increases in health care costs are undoubtedly
attributable to remarkable but expensive improvements
in health care technology and in expanded health care
coverage for people previously underserved. But spiralling
health care costs are also fueled by severe economic
distortions in the health care financing systems.

Prior public policy decisions are responsible for
a non-competitive health care environment. Heavy regulation
of alternative delivery systems such as health maintenance
organizations (HMOs) have made it nearly impossible for
these systems to operate on a competitive basis. Cost-plus
reimbursement under Medicaid and Medicare encourages
doctors and hospitals to increase the volume and quality
of hospital services without considering cost. The federal
health insurance tax subsidy program, costing $13 billion
annually, promotes adoption of health policies without
full regard for costs. Regulatory programs such as the
health system agencies (HSA) and professional standards
review organizations (PSROs), while successful in some

areas, have not yet demonstrated nation-wide success in
holding down health care costs.

An Anderson Administration will reform federal financing,
and encourage market-oriented incentives in order to
reward cost-conscious behavior, contain rising health care
costs, and respond to real health needs in the most
appropriate and caring manner. Specifically, an Anderson
Administration will:

● Phase out retroactive cost-plus reimbursement under
  federal programs and replace it with prospective
  rate or fixed-premium financing. This will eliminate
  much of the expensive cost accounting and cost-reporting
  practices now imposed on hospitals, nursing homes,
  home health agencies, and health maintenance organizations,
  giving providers the incentive to contain costs rather
  than rewarding excessive spending;

● Amend Medicare and Medicaid to allow participants to
  choose among competing health care options. This
  will promote flexibility, by allowing participants
  to select according to their needs, whether that be
  through prospective financial arrangements with
  hospitals or ambulatory care facilities, or through
  fixed-premium financing like a health maintenance
  organization;

● Make employer health insurance tax deductibles contingent
  upon the offering of several qualified competitive
  insurance plans to encourage private sector competition.
  Employers should be required to make the same dollar
  outlay for health benefits per employee, regardless
  of the plan's cost, thus encouraging employees to
  make cost-effective selections and insurers to
  monitor the cost and efficiency of health care
  providers. Appropriate exemptions for small businesses
  should be allowed; and

● Eliminate unnecessary and inefficient health system
regulations as the principles of competition take effect.
Federal funding for the health systems agencies and
professional standards review organizations programs
should be maintained. These regulatory programs were
established in response to the failure of marketplace
mechanisms to curb rising health costs. As competition
is brought back into the health system, however, these
regulatory activities can be phased out.

These reforms are designed to create incentives, control

costs, deliver services efficiently, and provide quality

services for all participants in the health care industry.

An Anderson Administration will endeavor to hold down costs

and provide quality health care simultaneously.

A second major problem is the lack of health care

coverage for 22 million Americans. Despite considerable

investment in medical care payments for the poor, these

populations still suffer from poorly coordinated and episodic

health care, and decreased access to medical care services.

An Anderson Administration will propose a responsible

federal health care policy to better insure access to adequate

health care and protection from impoverishment. Specifically,

an Anderson Administration will:

● Increase the supply of medical personnel to underserved
areas through increased funding of the National Health
Service Corps. The NHSC has been successful in placing
physicians, dentists and nurses in underserved areas
where many have remained to practice.

● Convert, where possible, urban hospitals with severe
financial predicaments to serve, in whole or in part,
as primary-care centers with federal assistance.

- Stimulate demonstration projects utilizing the Independent Provider Association (IPA) model for rural area physicians, linking them to existing central urban HMOs. By facilitating the specialty services through the urban HMO, IPAs can "subcontract" the delivery of services to rural patients through existing solo practice or small-group physicians;

- Expand the Medicare and Medicaid programs to include provision of mental health services; and

- Expand, in gradual steps, the Medicaid program to provide adequate coverage for the poor and working poor not yet covered, including coverage of low-income intact families, childless couples, and singles, as more efficient practices free up resources for such growth in beneficiary population.

To better insure access to catastrophic coverage for working men and women, the Anderson Administration will propose legislation requiring private-sector employers to offer a catastrophic insurance option in order to qualify their health plans for federal tax deductions.

Our health care system also lacks effective, long-term care services for the elderly. Federal programs frequently foster unnecessary hospitalization, which not only has serious financial impact on the individual and the government, but also creates a class of demoralized and dependent senior citizens. We must shift our emphasis from institutionalization to home health care. Approximately 2.5% of the federal health care budget is spent on home health care, compared to 20% spent on nursing home care, yet it is estimated that many of the 1,100,000 nursing home residents could be cared for more

cheaply, humanely, and appropriately by alternative health
care services.

An Anderson Administration will propose a comprehensive
federal policy supporting long-term care needs of older Americans
that is directed toward optimal health care maintenance through
prevention, care, and rehabilitation. We must provide the
necessary care to allow older Americans to remain financially
secure and productive participants in their community.
Specifically, an Anderson Administration will:

- Provide, as part of the Medicare program, a number of
  home health services: 1) homemaker and healthaide
  programs to provide such services as meal preparation,
  cleaning, and personal care; 2) adult day care centers
  for the elderly who need full supervision, but are
  cared for at night and weekends by relatives; 3) respite
  services to allow families to leave elderly members
  in care of competent individuals during vacations;
  4) patient education to encourage the elderly toward
  greater self-reliance and self-sufficiency;

- Allow tax credits for families caring for elderly
  relatives to assist them in meeting rising costs for
  goods and services for the elderly individual;

- Extend Medicare benefits to cover services provided
  by alternative health care professionals, such as
  nurses and physician's assistants;

- Extend Medicare benefits to cover eyeglasses, dentures,
  and hearing devices;

- Promote provision of low-cost housing communities
  through tax credits, low-interest loans, or direct-
  funding incentives; and

- Expand the Institute on Aging's research budget at
  NIH beyond the current 2% level.

An Anderson Administration will propose these reforms
to insure greater security and fulfillment for elderly
Americans. We must begin to take a step away from viewing
the elderly as a burden and back toward seeing them as sources
of wisdom and guidance.

Our present health care system also places disproportionate
emphasis on the treatment of illness and lacks appropriate
emphasis on preventive health care and health research. This
practice is cost-inefficient and discourages proper health
maintenance. We must place increased emphasis on protecting
the healthy populations of our country from illness and on
encouraging their continued good health. Health
research must be recognized as a legitimate operating
cost of the health care system.

An Anderson Administration will support programs to
promote and extend good health to all Americans. Specifically,
an Anderson Administration will:

- Continue enforcement of clean air, clean water, solid
  waste, and toxic substance standards;

- Increase funding for prevention and treatment of drug
  and alcohol abuse, and mental illness;

- Pursue handgun control and automotive safety initiatives
  to reduce the loss of life and disability resulting
  from handgun and car accidents;

- Support a Child Health Assurance Program to extend
  care to low-income children and pregnant women,

Preventive health care and early detection of disease
for these groups would do much to eliminate birth
defects and decrease the incidence of many chronic
debilitating diseases;

● Provide adequate funding for all forms of biomedical
and health care research particularly in the area of
prevention. The results of research relating health
to lifestyle, diet, and the environment must be
adequately disseminated to the public, so that
enlightened personal decisions can be made;

● Make tax monies to professional health care education
facilities that are heavily dependent upon federal
financing contingent upon instruction on preventive
medicine, nutrition, and epidemiology as part of their
core curriculum; and

● Continue support of OSHA and encouragement of innovative
and economic ways of achieving safety and occupational
health standards.

The measures outlined above form a health care policy

that is fiscally responsible, incentive-based, and targeted

on the gaps and weaknesses that currently exist in our

fundamentally strong, private-sector based health care

system. To curb escalating health care costs, we propose

competition among health care options in the private and

public sector. To reduce the gaps, we propose to extend

Medicaid eligibility for the poor and support National Health

Service Corps for under-served inner city and rural citizens.

To care for the elderly, we extend home health care coverage

and other Medicare provisions. And finally, we change the

focus of health care to preventive measures like the Child

133

Health Assurance Program.   These measures stop short of

comprehensive national health care, but they address the

most critical needs of the American health care system in

an affordable fashion.

WELFARE REFORM

Welfare reform remains one of the great unfulfilled promises of government. The existing patchwork of public assistance programs is fragmented, irrational, wasteful, duplicative and inefficient. Repeated efforts at comprehensive welfare reform have failed under both Democratic and Republican Administrations.

The continuing failure to enact the necessary reforms has manifested itself in several forms. State and local governments which have sought to meet legitimate public assistance needs have been burdened by escalating costs, despite honest attempts to eliminate welfare fraud. States and localities that have permitted inflation to erode benefit levels have fared better financially, but welfare recipients in those states have suffered from increasingly inadequate support levels.

In many states, Aid for Families with Dependent Children (AFDC) benefits have been limited to one-parent households, forcing the breakup of families when fathers leave home to retain benefits for the children. In nearly all states there remains substantial work disincentives with welfare recipients confronting high "effective" marginal tax rates.

Transferring all responsibility for public welfare programs back to the states is not an appropriate means of

dealing with the problems. We must seek to utilize the
greater administrative efficiency that can be realized by
large-scale delivery programs at the federal level with the
greater equity and savings that can be realized at the local
level by closer supervision and oversight.

Our task is to devise a more rational public assistance
delivery scheme. Experience has demonstrated that welfare
reform is best addressed by a series of selective reforms,
rather than by attempting to secure immediate comprehensive
reform. Adoption of the Social Welfare Reform Amendments of
1979, approved by the House of Representatives last December,
would be a good first step towards reform of public assistance. The bill would:

● establish a national AFDC minimum benefit level equal to
   65 percent of the poverty level for all families with
   children;

● raise income limits in certain states and provide a system
   of declining cash welfare supplements to recipients until
   the income ceiling is reached;

● require states to offer Aid for Families with Dependent
   Children (AFDC) benefits to families with two parents,
   one of whom is unemployed, providing the family meets
   an income and "unemployment test";

● decrease the non-federal funding share of AFDC benefits
   by 10-30 percent, depending on the nature of the benefit
   provided; and

● liberalize the Supplemental Security Income (SSI) program
   for the aged, blind and disabled, by permitting a husband
   and wife who separate to qualify for individual benefits
   earlier; and "cash out" foodstamps for certain classes
   of SSI recipients.

We must, however, go beyond these reforms in our efforts
to provide a more responsive and cost-effective delivery
system. Public assistance should be tied to both work incentives and work requirements for the able-bodied. Our principal objective must be the provision of private sector employment. While public sector employment programs will continue
to play an important role in job-training and temporary
employment, special attention must be directed at longer-term,
private sector job opportunity.

We support an expansion of the Supportive Work Program,
based on the recent successful demonstration project, in conjunction with the WIN program for AFDC recipients. We also
endorse further expansion of the Earned Income Tax Credit for
the working poor. These and other initiatives, including
proposed changes in the benefit reduction formula, would go
a long way toward increasing work incentives; but renewed
emphasis must also be placed on job creation. We support
retention of the Employment Tax Credit, which encourages new
hires of disadvantaged workers, and expanded reliance upon
the private sector jobs initiatives under Title VII of CETA.
We must recognize, however, that the greatest provider of
jobs for the disadvantaged in this country has always been a
growing and vibrant economy.

If welfare costs are to be contained without sacrificing
benefit levels for the truly needy, we need continuing

administrative improvements in welfare programs, including
standard procedures for the periodic determination of income
and eligibility, and expansion of electronic management
information systems. We support the use of innovative new
approaches, like the National Recipient Systems (NRS), to the
problem of erroneous payments.

Food Stamps

Despite some of the earlier problems associated with the
program, the Food Stamp Program remains a vitally important
element of our public assistance delivery system. Food Stamps
have provided timely and critical assistance to millions of
Americans whose household budgets have been disrupted by
temporary or permanent layoffs or whose incomes have suffered
due to age or physical handicap. As a compassionate and
humane society, we cannot ignore the legitimate nutritional
needs of those who would otherwise go hungry. We shall continue to support full and adequate funding of the Food Stamp
Program.

138

SENIOR CITIZENS

Senior citizens desire to live a useful and secure life. Yet, for many, this goal remains elusive despite new federal initiatives and expenditures which consume one-fourth of the current federal budget. An estimated nine million older Americans now live in poverty, lacking wholesome food, adequate housing, and proper health care. For those living in isolation, a sense of being unneeded and unwanted robs their later years of meaning and dignity.

An Anderson Administration would be committed to meeting the real needs of older citizens, strengthening effective programs and initiating reforms as experience dictates. Before recommending any additions, however, we would insure that ineffective programs are eliminated.

An Anderson Administration would remove the barriers discouraging productive activity by the aging by:

● liberalizing the Social Security "retirement test", which limits outside earnings from part-time and temporary employment; and

● tightening loopholes in the Age Discrimination In Employment Act and enforcing current provisions to eliminate early mandatory retirement.

In the vital area of health care for the aging, reforms in the Medicare system could both improve care and reduce cost by eliminating unnecessary institutionalization. Older persons not needing intensive care in high-cost facilities could receive appropriate personal attention from their families or neighbors assisted by local supportive services. To encourage this approach we would:

- modify provisions which tax Social Security recipients living with their families, rather than in institutions;

- propose income tax deductions for families which care for relatives in their homes; and

- provide supportive services such as geriatric day care, homemaker services, nutrition programs, and sheltered living arrangements to allow the aging to remain in their communities at reduced cost.

The Medicare program would be revised to include home health services:

- homemaker and health-aide programs to provide services such as meal preparation, cleaning and personal care;

- adult day care centers for aging persons requiring full-time supervision who receive care from relatives on nights and weekends;

- respite services to allow families to entrust aging family members to the care of competent individuals during vacations; and

- patient education to help ill persons achieve greater self-reliance and self-sufficiency.

We would also encourage the development and use of health maintenance organizations (HMOs), which offer health services for predetermined annual fees. Prospective payment encourages preventive care and discourages unnecessary medical procedures.

We would support legislation to end fraud and abuse in
the sale of private health insurance purchased by many aging
persons to cover the gaps in Medicare coverage.

Lack of adequate, affordable housing plagues many aging
persons. We favor increased support of public housing for
older persons and pledge to continue to aid the aging in
coping with rising energy costs.

Social Security Financing

The Social Security system is a public trust. It must
be protected and preserved. We cannot allow potential
insolvency to jeopardize the benefits of those who have
contributed to the system during their working years.

Despite a series of scheduled payroll tax increases
approved by the Congress in 1977, it is evident that neither
the short-term nor the long-term financing questions have been
resolved. It is anticipated that the Old Age and Survivors
Insurance Trust Fund will approach insolvency within a few
years.

The recurring problems with Social Security financing
require close Congressional scrutiny. The 1977 amendments
corrected one flaw in the Social Security program (the method
for indexing benefits), which contributed to the long-term
instability of the trust funds. There are, however, other
problems. One factor is the increase in the number of

retirees relative to the number of contributing workers.
The changing beneficiary/contributor ratio means that more
benefits will have to be paid out while contributions to
the trust fund decline. The second factor is inflation.
Social Security benefits are indexed to inflation to maintain
the value of the benefits. In recent years, however,
inflation rates have exceeded wage increases, resulting
in a further depletion of the funds.

The short-term financing problems of the Old Age and
Survivors Insurance Trust Fund can be resolved by either
reallocating a portion of the payroll tax from the disability
and health insurance trust funds, or allowing the OASI Trust
Fund to borrow from one of the other two funds.

The longer-term problems of the Social Security system
require a more fundamental adjustment. When the "baby boom"
generation reaches retirement age, the ratio of beneficiaries
to contributors will rise sharply, requiring correspondingly
sharp increase in payroll taxes in order to keep the Social
Security system solvent. The problem can be avoided, either
by substantially reducing benefits at that time or by gradually
increasing the retirement age beginning in the year 2000. It
would be unconscionable to postpone such a decision until
that date. Individuals must be allowed to plan for their
retirement future with the confidence that last minute changes

in Social Security will not disrupt their plans.   An
Anderson Administration will urge Congress to resolve this
question so as to better facilitate retirement planning by
young Americans.

The problems associated with rising Social Security
payroll taxes -- lowered employment and higher prices --
can be resolved in part by alternative financing, including
the use of revenues from higher gasoline taxes.   A 50 cent
a gallon increase could generate enough revenues in 1980 to
reduce the employee's contribution by 50 percent.   Such a
trade-off, if coupled with other forms of relief, could
satisfy an urgent conservation need and reduce the adverse
economic impacts associated with payroll taxes.

THE FAMILY

American families, while evolving in diverse ways in recent years, remain a cornerstone of American society. However, complex forces have recently confronted the American family. Spiralling inflation, discriminating tax structures, conflicting welfare policies, and declining educational experiences are indicative of the challenges confronting family life in the 1980's. The many social tensions a family must face include the problems of material health, family planning, day care, and child welfare. In addition, the malaise in single parent families living in poverty deserves special attention. This broad catalogue of problems and needs includes abortion, adolescent pregnancy, health care, protection of the elderly, housing discrimination, unemployment, alcoholism and drug abuse, domestic violence, and flexible working schedules.

Given the diverse ideological opinions held as to the meaning of a family, it is unwise for the government to think in terms of a "family policy". The government, however, should recognize the impact that its laws and practices have upon our social institutions, and try wherever possible to see that these laws and practices do not actively discriminate against the initiatives of the family. An Anderson Administration will support:

● The elimination during the next few years of the "marriage tax" which discriminates against working spouses whose combined incomes are taxed at a proportionately higher rate than if they were single.

● Elimination of inheritance and gift taxes in transfers between spouses.

● Individual Retirement Accounts (IRA) for homemakers.

● Government assistance for displaced homemakers.

● Gradual revision of the federal welfare laws to eliminate discrimination against two-parent families.

● Reform of the federal health care system as set forth elsewhere in the platform.

● Elimination of the existing biases against intermediate care facilities and home-care treatment in federal health care programs.

● Support for added tax deductions for wage earners in families that care for relatives instead of institution-alizing them.

● Support for federal funding for child care for children whose parent or parents are employed and cannot afford privately funded child care.

● Support for increased child care facilities for welfare mothers who want to work or training for work.

● Recognition in our laws that the role of the homemaker is of equal value and dignity with that of the providing spouse.

● Reform of child support and alimony enforcement machinery.

● Elimination of discrimination against women as set forth elsewhere in the platform.

● Support for Child Health Assurance Plan (CHAP) to provide preventive health care for children.

CONSUMER AFFAIRS

Fundamental to the functioning of a sound and stable domestic order is the protection of the health and safety of the American consumer. The American marketplace was founded upon the premise that the consumer is sovereign -- we must continue to adhere to this principle. While we must uphold essential health and safety standards, we must also recognize that the American consumer does not benefit from an excessively regulated economy. We must protect the recent gains made in protecting the basic rights of the American consumer.

We must take the following steps to ensure the basic rights of consumers:

- support the improvement of management coordination and effectiveness of agency consumer programs through the efforts of the existing Inter-Agency Consumer Affairs Council and the implementation of government-wide standards for these consumer programs;

- continue support for essential food safety and drug statutes;

- preserve product disclosure requirements:

- protect consumers against dangerous products with appropriate standards for auto safety, clothing flammability, new drugs and chemicals, and food and children's products;

- support the right of a fair hearing for consumers and public participation in government proceedings;

● enforce legislation prohibiting debt collection agencies
  from engaging in unfair collection practices;

● enforce truth-in-lending and fair credit reporting laws;

● support for legislation to overturn the Illinois Brick
  case to provide indirect purchasers the right to seek
  redress against a manufacturer;

● eliminate abuses in the sale of credit life insurance;

● eliminate fraud in sale of health policies to the elderly;

● support a nation-wide program under the Elementary and
  Secondary Education Act to alert consumers of their
  rights, enhance their ability to make rational and well
  informed choices, and to inform them of their opportunity
  for participation in government decision-making;

● enforce anti-trust laws to protect consumers and assure
  an efficient and productive marketplace; and

● enforce anti-redlining laws.

VETERANS

Our veterans have risked their lives to defend our nation's interests, and deserve our deepest respect. We must be willing, as a nation, to show our appreciation of veterans of our foreign wars.

The Veterans Administration was established to insure that our veterans would be treated properly. Yet, despite its resources, despites its manpower, the Veterans Administration often fails to fulfill its responsibilities. Too frequently, veterans are turned away from V.A. Hospitals; they are denied the medical care they need and deserve. An outside evaluation team should make a thorough review of the Veterans Administration and recommend pressures for reorganization and improvement.

One of the Veterans Administration's most glaring failures has been its response to Vietnam veterans. We recognize the unique problems facing these veterans, victims of a war that left many of them physically, psychologically, and emotionally shattered. In general, Vietnam veterans have a higher unemployment rate than non-veterans, and 20 percent earn less than $7,000 per year. It has been estimated that 25-30 percent of all Vietnam veterans suffer from high-level readjustment problems, including drug addiction, alcoholism, and chronic depression.

The most serious effects of the Vietnam War, however,
may not be realized for many years. It is now known that
the herbicide code-named "Agent Orange", which was used
extensively in Vietnam, contains a deadly chemical which
may product cancer, anemia, and hemorrhaging in those exposed
to it and birth defects in their children. Thousands of
American soldiers and Vietnamese were exposed to this deadly
herbicide. Today many veterans face the uncertainty of
not knowing whether the delayed effects of Agent Orange will
claim them or their offspring as victims.

We believe that the plight of the Vietnam veterans can
no longer be ignored. We strongly support the enactment of
comprehensive legislation to improve our nation's treatment of
Vietnam veterans, such as the Vietnam Veteran's Act currently
proposed by Senator Heinz.

An Anderson Administration will:

● Extend the limitation date for Vietnam veterans' education benefits with a 10-year extension for theater
veterans and a 3-year extension for era veterans. Educational benefits should be adjusted to reflect the
cost of living. The limitation of state matching
requirements will be eliminated;

● Require the Veterans Administration to undertake a
major outreach program to contact the victims of Agent
Orange poisoning. This program should include evaluation, treatment, and compensation, where due, for both
veterans and their children;

● Authorize the Veterans Administration to pay the
administrative start-up costs needed to establish state-
run programs providing direct housing loans at an interest rate below the prevailing market rate;

- Provide for necessary personal counseling of Vietnam veterans. There should be no fixed deadline on this counseling. Theater veterans should be able to take advantage of non-V.A. facilities, such as community health centers or private mental health services. An outreach program should be employed to contact those Vietnam era veterans who have become disenchanted with the current Veterans Administration; and

- Implement programs, under the auspices of the Veterans Administration, to reimburse employers for wages and other training expenses incurred for veterans. These reimbursements would be available up to the value of the monthly educational entitlement available to the veteran.

These proposals will cost money. To neglect our veterans, however, could prove even more expensive, both to society and to the military. Our past practices have led to great attrition from our voluntary army; recruitment of qualified and competent people is becoming increasingly difficult. A major effort must be made to reverse our past decade of neglect.

PRIMARY AND SECONDARY EDUCATION

Public education is an investment in America's future --
an investment of even greater value to the nation than our
capital plant and equipment. We must upgrade our investment
in our human capital, just as we seek to rebuild our physical
capital.

Despite a rising federal dollar investment in primary
and secondary education, there is a growing concern about
the rate of return on those federal dollars. The question,
"Why can't Johnny read?" is asked with concern at the third
grade level. At the high school level, it is asked with
dismay.

Governor Reagan proposes to abolish the Department of
Education. We propose to make it work. This is no time to
sound the retreat on public education.

Over the past four years, federal aid to education has
increased by 73 percent. An Anderson Administration pledges
to make better use of those dollars.

Education and Regulatory Reform

The federal government, in recent years, has assumed
a larger and larger role in local education programs,
resulting in waste and duplication of effort. Grantsmanship

151

has replaced scholarship at the local level in the scramble for federal dollars. The Anderson Administration will work for formula federal aid to local school districts to take school boards out of educational finance and back to educational excellence.

We must work to redefine the federal role in primary and secondary education. There must, of course, be oversight of federal dollars, but such oversight should not be intrusive or destructive of local school matters. The federal government should serve as a catalyst -- providing the funds which can help public school systems achieve their goals, rather than dictating those goals.

To assist in the task of redefining the federal role, we propose to appoint, with Congressional authorization, a Presidential Commission on Primary and Secondary Education. The Commission's mandate will expire 18 months after its authorization, after providing recommendations on ways to:

● reduce the federal paperwork burden on local schools;

● evaluate better the financial needs of public schools;

● restore state and local initiative;

● minimize unnecessary federal intrusion; and

● harmonize federal and state regulation.

Federal Aid to Primary and Secondary Education

The creation of the new Department of Education affords the opportunity to review the full range of federal education programs in a coherant and comprehensive fashion. The new department should review the proper role and mix of categorical and block grant programs. In a number of areas, including special education, categorical grants play an essential role in assuring federal objectives. In the absence of a compelling federal interest in program supervision, federal assistance should take the form of block grants in order to minimize paperwork and maximize local initiative.

Federal aid to education must continue to play a leading role in assuring that school districts with insufficient local resources can provide equal education opportunity. Federal assistance must put a greater emphasis on reducing the   intra-state disparities that still exist.

An Anderson Administration will continue to support the Title I concentration grants for remedial instruction of low income and disadvantaged students. We also reaffirm our support for the Headstart Program and related program initiatives.

An Anderson Administration will oppose tuition tax credits for primary and secondary education. Tax expenditures of this nature would drain much needed resources from public education needs at a time when the public school system's long-standing role as the principal provider of quality education is endangered. An Anderson Administration, while

153

recognizing the important role of private primary and
secondary institutions, is committed to preserving the
traditional importance of free public education.

We recognize the special education needs of the disadvantaged or the specially situated. We reaffirm our
commitment to quality education for all and for federal
support of special education initiatives, including
targetted assistance for low income and low achieving
students and bilingual education programs for those who
possess limited English language skills.

Special attention must be directed at the problems
associated with federally mandated education requirements.
An Anderson Administration is committed to reducing federally
imposed education costs by increasing the federal funding of
those costs. The federal government must shoulder the fiscal
responsibility for its own legislative mandates.

Education of the Handicapped

There are an estimated 8 million handicapped children
under the age of 21 in the United States. Nearly half of
them are enrolled in programs that fail to address their
special problems. Many of those problems remain undiagnosed.
As a consequence, many of these children are wrongfully
labeled as "slow learners" or characterized as having

"attitude problems." The Department of Education, under an
Anderson Administration, will encourage more extensive
testing at the pre-school or first grade level in order to
better identify hidden handicaps.

We reaffirm our commitment to the Handicapped Childrens
Act of 1975, P.L. 94-142, which requires that handicapped
children be educated with the unhandicapped. We will support
additional federal funds for the supplemental training of
the classroom teachers needed to meet the federal requirements.

An Anderson Administration will also focus on the transitional problems that many handicapped students meet when
they seek to move from the classroom to the workplace. Better
linkages are required between special education programs and
private sector affirmative action employment programs.

Vocational and Technical Education

Despite an unemployment rate of nearly 8 percent, many
skilled jobs in this country still go unfilled for lack of
qualified employees. The paradox of high unemployment and
unfilled jobs illustrates the continuing need for federal
support of vocational and technical education. Vocational
programs can serve not only to improve the employability
of program participants, but also make education more relevant to disillusioned youth.

An Anderson Administration will encourage a vigorous
vocational and technical education program, tied to comprehensive career counseling programs. We pledge continuing
efforts aimed at upgrading technical equipment and facilities and encouraging private industry to establish work-
study programs at the school level.

Gifted & Talented

The creativity and intelligence of American children
are our most valuable natural resource. Our most promising
investment in the future is in the gifted and talented
children who excel through a combination of ability and
perseverance, and test the limits of our traditional educational resources.

The federal government has a special responsibility to
these children, and to the school systems which must continually challenge and motivate them. Ironically, these students,
who have the greatest potential to benefit from education
have the highest drop-out rate. Many schools lack the
facilities and personnel to identify and provide for the
special needs of the gifted. Currently, only 12% of the
2,000,000 to 2,500,000 talented children in the United States
are receiving special attention, and interstate differences
in participation are profound. We are mandated to reduce the
inequities and to guarantee that every gifted child is inspired

to actualize his or her potential.

- John Anderson would direct the Department of Education to develop programs to serve gifted and talented students in every state.

- Federal funding can also be used to assist in the development of cooperative programs between private and public secondary and post-secondary schools and to improve programs now established by various public institutions, such as the National Science Foundation.

- The private sector can and must participate in the education of these unique students. By opening the arts, business, and industry to the inquisitive and creative minds of talented students, we can provide them with invaluable opportunities for discovery and learning.

Bilingual Education

We have an obligation to deliver a fair and equitable education to all residents of this nation. We must strengthen our commitment to bilingual education. Bilingual programs should not simply be transitions toward a single language education, but rather should be jointly designed by government and community representatives with minority participation to maintain and cultivate a student's multiple linguistic capability.

Under an Anderson Administration, the Department of Education would be required to provide appropriate guidance to state and local governments and school boards for the joint development of responsive and effective bilingual education programs. The federal government will provide funding to cover the additional costs of mandated programs.

Literacy

At present, estimates indicate that between 20 and 30 million adults lack the fundamental skills necessary to read a newspaper or fill out a job application. We believe that without the ability to read, an individual is deprived of the ability to pursue his or her basic rights. Without reading skills, an individual has little opportunity for employment. Illiteracy prevents the people who need the greatest voice in government from having much of a voice at all.

Illiteracy contributes to an increased inefficiency of the American worker. Education programs of the past have failed to address the needs of the illiterate. We need to attack the problem where it begins -- in our primary and secondary schools.

Success rates in adult education have been low and only a small percentage of the illiterates in this nation have even been reached by such programs. This nation cannot afford to hire the individual tutors that literacy training requires. It must be up to individual communities to muster the resources and manpower necessary for literacy training.

An Anderson Administration will direct the Department of Education to undertake experimentation with community-developed and community-run literacy programs. Such programs should involve all appropriate resources in a region; the

local school system, colleges, the private sector, local
government, and the community. The Department should also
have the responsibility for informing the nation of the
severity of the literacy problem and devising methods to
convince those who are illiterate to seek aid.

HIGHER EDUCATION

In the 1960's and 1970's, our federal and state
governments invested heavily in the expansion of higher
education. They created an educational system unparalleled
in human history, an asset of priceless value. Our modern
institutions of higher education not only provide educational
opportunity, they also are centers of scientific research,
and have a major impact on economic growth in a technologically
oriented society which requires the services of skilled
professionals. Most important to our democratic society,
institutions of higher learning are a primary mode of social
and economic mobility.

In the 1980's, we enter a critical period for our
higher education establishment. The expansion of the last
two decades has halted. By 1983, enrollment in higher
education will peak, and then decline by 15 percent by 1990.
As with any sector when it enters a static period, our nation's
universities and colleges face a period of disruption. These
institutions must retrench, rebuild, and revitalize to help
our nation face the demanding years ahead. Just as the
steel and other basic industries in our country face a time
of rebuilding, so too do our educational institutions.

The federal government has a crucial stake in sustaining the educational establishment. Hundreds of programs in a variety of federal agencies have invested in higher education: its academic quality and fiscal health; the vitality of its research and scholarship; and the availability of educational and self-development opportunities.

The federal government has supported our institutions of higher education by grants to students, faculty members, and to the universities themselves. As we look toward the 1980's and beyond, we must continue and strengthen all three means of support.

Federal financial aid to students in higher education is not a coherent program. It is a complicated mixture of programs reflecting different national commitments and goals developed over the past 36 years. Many of the programs are inadequately funded, and others are misdirected.

Our primary objective in providing grants and loans should be to increase access to higher education by lowering financial barriers to all members of society. We must encourage the provision of quality educational services, and promote traditional values which may have been ignored by efforts to rectify past inequities. There are no simple solutions to the weaknesses in the current federal financial aid programs.

161

We can identify problem areas but much research is necessary

to develop comprehensive solutions. An Anderson Administration

will make a commitment to develop these solutions, and will:

- Develop a more rational, equitable, and widely available
  loan program to provide needed aid to middle income families.
  Currently, there are numerous loan programs, each with
  different repayment terms and degrees of availability;

- Gradually increase the Basic Educational Opportunity
  Grants (BEOG) to reflect changes in the costs of education;

- Liberalize the half-cost rule, which presently limits
  grant assistance to $750 annually for disadvantaged
  students attending a tuition free constitution;

- Support renewed emphasis on self-help College Work-Study
  Program;

- Encourage and increase funding of the TRIO programs:
  Talent Search, Upward Bound, Special Services for
  Disadvantaged Students, Educational Opportunity Centers,
  and Educational Information Centers--that deal with special
  problems and difficulties of access for the educationally
  disadvantaged ;

- Develop targeted post-enrollment remedial programs for
  students coming from disadvantaged educational environments;

- Establish both an undergraduate and graduate Merit
  Scholarship Program at an estimated cost of $80 million; and

- Maintain real spending on Supplemental Educational
  Opportunity Grants (SEOG) and State Student Incentive
  Grants (SSIG), currently funded at $440 million annually.

In addition to student financial aid, we must recognize

the importance of subsidizing basic research in our institutions

of higher learning. These centers play a significant role in

the research and development needed to advance the technological genius and cultural heritage of our society. Recognizing

this role, an Anderson Administration will:

- maintain real levels of support for the humanities;

- modestly increase funding for foreign language and area
  studies programs as described below;

- increase support for engineering research;

- increase support for quality scientific equipment,
  instrumentation, and facilities through a four-year
  phase-in program;

- upgrade research laboratories and equipment at universities and colleges with a five-year program of grants;

- create a fund for competitive post doctorate and research
  fellowships; special attention will be given to people
  out of universities for several years;

- increase support for research libraries collection
  development and collection preservation;

- improve the administration policies federally sponsored
  research to assure that regulations do not unduly restrict
  research programs;

- encourage both stability and predictability of resources; and

- encourage flexibility by federal regulators and auditors
  in the exercise of financial oversight; and recognize
  that efforts to document fully and precisely how every
  federal dollar is spent are often counter-productive;

Our nation has lead the world in the quality of our

medicine and medical professionals. As we renew our emphasis

in comprehensive health care, we must continue to provide

quality educational and research resources. The federal

government can play a crucial role in sustaining these

capabilities. An Anderson Administration will:

- support House Resolution 3633 Nurse Training and
  Health Programs Extension Act, providing continuing

163

capitation funding for nursing education, and
increased funding for the training of nurse
practitioners and nurse midwives;

● increase funding for the National Health Service Corps;

● encourage the training of more health professionals, including
   physicians' assistants, nurse practitioners, paramedics,
   physical therapists, and midwives; and

● support predictable, long-term funding for biomedical
   research.

Federal involvement in higher education has resulted
in numerous restrictions, changes in institutional procedures,
and additional costs and burdens. Indiscriminately applied federal
regulations have hampered our institutions of higher learning,
impeded freedom of action and restricted self-management.

More care must be taken in the application of regulations
to insure they do not unfairly impinge on the role of educational
institutions. An Anderson Administration will not retreat
from a forceful policy of affirmative action and environmental
concern. But within these constraints, we must reexamine
the effect of government regulations. Specifically, an Anderson
Administration will propose to:

● subsidize compliance costs with a modest grant program;

● develop a comprehensive regulatory policy;

● take greater efforts to assess the impact of grant
   compliance requirements before their enactment; and

● increase flexibility in fund management for research.

International studies programs in our nation's institutions
of higher learning are currently in a state of decline.
America's ability to understand and deal effectively with both

friends and foes depends heavily on trained and educated
people knowledgeable in international affairs and competent
in foreign languages. But the network of institutions and
programs created in the 1950's and 1960's through the combined
efforts of the government, private foundations and the universities
has been seriously eroded. Federally funded foreign language
and area fellowships declined from a peak of 2,557 in 1969
to 828 in 1978. Federal expenditures for university-based
foreign affairs research declined from $20.3 million to $8.5
million, or 58 percent in constant dollars. At a time when
America's needs for competence in international studies and
foreign languages is becoming increasingly complex and urgent,
our ability to respond to these needs is decreasing precipitiously.

In a nation as large and pluralistic as the United States,
only the federal government can provide the leadership and
resources essential to improve substantially our foreign
language and international studies capabilities. An Anderson
Administration will establish long-term, enduring policies
to:

- provide financial support for existing international
  studies programs at our universities and colleges and
  encourage the creation of new centers to correspond to
  national needs;

- provide funding for language teaching and support
  research designed to discover more adequate and effective
  language teaching techniques at all levels of instruction;

- increase support for foreign area and global issues
  research; and

- strengthen and expand our various international affairs
  programs at the community level, especially through the
  resources of our vast community college system.

The diversity and special services of minority-oriented
institutions of higher learning are essential to rectifying
past inequities. An Anderson Administration will:

● continue to support black colleges and universities;

● fully support the maintenance and development of American
  Indian community colleges. We are opposed to the transferring of schools under BIA control to the Department
  of Education. We recognize the need for community
  members to become further involved in the running of
  their schools. Decisions on the creation or termination
  of schools should not be made without tribal consent.

THE ARTS

Our nation has always been distinguished by its rich and full artistic culture. The arts, in their popular as well as their professional forms, have played a key role in enriching the lives of all Americans. John Anderson affirms the essential role the arts play in American society.

John Anderson believes that the federal government should be a strong supporter of the arts. Yet, we must be careful in choosing the form of this support. The government should foster the development of the arts without controlling their content. Government support of the arts should consist primarily of creating an environment that, while encouraging a balanced development of all arts, allows the mechanisms of private and popular selection to play a predominant role.

John Anderson cites the following areas in which the government can assist the arts:

NATIONAL ENDOWMENTS -- Funding for the National Endowments for the Arts and the Humanities should keep pace with inflation. The President should monitor the Endowment's operations to insure that the public has access to the Endowment's programs, and to insure that their funds are being spent wisely.

WHITE HOUSE CONFERENCE ON THE ARTS AND HUMANITIES -- John Anderson has supported efforts to hold a White House Conference on the Arts and Humanities. He will continue to help to arrange this Conference, which would provide a needed opportunity to discuss the future of American arts.

CULTURAL HERITAGE PRESERVATION -- The federal government should
take measures to assure that the nation's cultural heritage --
its monuments, artifacts, works of art, languages, and cultural
traditions -- is protected and preserved.

ART BANK -- John Anderson supports the bill to create a National
Art Bank within the National Endowment for the Arts. The funds
for this Art Bank would be used to purchase works of American
art, which would then be leased for exhibition in government
buildings, hospitals, and civic centers. The Art Bank would
benefit all Americans by increasing exposure to American
artists, and bringing the best of contemporary American art
to all regions of the country.

PRIVATE SUPPORT -- Private financial support is the element
essential to the well-being of our national arts. The federal
government offers a tax credit to those private individuals
and corporations contributing to the arts. The Anderson
Administration would encourage the private sector to take
maximum advantage of this tax credit.

The challenge grant program, which provides matching
funds for contributions from the private sector, has proven
very successful. Anderson strongly supports this method
of giving financial assistance to the arts.

A patron awards program is a third measure that could
be used to foster contributions from the private sector.
Individuals and corporations who provide essential support
to the arts deserve to have their support publicly recognized.

FAIR COMPENSATION -- John Anderson would investigate improvements
in copyright and patent laws to insure that artists receive proper
compensation for their work. He favors tax credits in those
instances where an artist lends his or her talents to public
performances.

TAXES -- John Anderson supports the Artists Equity Tax Act,
and endorses the clarifications of the bill's language that
have been suggested by the Authors League of America. This
bill would modify our tax laws to: (1) encourage donations
of art into the public domain, and (2) eliminate unfair tax
burdens on artists and their heirs.

While recognizing the costs of these programs to foster
the arts, John Anderson believes we must remember the arts'
proven role in economic renewal and development. The
establishment of art centers leads to improved property values,
the growth of ancillary industries, with an accompanying
increase in tax revenues. The arts could prove particularly
useful in urban renewal programs, as they would help to attract
people back into the cities. It is clear that the arts play
an essential role in the well being our our nation.

ENVIRONMENT

The protection and preservation of the Earth's biosphere
is vital to human survival. It is therefore necessary to
ensure that our environmental initiatives of the past decade
are not abandoned. We need to encourage a new ethos in our
society that is built upon a greater respect for the environment
and a greater willingness to protect it.

The Anderson Administration will accept the challenge
offered by continuing threats to the environment by ensuring
strong enforcement of our present environmental laws, and by
enacting additional environmental legislation when necessary.

The Anderson Administration will be willing to accept
the economic costs related to the protection and preservation
of our air, land, and water against pollution, exhaustion,
and depletion. We will ask the same of all our citizens.
Our values cannot be oriented to short-term measures taken at
the expense of future generations.

The nation's environmental standards were enacted to
protect the health and safety of the American people and to
ensure the quality of our lives and the lives of our children.
We will exert our best efforts to meet our national commitment
of protecting our environment. We will not relax these
standards.

The following are important issues where an Anderson
Administration will take new initiatives.

Oceans and Coastal Areas

The United States continues to neglect its connections
to the seas. The rapid deterioration of our nation's
coastlines and waters is visible in oil-stained tidal pools,
quarantined shellfish beds, the depletion of shorebird populations
and the loss of 300,000 acres of wetlands and 6,000 acres of
fragile barrier islands which protect the Atlantic and Gulf
Coasts.

Dumping of sewage sludge, catastrophic oil spills, chronic
oil spills, and development of offshore oil and gas threaten to
turn portions of our seas into large polluted sinks with
barren underseas plains.

Once considered useless, our coastal wetlands are now
seen as invaluable endangered resources. They provide vital
habitat for waterfowl, other coastal wildlife, food for
commercially valuable fish and shellfish, natural waste
treatment for tons of sewage effluent, storage for flood
waters and the recharging of groundwater supplies. These valuable
wetlands are being altered, polluted, and plundered by the
pressures of energy siting, escalating demand for shipping
channels, commercial development and second-home development.

Fish are in great demand as a source of protein; new
sources of continental shelf oil and gas are urgently required
to meet energy needs; seabed nodules are about to be mined

for strategic minerals; global shipping grows; ports and

harbors have become busier. Along the attractive coastal

rim, urban populations concentrate more heavily and seek

recreational joys from both water-related sports and esthetic

surroundings. Finally, well over 100 nations face the sea,

and they are exploring the potential of the oceans in

contributing to their future.

    To protect our oceans and coastlines from rampant resource

exploitation, the Anderson Administration will institute the

following programs:

● It will actively lobby for the passage of "Oil Spill
  Superfund" legislation which would provide funds
  for rapid clean-up and damage compensation. Under
  our program:

    -- Revenue for the superfund will be obtained through the
       taxation of companies involved with the transport and
       storage of oil that could result in the pollution of
       our country's waters.

    -- Administration of the superfund will be by the
       EPA.

    -- Use of superfund monies will be for:

       - the clean-up of oil spills.

       - immediate compensation for damages caused by
         the oil spill.

       The superfund will have the ability to sue the
       polluter to recover funds disbursed for damages,
       and the tax will be adjusted on a biennial
       basis in light of actuarial calculations.

With increased shipping of petroleum and hazardous cargo, and

with increased size and decreased maneuverability of ships,

greater attention is necessary to reduce risk to the
environment and to assure safety for human life.

● The Anderson Administration will direct the Coast Guard
to strengthen traffic management systems and to devise
means to enforce safety regulations more strictly.
Additionally, new incentives and penalties will be
provided to the shipping industry itself, so as to
facilitate its assuming greater responsibility for
operations. The Anderson Administration will also
ask Congress to increase Coast Guard funding to cover
the costs for these new programs.

● The Anderson Administration will direct the Department
of Transportation to research ways and means to accommodate
increased maritime traffic, while reducing risk.

● Sophisticated technology required for Arctic hydrocarbon
exploration has not been tested and is still only in
the developmental stage. Under the Anderson Administration,
leasing in the Beaufort Sea will proceed only after
technological methods are proven -- and the annual review
of the leased areas is comprehensive and conclusive enough
to determine whether oil and gas exploration is having a
detrimental impact on species such as the endangered
Bowhead and Gray whales. Exploration in other Arctic
areas such as the Chukchi Sea, Norton Sound and Navarin
Basin will not proceed until the effects of Beaufort leasing
is known, and consideration will be given to limiting
exploration only within the barrier islands.

● The Anderson Administration will require the following
safeguards before any drilling is allowed to occur on
Georges Bank, the world's most abundant fishery:

    --   The barging of drill muds and cuttings off-site
         away from spawning areas except when meteorological
         conditions make this more hazardous than on-site
         disposal. Many of these materials contain toxic
         substances.

    --   The reinjection of formation waters into the drilled
         cavity. These are waters associated with oil and gas
         reservoirs which are usually separated from oil and

gas, and dumped overboard. Benzene, toluene, xylene, and ethyl-benzine are some of the materials found in these waters, and they are also the most toxic to marine organisms. The dumping of those materials could have a disastrous effect on fish larvae which circulate near the surface areas of the water columns.

-- Improvement in the composition and authority of the Biological Task Force established to monitor the effects of oil and gas actively on biological resources.

-- Leasees will be required to factor costs of safeguards into their costs of production in determining the feasibility of a particular tract. If the tract is subsequently determined to be economically infeasible, the developer will not be allowed to waive the safeguards, rather, the tract will be deleted.

• Existing legislative and administrative authorities under the Federal Water Pollution Control Act (Section 404) will be strictly enforced, and federal agencies will encourage and solicit local support and aid in this enforcement.

• The 1972 Coastal Zone Management Act is due for Congressional reauthorization. The Anderson Administration would seek to have this Act reauthorized by Congress and strengthened with more effective management incentives and enforcement tools. The following points should be included:

-- The CZMA should provide stronger incentives and penalties for states to develop and adopt their own management plans.

-- Periodic reports should be required from state and federal governments on the coastal areas, including reviews of state management plans.

-- Incentives for states to identify and preserve coastal areas of national significance.

-- Funding for additional beach access.

● An Anderson Administration would address the issue of reducing federal funding for projects in high hazard areas especially on flood plains, wetlands, and barrier islands.

● An Anderson Administration would support a strong, viable Marine Sanctuary Program.

● Recent proposed changes in Section 404 of the Federal Water Pollution Control Act giving the Army Corps of Engineers more authority in the permitting process would be opposed by an Anderson Administration. (We favor the present procedure in which EPA has final veto over the Corps permits in the case of fragile areas.)

● An Anderson Administration will require a review of our major ports in order to establish what are our national needs for ports and how established infra-structure can meet these needs without encouraging additional construction at the expense of our wetlands.

● Through the United States Law of the Sea conference, the Anderson Administration would encourage adoption of environmental standards that would better control ocean pollution, the dumping of waste and the continuing disposal of radioactive materials on an international basis.

175

Public Lands

To fill the resource demands of a continually growing
consumer population, many people wish to exploit the vast
tracts of resource rich public lands in the West, and the remote
undeveloped spots in the East. We must recognize that once we
begin the exploitation of our public lands, however, that we
are creating irreversible change. For this reason, it is
in the best interest of the American people to hold portions
of our natural lands in safekeeping, forever to be free from
the threat of exploitation. Other federally owned lands can
provide large amounts of valuable timber, minerals, and
grazing land, if they are carefully managed. The next
administration will have to address the following land
management and resource preservation topics:

Alaska Lands

The Udall-Anderson Alaska Lands Bill (H.R. 39) passed
the House of Representatives due in large part to intensive
support by its primary minority co-sponsor, John Anderson.
If enacted into law, this measure will protect approximately
128 million acres of unspoiled Alaska lands; of these, 67
million acres will be given "wilderness" designation. More
recently, the Senate passed its own version of the Alaska
Lands Bill, proposing the protection of approximately 100
million acres, but excluding some prime regions that are
protected by the House bill.

● Our Administration will exert its best efforts to secure enactment of a strong Alaska Lands Bill, as introduced by John Anderson in the House of Representatives.

Sagebrush Rebellion

The Bureau of Land Management of the Department of Interior manages the nation's "unappropriated, unreserved lands". This now amounts to about one-fourth of the land area of the United States. Ninety percent of these unreserved lands are west of the Rocky Mountains. There is currently local political pressure to enable states to assume management of these lands.

It is, however, also argued that states will find it too expensive to manage the lands and will succumb to over-whelming pressures to sell it. (It would cost Idaho $51 million to manage 20 million acres of national forest lands at the current level of management by the federal government.) With the zeal to develop these areas, environmental concerns could easily be overlooked or ignored.

● The Anderson Administration will work to have federal lands remain in the possession of the federal government to ensure they are managed in the best national public interest, according to principles of conservation and multiple use of all resources.

Forestry

More and more pressure has come from the timber industry
and building trades to cut more heavily in our national forests
as lumber shortages increase. Yet, we currently export logs
to Japan. The hard choice here is between the preservation of
an important and substantial part of the environment and the
accummulation of needed export revenues. In an area as
important as the national forests, we must allocate our resources
more wisely. We must have respect for the land that extends
beyond our time. Broad interests definitely should be
represented in the preservation of national forests.

* The Anderson Administration will vigorously enforce
  the multiple use/sustained-yield policy set forth
  in the National Forest Management Act of 1976.

* The Anderson Administration will require the Forest
  Service to review its timber pricing policy to bring
  it in line with sound business practices, since the
  subsidizing of timber prices discourages private
  forest investment and other uses of the forests. More
  emphasis will be placed on private timber farms by the
  Forest Service to increase its cost-sharing and
  assistance programs.

RARE II Process

Through the RARE II (Roadless Area Review and
Evaluation) process, the Forest Service has reviewed 62
million acres of roadless lands in the national forest
system. The Forest Service has recommended 15.4 million

acres as wilderness, 35 million acres be managed for multiple
use (logging, grazing, recreation), and 10.8 million acres
be studied further.

● Under the Anderson Administration, wilderness designations
will be increased and areas not previously studied will be
re-evaluated for their wilderness potential.

Urban Parks

To improve the urban environment and to assist urban
areas maintain and protect their valuable parks, an Anderson
Administration will:

● Encourage the National Park Service to attend to the
special needs and problems of parks and public
recreational areas within the urban setting.

Air and Water Quality

In recent years the energy needs of our country have been
the primary issue in the minds of our government officials and
the general public. Since this issue receives focused attention
and efforts, other domestic programs and issues at times go
lacking or are even submerged. Environmental concerns are
often considered hinderances to energy development and industry
is continually attempting to have standards eased. Auto
manufacturers plead to have auto emission standards relaxed
as a way of attaining adequate mile-per-gallon ratings. The
increased use of coal and synthetic fuels bring with it the
potential of vitiating the nation's air quality. Emissions
from increasing fossil fuel combustion combine with accumulations
of carbon dioxide to form acid rain that has fallen on the
Northeast depleting fish in mountain lakes, affecting
crop production and forest yields.

Our water quality and reserves are also declining at a
dangerous rate. Our ground water is being contaminated by
abandoned waste dumps, unsafe landfills, polluted streams,
and oil and gas well drilling techniques.

Some suggest we submerge environmental concerns to solve
the energy, productivity, and economy issues. We must put
in place policies and programs that will answer the needs
of the future and not be oriented to short-term concerns

without reference to what the consequences might be for
future generations.

- The Anderson Administration will establish the strict
  enforcement of the Clean Air Act of 1977 and the Water
  Pollution Control Act of 1972 as national priorities.

- Through the EPA, the Anderson Administration will seek
  to reduce further industrial emissions and require the
  installation of best available control technology on
  existing coal-fired power plants.

- The Anderson Administration will lobby against attempts
  to weaken standards or postpone the deadlines for reducing
  carbon monoxide and hydrocarbon levels in automobile
  exhausts.

- The Anderson Administration will direct the EPA to phase
  out the substitution of taller smoke stacks for emission
  controls.

- The Anderson Administration will seek to retain the
  section of the Clean Air Act that prohibits any "significant
  deterioration" of pristine air in our national parks and
  wilderness areas. (Removal of this provision would have
  allowed a giant coal-fired plant to be erected only nine
  miles from a major park in Utah.)

- The Anderson Administration will direct the EPA to
  institute an exhaustive study of the effects of acid
  rain and methods for its prevention. (For further
  discussion of acid rain, see the Energy plank.)

- A national program of water conservation will be
  initiated by the Anderson Administration. Environmental
  values will receive top priority in planning of water
  programs and projects.

- Through the EPA, the Anderson Administration will
  strictly enforce federal standards for carcinogens
  in drinking water. If standards are not met by the
  utility or municipality serving a community, the
  consumers will be notified, and the utility required
  to meet the standards using appropriate technologies.

181

Wildlife

Ninety percent of all species which ever lived on Earth have now disappeared; almost all of them died out naturally. Recently, this process has changed. Man's actions now account for the extermination of numerous species. In 300 years man has eliminated 150 known species of mammals and birds, and an unknown number of reptiles, amphibians, and fish. Pressures from an increasing world population seeking room to live and resources necessary to support an ever rising standard of living are depleting the habitat of our wildlife.

A concern for wildlife conservation can seem frivolous in today's world, yet man has a tremendous self-interest in ensuring ecosystem stability and protecting the Earth's gene pool. Any reduction in the diversity of resources reduces our ability to respond to new problems and opportunities. In order to protect the wildlife of our lands and seas, the Anderson Administration will:

- Strengthen the National Wildlife Refuge program by limiting the secondary uses of the refuges: grazing, timber harvest, hunting, trapping, predator control, and pesticide use.

- Expand and strengthen the current embargo on the import of products derived from endangered wildlife.

- Exercise the influence of the United States to encourage other countries to terminate the wholesale slaughter of whales, porpoises, seals, and other wildlife.

●   Enforce international whale conservation efforts
through sanctions under the Pelly amendment to the
Fisherman's Protective Act, which provides that any
nation which undermines an international conversation
treaty will have its nation's fishing products embargoed
from entering U.S. ports under the direction of the
Department of Commerce. Where a nation was in violation
of an international conservation treaty and certified
under the Pelly amendment, the Anderson Administration
would employ the Packwood/Magnuson amendments to the
Fishery Conservation and Management Act, which can
expressly limit the amount of fishing allowed within
the U.S.-200 mile limit.

Water Projects

Due to the pork-barrel nature of Army Corps of Engineers and other federally funded water projects, legislation in this area is often given a cursory review by Congress and usually passes with ease. As a result, many water projects are constructed without proper attention to their environmental impact.

The insatiable desire for ever cheaper electric power, without attention to cost-benefit ratios, will bring about the construction of numerous hydro-electric dams on previously free-flowing rivers and streams. This could have many adverse effects such as the destruction of valuable fish and wildlife habitats, the inundation of productive farmland, the displacement of rural populations, and loss of irreplaceable scenic and recreational areas.

The wetlands of our country are also in jeopardy. Land developers are now turning to areas that were previously difficult to develop, but are now attractive due to escalating land costs. Now that the technology and machinery exists to drain our marshes and wetlands easily, we are faced with the prospect of the destruction of these valuable ecosystems that provide habitats for many forms of flora and fauna. Wetlands are also a valuable component in our water cycle, providing natural waste treatment and a means by which we can store flood waters to recharge our groundwater supplies.

To assure that federal water projects respect environmental concerns the Anderson Administration will do the following:

- Direct the Army Corps of Engineers to place a strong emphasis on the preservation and restoration of our nation's wetlands.

- Pay careful attention to proposed federal water projects to see that their cost-benefit ratios do not underestimate environmental impact. An example of a project that proves to be very cost-effective and that the Anderson Administration will support is the Charles River Watershed Project in North Carolina. This project establishes good flood-plain management and protects valuable wetlands.

- Re-evaluate the cost-benefit ratios of all navigation projects for barges that are less than 40 percent complete to determine if they are still profitable. If they no longer pass this profitability test, then the Administration will halt their construction.

- Decrease federal funding of water project costs to encourage the states to assume a larger share of project costs.

- Federal water project aid will be made conditional on state implementation of groundwater management laws.

Toxic Substances

Through the manufacture of chemical substances, our
nation generates 77 billion pounds of hazardous waste each
year. Such waste threatens our air, rivers, and ground
water resources. The serious toxic contamination discovered
in the Love Canal area of New York has understandably resulted
in public suspicion, fear, and anger. Such reaction is not
unwarranted. There is convincing and sobering evidence
that chemical wastes until recently have been disposed of
illegally or carelessly in a way that assures they will
ultimately find their way into the environment. In many
instances these chemicals once released cannot be controlled.

The U.S. government through EPA has the framework to
control chemical products and wastes. (The Toxic Substances
Control Act authorizes the government to collect information
on chemicals that may damage health or the environment and
to control them where necesssary.) The Resource Conservation
and Recovery Act provides for government control over hazardous
wastes from their point of generation to final disposal.

Thus the U.S. government is beginning to collect information
on all aspects of waste generation and to dispose of (or
store) the wastes securely. There is growing public concern
that the federal government's present level of commitment is
not adequate for the task.

In many instances, the failure to take swift measures endangers the public's health. As a matter of public policy, we cannot delay action while we await conclusive evidence of toxic-related cancer, abortion, fatalities, and birth defects.

Federal policy must be focused on the prevention of toxic disasters. The following policies will be implemented to address this national environmental crisis:

● The Anderson Administration will more aggressively enforce the Toxic Substances Control Act and the Resources Conservation and Recovery Act. This calls for rapid promulgation of the rules by the EPA and for the expansion of testing and monitoring. Within legislative mandates, the Anderson Administration will expand the existing testing and monitoring procedures.

● The Anderson Adminsitration will work toward enactment of a "Toxic Waste Superfund" program for the clean-up of improperly disposed of toxic materials.

  -- The superfund will be built on taxes levied on the principal hazardous waste generating industries.

  -- The industries to be taxed will be identified through a study by the EPA.

  -- The individual tax rates will be determined by the quantity of waste produced by the company.

  -- The "Toxic Waste Superfund" will be administered by the EPA.

  -- The superfund will be used for:

     - the clean-up of improperly disposed of toxic materials.

— Compensation to innocent victims as a
remedy of last resort. It must be noted that
a polluter is liable for injuries incurred as
a result of its improper disposal of toxic waste.
If the polluter is unknown, or if liability for
damage cannot be expeditiously established, then
the EPA will be able to award compensation to the
victim if it can be proven that injuries resulted
from the improper disposal of toxic wastes.

● The Anderson Administration will promptly convene regional
councils of governors and mayors to develop sensible
regional solutions to the disposal site problem. These
councils would make the hard choices that are needed,
assisted by technical experts from federal, state,
and local agencies, with input from private citizens.

● The Anderson Administration will direct the EPA to
grant funds to be used to help the councils ensure
that these priority disposal sites are managed with
the greatest care and skill. This would include provision
of technology development funds where appropriate in order
to pioneer new and more effective disposal techniques.

● The Anderson Administration will institute temporary
emergency bans on the usage of toxic substances, herbicides,
and pesticides where there is extensive evidence and
confirmatory information that the substance is causing
serious adverse health effects on people and the
environment. (The EPA imposed an emergency ban on
the use of both 2,4,5 -T and Silvex. They took the
action due to evidence that these herbicides caused
cancer, birth defects, and miscarriages. We support
this emergency ban.)

● The Anderson Administration will examine in detail the
problem of the transport of hazardous chemicals. It
will act quickly to reduce the danger to the public
from this source. Safe traffic routes will clearly be
a major component of this initiative.

IV.   GUARANTEEING RIGHTS AND PROMOTING JUSTICE

Prosperity without justice, and security without basic rights, are incomplete. Indeed, any society that long denies basic rights and just treatment to all its citizens diminishes its unity and strength, and sows a crop of bitterness and rage. It is both the obligation and the interest, of every society to deal fairly with all.

In modern American society, however, it must be remembered that economic well-being is considered a basic right of all Americans. Action in the field of civil rights today, therefore, has these basic priorities:

First, we must seek to provide employment opportunities for all. This is the purpose of our proposals here and elsewhere in the platform in the area of jobs.

Second, we must transform our laws so that they cover and protect all equally. This is the purpose of our proposals in the area of civil rights.

Third, we must ensure that all the laws we have are enforced fairly and equally. This is the purpose of our proposals in the area of criminal justice.

JOBS AND JUSTICE

A just and progressive civil rights policy must be founded not only upon the enactment and enforcement of civil rights legislation, but must also be founded upon an economic policy that provides opportunities for employment and advancement.

Throughout this program we have set forth proposals that
affect the employment status of minorities. These include
strengthening Title VII of CETA, enacting a Youth Energy
Projects Act,   supporting the Youth Act of 1980, stimulating
small businesses in declining areas, establishing urban enterprise
zones, and rebuilding neighborhood confidence by promoting
policies that encourage local initiative. We have proposed
urban housing programs to increase the supply of low income
housing, encouraging self-ownership, and removing restrictions
on the use of HUD funds for the restoration of existing
residential structures. We have proposed low income energy
assistance needed to help families unable to meet skyrocketing
residential energy and weatherization costs. Our investment
proposals include tax credits for firms that renovate their
existing structures (largely relevant to urban areas). We
have proposed a job-creating Urban Investment Trust Fund to
rebuild the basic infrastructure of our cities and a job-
creating Community Transit Trust Fund to renovate and rebuild
our transportation network. Jobs will be a central concern of
an Anderson Administration.

In addition to these and other programs outlined in this
program, we propose a strong initiative in the field of minority
business.

The ownership of businesses and other capital assets is
the best way in which members of minority groups can gain their

deserved share of the American economy. However, minority-
owned businesses face not only all of the problems of finance,
overregulation and marketing facing all small businesses,
but also the additional problems caused by a long history of
discrimination. Thus, it is necessary to provide additional
assistance to Black, Hispanic, American Indian and other minority
entrepreneurs. Such assistance should be carefully tailored
to provide help to businesses that create long-term productive
jobs and stimulate economic growth. We endeavor to:

●   Place additional emphasis in the Minority Business
     Development Program upon assisting minority entrepreneurs
     in growth industries, such as energy production and con-
     servation, electronics and communications.

●   Implement legislative setaside provisions for minority
     businesses, especially in areas that can improve the
     productivity of the minority community and the economy
     as a whole, including funds allocated for research and
     development activities.

●   Expand the Minority Business Technology Commercialization
     Program of the U.S. Department of Commerce in assisting
     minority entrepreneurs to participate in the process of
     the commercialization of new technologies, including
     those resulting from our space program.

●   Make the programs of the Small Business Administration
     more effective through streamlined procedures,
     monitoring of results and closer working with
     minority-owned banks.

                          CIVIL RIGHTS

     John Anderson's commitment to civil rights has never
wavered throughout his years of government service. A vocal
supporter of every major piece of civil rights legislation
from the 1964 Civil Rights Act to the 1980 Fair Housing

Act, he has remained steadfast in his loyalty to the principles
of equal education, open housing, and employment for all.
Governor Lucey has an equally long and distinguished civil
rights record.

Although many are willing to make the claim that the battle
for civil rights has been won and is over, we disagree. We
are willing to applaud the progress thus far, but as long as
we fail to see an Equal Rights Amendment ratified, as long
as previous commitments to the rights of American Indians,
Hispanics, Blacks, and other minorities are not honored; as
long as we fail to extend those same commitments to the rights
of the handicapped, immigrants, and others; as long as our
fair housing laws are wantonly abused; and as long as groups
such as the Ku Klux Klan and the Nazi party not only survive
but actually gain nominations for public office, we are
unwilling to call for a truce in the struggle for civil rights.

In most instances, the legislation necessary for the
guarantee of civil rights is already in existence. Unfortunately, many of these laws, some of which have existed for a
century, and some for two decades, are not being seriously upheld or
enforced. Existing laws and statutes must be upheld and,
if necessary, revised to enhance their enforcement. Only
when we strictly enforce laws such as the Civil Rights Acts ard
uphold our fair housing laws will we realize an effective commitment
to civil rights.

Housing

Title VIII of the 1968 Civil Rights Act declared that
"it is the policy of the United States to provide, within
constitutional limitations, for fair housing throughout the
United States." But despite this, many Blacks, Hispanics,
and other minorities are still denied equal housing opportunities.

We believe steps must be taken immediately to insure
equal housing opportunities for all.

● The Anderson Administration will seek immediate enactment of Fair Housing legislation, if H.R. 5200 is not
enacted during the 96th Congress.

In 1968, John Anderson cast the deciding vote in the
Rules Committee which brought the Open Housing bill to the
House floor, and he helped lead the fight for its passage.
We recognize that the original bill must be strengthened.
Thus, we support the legislation currently before the Con-
gress which would authorize HUD to order violators to cease
discriminatory practices, and to assess civil penalties
against those accused of violating the Fair Housing Act.

We believe adequate funding must be provided to enable
HUD to conduct community-wide compliance reviews, monitor
compliance agreements, and establish a viable program for

interagency coordination with regard to fair housing. We
must increase funding for the Department of Justice in order
to ensure adequate prosecution of Title VIII violators.

Affirmative Action

The mandate of our civil rights legislation cannot be
fulfilled simply by prohibiting practices intentionally
designed to deny opportunities, We believe that
we must make an honest and positive effort to
enforce the equal protection clause of our constitution
through the establishment of affirmative action programs.

We cannot be lax either in the monitoring or in the
enforcement of affirmative action programs. Such programs
have been in effect for only a brief interval of time compared
to the years of oppression that preceeded them. Over a
century ago, the Supreme Court stated that when a person emerges
from slavery to citizenship, he "ceases to be a special
favorite of the laws." Such thinking, similar to the growing
revisionism of today, helped to usher in a century
of enforced segregation and discrimination. An Anderson
Administration will never accept such a reactionary and unjus-
tified view. It will be prepared to use the threat of termi-
nating federal funds to offending institutions and municipalities much more extensively than previous administrations
have been.

We also believe that the federal government should set
the example in the application of minority hiring practices.
An Anderson Administration will require full accountability
from all government departments and agencies with regard
to the implementation of affirmative action. We believe
that the true test of an administration's intentions lies in
its ability to place minorities in all branches of government,
not just in those sections of government concerned with
minorities. An Anderson Administration will seek to place
minorities in all foreign as well as domestic branches of
government.

Education

Since the <u>Brown vs. The Board of Education</u> decision,
school districts have struggled with the problem of properly
integrating their schools. We favor federal support for
communities to devise their own method to attain school
desegregation. Those methods include redrawing zone boundaries,
pairing and clustering of schools, and cooperative arrangements
between school districts where feasible. However, if these
strategies fail to achieve integration, we favor an
intelligently devised busing plan as a last resort.

The Anderson Administration will absolutely oppose any
attempts to pass a constitutional amendment prohibiting
busing.

Busing

    We recognize that court-ordered busing is the result of community failure to design a local remedy for school desegregation. An Anderson Administration will seek to enact the National Educational Opportunity Act introduced in the 95th and 96th Congresses by John Anderson. This legislation would provide federal funds to encourage local cooperation in enacting school desegregation programs.

AMERICAN INDIANS AND ALASKAN NATIVES

The obligation owed to American Indians and Alaskan
Natives by the federal government is not discretionary, but
is based on prior legal commitments established through
judicial and legislative pronouncements. However, in many
instances, the federal government has failed or is failing
to meet this nation's obligations to American Indians and
Alaskan Natives.

- We have always been strong supporters of sovereign
  tribal rule, as guaranteed to American Indians and
  Alaskan Natives by treaty, Supreme Court decisions,
  Congressional policy and Executive Order. Under an
  Anderson Administration, treaties will not be abro-
  gated without the consent of all parties involved.

- We believe that a strong Bureau of Indian Affairs is
  necessary to adequately protect the interests of
  American Indians and Alaskan Natives within the federal
  government. Any reorganization of the Bureau should
  seek to distribute more power toward both the Agency
  and tribal level.

- The federal government must work with American Indians
  and Alaskan Natives to plan, develop and implement
  realistic economic development programs which will
  improve and strengthen their economic position and which
  will bring long-term employment opportunities to their
  people. Where Tribal and Alaskan Native lands contain
  considerable amounts of coal, uranium, natural gas and
  other natural resources, the federal government should
  not be permitted nor should it permit private industry
  to exploit these resources in a manner detrimental to
  those Tribes and Alaskan Natives.

- We support the efforts of the Bureau of Indian Affairs'
  Federal Recognition Project.

- An Anderson Administration will order enforcement of
  the Voters Rights Act and the Bilingual Education Act
  to assure that American Indians and Alaskan Natives
  will receive voting information as well as sufficient
  educational materials in their native languages.

0   Life expectancy for American Indians and Alaskan Natives
     is low. We propose an expansion of programs involving
     tribally controlled paraprofessionals and grassroots
     health services with an emphasis on preventive medicine.

PUERTO RICO

The islands of Puerto Rico should be entitled to political

self-determination. We support any decision the people

of Puerto Rico make in a referendum whether the decision

includes becoming a state, maintaining its status as a commonwealth

or establishing independence.

SEXUAL ORIENTATION

We believe that discrimination due to sexual orientation

should not be tolerated by the federal government. An Anderson

Administration would work to enforce the repeal of that section of th

Nationality and Immigration Act which excludes individuals

from immigrating solely on the grounds of sexual orientation.

We would issue an executive order barring discrimination based

upon sexual orientation within the federal government. An

Anderson Administration would encourage Congress to extend to

the Civil Rigths Commission the power to investigate acts of

discrimination against individuals based upon their sexual

orientation.

DISTRICT OF COLUMBIA

We applaud past efforts to grant the District

representational rights. We support ratification of the

amendment which would grant D.C. voting rights in Congress.

IMMIGRATION

Immigration policy raises a number of difficult issues. We seek to balance the aspirations of the poor, hungry, and jobless in other lands while protecting the most disadvantaged members of our own society from special burdens.

An Anderson Administration will create an executive task force to review and, where appropriate, to implement the recommendations of the Select Commission of Immigration and Refugee Policy as soon as its report is made public. In so doing, it will constantly keep in mind the contributions made by generations of immigrants.

The two thousand mile border we share with Mexico presents unique problems, but unique opportunities for mutually beneficial cooperation as well. The immigration of undocumented Mexican workers affects the interests of many parties, not just those of our two governments. It affects local communities on both sides of the border; it affects the American worker as well as the undocumented Mexican worker, and it affects our own Hispanic-American community.

We believe that any attempt to close the border would be detrimental to our relations with Mexico. We are opposed to any policy which requires the carrying of work cards. Such a policy is inconsistent with this nation's fundamental commitment to civil rights.

We must deal with the issue of Mexican immigration
within the context of other border issues. The existing
mechanisms for handling specific problems in the border region
have not been satisfactory. Therefore, an Anderson Administration would propose the creation of a joint Mexican-American
commission to promote cooperative border development in an
integrated fashion as described elsewhere in the platform.

HANDICAPPED

While significant strides have been made toward ending
discrimination against the handicapped, much remains to be
done in terms of increasing employment and education opportunities, while also promoting freer access to public buildings
and services. Several tasks remain to be done.

- We must work to eliminate discrimination against the
  handicapped in housing by amending Title VIII of the
  Civil Rights Act to bar such discrimination.

- We must insure compliance with Section 504 of the Rehabilitation Act of 1973 to increase the accessibility of
  public facilities for disabled Americans.

- We must accelerate the spending of monies already
  authorized for independent living demonstration projects.

- We must expand federal vocational and educational
  training provisions to include independent skill training
  programs for the disabled.

- We must provide appropriate tax relief for private
  employers who remove architectural or other barriers to
  the hiring of the handicapped.

JUSTICE FOR AMERICAN WOMEN

The time has come for all our institutions and leaders to seek justice for American women.

Full partnership for women in our society is essential to our self-respect as a nation and our moral standing as a world leader. In addition, rebuilding our nation depends on our capacity to utilize all the creativity, leadership, and technical skills available. Justice for women is not a luxury; it is a necessity.

The women's movement of this generation is a vital force in our society. Thousands of the ablest women are enlisted in this cause and have achieved great gains.

Federal legislation prohibiting discrimination in education, employment, credit, and housing has been passed. The Equal Rights Amendment has been ratified by 35 states representing 72 percent of the population. Thirteen states have added effective ERA's to their state constitutions. The Supreme Court has made tentative but ambiguous steps in the direction of interpreting the fourteenth and fifth amendments to extend to women equal protection of the laws.

Women of means can get legal, safe abortions.

Improvements have been made in marital property, divorce, and inheritance laws in a number of states.

The number of women mayors, city council members, and state legislators has steadily grown.

Half our college undergraduates are women, and 25 percent of our law and medical school enrollment.

Participation of girls and women in sports has skyrocketed.

Opportunities for women in non-traditional training and jobs have been opened up.

Government funding of child care facilities for low income women has increased.

Women have made gains in full acceptance in the military services, particularly in non-traditional occupations.

Some shelters for victims of rape and battered women have been established, and some federal government funding is being provided.

These gains came against great opposition and at great cost in time and money to literally thousands of women and many supportive men.

In spite of the impressive victories already won, women are nowhere near achieving full partnership in any of our institutions, including the family.

The ERA, which would provide legal equality, has not been ratified.

The ERA is sorely needed because federal law and most state laws are based on the English common law, under which

married women were chattel under the control of their husbands.
They were considered incompetent to control their children,
their property, or their own lives. Although many piecemeal
reforms have been made, the laws are still riddled with ves-
tiges of the English common law. For example, one state code
reads as follows: "The husband is the head of the family and
the wife is subject to him; her legal civil existence is
merged in the husband, except so far as the law recognizes her
separately, either for her own protection, or for her benefit,
or for the preservation of public order."

Under another state code, a widow may forfeit any rights
in her deceased husband's estate if she is guilty of "misconduct." There is no smiliar provision applying to a widower.

In a number of states, a wife may not receive alimony if
she is at fault. A husband, however, is not penalized for
being at fault.

In several states, profits from a business run jointly by
wife and husband are the property of the husband.

The ERA is needed to insure that states and the federal
government make a systematic effort to review and revise their
codes to eliminate such laws as these.

Many other problems remain:

- stumbling blocks have been put in the way of those seeking reform of domestic relations laws to accord homemakers the value and dignity they so richly deserve;

- over one-half of divorced mothers are supporting their children without assistance from the father and only 4.6 percent of divorced women receive any alimony;

- the right to choose whether to bear children is not available to many poor women, and sterilizations without informed consent are still being performed;

- women still earn on the average 59 percent of what men earn, and 80 percent of women in the labor force are still employed in the sex--segregated low-paid occupations. Many of these occupations pay less than traditionally male jobs with less responsibility and requiring less skill and education. Too many of the children of working mothers have inadequate care. Only 1.6 million licensed day care slots are available for 6.9 million children under 6 with working mothers.

- our university faculties have been very resistant to employing and promoting women. Although there are many more women Ph.D.'s than 15 years ago, the percentage of women faculty in universities has not improved significantly. Most of the improvement has come at four-year and two-year colleges in lower ranks.

- little progress has been made in participation of women in non-traditional vocational education programs;

- most battered women still have no refuge from violence, particularly women in small towns and rural areas;

- the domestic relations laws of most states and the tax laws of the federal government are not based on the premise that the contributions of homemakers are equal in value and dignity to that of the providing spouse;

- the federal government does not direct a fair share of employment and training opportunities to women;

- many federal government programs, such as alcohol and drug abuse programs, have not provided benefits to women in proportion to their needs. Health research has focused on women's reproduction leaving women out of studies on other aspects of health. In some programs, data are not kept by sex so that assessment of the impact on women cannot be made.

The Anderson administration will strive to create a climate that will encourage all our leaders and institutions to join the effort to bring women into full partnership in our society.

Equal Rights Amendment

The Anderson administration will strongly support the Equal Rights Amendment by giving its ratification a high priority. We will develop a joint strategy with state sponsors in unratified states and do our part to implement it. We will publicize the truth about the ERA and expose the distortions that are prevalent. We support the boycott of unratified states and urge private organizations to do so.

Reproductive Freedom

The Anderson administration will:

• oppose government intrusion or coercion in the most private of decisions -- to bear or not to bear children. We support freedom of choice for the individual;

• oppose any constitutional amendment prohibiting abortion and urge that federal programs providing funding for medical care of pregnancy and childbirth should include funding for abortion;

• strictly enforce federal regulations to insure that sterilization is voluntary;

• increase government funding of family planning services, including services for teenagers; and

• increase research to find more effective methods of contraception, with the hope the time will come soon when no woman finds it necessary to have an abortion.

Appointments

Recognizing that highly qualified women are not as visible as highly qualified men, the Anderson administration will make a systematic effort to identify women for key positions, using the many women's organizations and other sources. Volunteer experience will be evaluated on its merits.

Enforcement of Anti-Discrimination Laws

Anderson's administration will vigorously enforce anti-discrimination laws and executive orders, giving special attention to university tenure and promotion practices. We will oppose amendments that weaken such laws, including amendments that would limit women's opportunities to participate in sports. Appointees to positions responsible for enforcing such laws will be chosen on the basis of their capacity and commitment to full enforcement.

Participation of Women in Government Programs

Anderson's administration will require that administrators of government programs collect data by sex and review the

impact of these programs on women and the participation of
women in policymaking. Corrective action will be required
in those services, such as employment and training programs
and alcohol and drug abuse programs, not enrolling women in
proportion to their numbers in the populations served.
Health research will include women in the populations studied
and women will serve on the committees designing studies and
selecting grantees. It will be the Anderson administration's
policy that women be equitably represented on all grant-awarding
and review boards, committees, and advisory panels.

Pay Equity

The Anderson administration will support research on
methods of achieving pay equity for women in traditionally
women's occupations and the development of guidelines and
legislation, if necessary, to promote this goal.

Child Care

The Anderson administration will support more extensive
child care funding for children whose parent or parents are
employed and cannot afford privately funded child care. We
will support increased child care facilities for welfare
mothers who want work or training for work.

Marriage

The Anderson administration will seek modification of federal laws to conform with the principle that the contributions of wife and husband are of equal value and dignity. We will:

- urge elimination of gift and estate taxes on transfers between marital partners;

- recommend elimination of the "marriage tax" by permitting two-earner families to file as if single;

- develop proposals for revision of social security laws to provide equity for homemakers and wives employed outside the home;

- support enactment of the Homemaker Reitrement bill of which John Anderson is a sponsor;

- support government assistance for displaced homemakers to help them enter or reenter paid employment;

- recommend legislation and appropriations to aid victims of domestic violence.

While the marital property, divorce, and inheritance laws are under state jurisdiction, the Anderson administration will create a climate that will encourage fair treatment of women.

Registration/Draft/Military Service

The Anderson administration opposes a peace time draft. If the Congress authorizes registration or a draft, we will urge inclusion of women.

The Anderson administration will support:

- repeal of laws prohibiting women in combat, leaving to the Armed Services discretion in assigning personnel;

• elimination of discrimination against women in the military services, and opening up of more military occupations
to women.

Health and Safety

Health insurance programs proposed by John Anderson's

administration or supported by it will include coverage of

women's health needs, such as care for pregnancy and pregnancy-

related disabilities and abortion. Coverage will be provided

for single-parent families and divorced and widowed women,

who too often have inadequate coverage.

Safety and Health Standards will protect the reproductive

health of women and men, and Title VII of the Civil Rights

Act will be strictly enforced in cases where women are indis-

criminately removed from positions involving contact with

toxic substances. The Equal Employment Opportunity Commission

and the Labor Department will be directed to issue **too**-

long-delayed guidelines immediately and proceed with enforcement.

Rural American Women

Women living in small towns and rural areas are particularly

handicapped by distance from educational institutions, employ-

ment and counseling services, day care, job training programs,

health services, battered women's and rape crisis centers, and

alcohol and drug abuse treatment ceters. John Anderson's

administration will endeavor in cooperation with representative organizations to modify federal programs as necessary to provide equity for farm women and other women living in rural areas and small towns.

Minority and Ethnic Women

Special attention will be given to the needs of minority and ethnic women in all programs to combat discrimination and in programs to provide services to support women.

International

The Anderson administration will:

- advocate ratification by the Senate of the U.N. Convention on Elimination of All Forms of Discrimination Against Women, attaching if appropriate reservations to insure consistency with United States laws;

- appoint more women to U.S. delegations, on governing bodies of international agencies, and in the U.N. system.

CRIMINAL JUSTICE

Criminal Code Reform

An Anderson Administration will support a studied, incremental approach to criminal code revision rather than an omnibus approach that may sacrifice essential civil rights in the process of legislative bargaining.

We should set clear priorities and concentrate on revision in areas of key concern. These include:

●   fair and uniform sentencing policies;

●   equal protection of rights for all, including aliens, in every appropriate area;

●   more extensive coverage of white-collar crime.

Police/Community Relations

A police department must have the cooperation and good will of the residents of a community if it is to act in an efficient and effective manner. For cooperation to exist, residents must believe that the police force is acting on their behalf and is not an enemy to be feared and avoided.

An Anderson Administration would introduce legislation to Congress which would specifically authorize the Attorney General to take civil action against offending government and police departments so as to eliminate

proven patterns and practices of misconduct in those departments. Anderson would also encourage efforts to increase
staffing for the Department of Justice in the criminal division with a special emphasis placed on minority recruitment
and hiring. Adequate staffing should also be provided for
civil rights enforcement in the U.S. Attorney's office.

We also believe that those suspected of violating the
law must be apprehended with a minimum of force. It
should be the trial, not the arrest, that renders judgement and determines punishment. The federal government
must use its powers of moral, legal and political persuasion to ensure that local justice is meted out in conformity with the standards of minimum force.

The Community Relations Service (CRS) which provides
mediation and conciliation as opposed to litigation can
be most useful in limiting racial tension. However, CRS
is understaffed and underfunded. An Anderson Administration will seek to expand the staff beyond the 111 it
now employs. Arbitration and mediation is a viable tool
in police and community relations as well as in intra-
community relations.

Prison Reform

There are approximately 314,000 offenders housed in
state and federal prisons. At present, prisons are largely
failing to rehabilitate those inmates and are instead
creating impediments to rehabilitation. One-third of all
prisoners released are back in prison within five years.

We support efforts being made by the courts to correct
unconstitutional prison conditions created by the neglect
of government officials. Such conditions can only prove
to be a counter-productive force in our society. In addition, an Anderson Administration would authorize the Attorney
General to institute civil suits on behalf of any inmate
unable to get redress for deprivations of his or her
federal constitutional and statutory rights.

We support legislation which would provide financial
assistance to states for use in expanding educational and
job training programs at correctional facilities.

Handgun Crime

The statistical profile of handgun crime constitutes
a litany of death:

●   handguns are used to commit nearly half of all the
        murders committed in the United States;

- during the peak years of the Vietnam War, more Americans were killed by handguns than were killed in action in Vietnam;

- almost three out of every four law enforcement officers killed are victims of handguns;

- every hour, one American is killed by a handgun.

Despite these tragic realities, small but influential elements of our society have successfully fought handgun crime controls. More than a decade after the Eisenhower Commission called for handgun registration and the eventual universal licensing of handgun ownership, these goals elude us.

Some state and local governments have enacted laws to regulate handgun sales, distribution, and possession. These controls have effectively reduced handgun crimes, but their piecemeal enactment has resulted in localized benefits. In the absence of uniform activity by the states and municipalities, the national handgun problem cannot be solved. The deadly facts showing high rates of homicide by handguns mean that comprehensive federal legislation is needed now.

Before assuming office, candidate Carter "committed" his Administration to handgun control. After taking office, President Carter either forgot his promise or intentionally ignored it. The Carter Administration has not proposed any gun control legislation to the Congress and the death toll from handgun crimes continues to mount.

The Anderson Administration will do what the Carter
Administration has failed to do: submit handgun legislation to both houses of Congress. The Anderson Administration will propose a Handgun Crime Control bill which will:

- Stop the manufacture, sale, and transfer of "Saturday
  Night Specials", the cheap handguns so widely used by
  criminals;

- Establish mandatory jail sentences for the commission
  of crimes with a handgun;

- Reduce illegal purchases of handguns by requiring
  purchasing licenses;

- Establish strict requirements for those who are
  licensed to sell or manufacture handguns;

- Develop a more effective tracing system to track
  down mis-used handguns and curtail illicit handgun
  traffic;

- Require manufacturers, dealers, and owners to report
  the theft or loss of handguns, and penalize those
  who fail to do so;

- Establish liability for illegal transfer of any handgun
  subsequently used to kill or injure another person;

- Improve enforcement of federal handgun laws;

- Require licenses to carry handguns outside the home
  or place of business.

The enactment of legislation embodying these proposals
will not eliminate handgun crimes completely, and it will
take years to eliminate illegal handguns from society.
Yet, the longer this legislation is postponed, the higher

the handgun death toll will climb. We must begin to enact
remedies immediately.

Right to Privacy

Our right to privacy and freedom from government intrusion
is one of our most fundamental rights. Now it is one of our
most endangered rights. Improved communications technology
allows increasing amounts of personal information to be
transmitted and stored electronically. Many life-altering
decisions are now based upon analyses of recorded data instead
of personal interviews. The use of microwaves in telephone
communications subjects our conversations to interception.
Electronic funds transfer systems are capable of centralizing
data on our financial transactions, but are also subject to
possible abuse.

An Anderson Administration will draft legislation which
more adequately protects our right to privacy. It will include
provisions enabling citizens:

- to have greater knowledge about data being collected
  about them;

- to have the opportunity to correct erroneous information;

- to be notified of adverse decisions based upon recorded
  information; and

- to protect consumers' private financial records from
  unauthorized disclosure.

Recent court decisions concerning First and Fourth
Amendment rights have increased the likelihood of government intrusion. An Anderson Administration will seek to
enact legislation proposed in 1979 by John Anderson to
prohibit law enforcement officials from obtaining search
warrants to seize notes, photographs, and similar materials
from groups or individuals not suspected of any criminal
activity, except when necessary to prevent death or serious
bodily injury.

Appointments

An Anderson Administration will work to increase the
number of minorities and women at every level of our judicial system -- as United States Attorneys, federal magis-
trates, federal judges, and United States Supreme Court
Justices.

We completely reject any ideological "litmus test" of
fitness for judicial positions as being wholly antithetical
to the ideals of an independent and impartial judiciary.

V. SECURITY POLICY

Foreign Policy

Introduction

The last two decades have seen a dramatic decline in the credibility and integrity of America's position in world affairs. We have witnessed the growth of Soviet military power, Soviet aggression in Afghanistan, and Soviet military and political thrusts in Southeast Asia and Africa. We have seen Americans taken hostage, our representatives abroad killed, and our embassies destroyed. We have seen a significant erosion of our own economic power, our industrial productivity and our scientific and technological base. With this decline has come a concurrent rise in our dependence on others -- on the Arab states for our oil, on the Third World for other vital raw materials, on the Europeans to rescue our currency, and on China to balance Russia.

We are drifting downstream, learning to cope with each new demonstration of our weakness, unable to take the measures necessary for our long-run survival as a free and independent society.

We need clear and coherent answers and thoughtful leadership to revive the wellsprings of our strength so that we can regain our independence and restore our international position.

The first priority for American foreign policy quite
simply must be to put our own house in order. Our economy and
our technological base have always been the principal sources
of our strength. Their decline is now the principal source of
our growing weakness. The call, elsewhere in this program, for
rebuilding our domestic strength is the starting point for our
international recovery.

The next priority for American foreign policy is to
restore and nurture our historic alliances, which have been
neglected in the pursuit of global power balances that play our
potential adversaries against each other. A common sense approach
to foreign policy will look to our alliance systems as the
bedrock of our long-range security.

The successful execution of these two prudent policies will
go far toward restoring our international posture. Relying
on these solid and secure foundations, we can better define
our relationships with the Soviet Union, China, and the Third
World.

The Soviet government will attempt to advance the
reach of Soviet influence, whenever it is considered timely
and promising. It will do so borne along by a large and
skilled population, by deep and powerful historic currents
of Russian nationalism, and by a comprehensive and flexible ideology. The Soviet Union is also beset with significant economic difficulties. It must contend with

East European states always probing the limits of Soviet domination,
and with a growing, united, and determined China. In dealing
with the Soviets, we must be militarily strong, but seek
whenever possible through negotiations to reduce fear and
uncertainty. We should also pursue an even-handed policy
between the Soviet Union and China, seeking to reduce
our reliance upon their mutual antagonism as a major factor in
our security position in Asia.

We must next re-examine our entire approach to the
Third World, an area in which the United States has suffered
great setbacks in the last two decades. We have treated Third
World countries more as clients and as suppliers than as
sovereign and independent states with their own needs,
interests, and destinies. Our foreign policy must enunciate
our ideals and promote our interests, but always within the
bounds of respect for the sovereignty and independence of
every nation, large and small.

We must also pay heed to human rights, not only to display
our moral concern but also to further human decency and to
relieve pain and suffering. A strengthened America will
launch a quiet offensive to help the refugee fleeing oppression, the Soviet citizen who wishes to leave his or her home-
land, political prisoners all over the world, and American
citizens languishing under barbarous conditions in foreign

jails. We must also reach out to the hundreds of thousands
of starving people in Cambodia, the Sahel, and other places
throughout the world.

To succeed in these tasks, we must pay more attention
to the conduct of our diplomacy. In recent years indecision
and disunity have characterized the conduct of American
diplomacy. There have been too many egregious examples
where at best communications broke down and at worst
important people with relevant viewpoints were deliberately
excluded from the decision-making process. An Anderson
administration will not tolerate such practices.

In formulating our policy, we must abandon the false
logic that dexterity is a substitute for genuine strength.
We must rediscover the meaning of the word commitment and
understand that flexibility for its own sake is a self-defeating
enterprise. We must recognize that America, as the world's
leading power, must set an example for others by providing
a focus for stability in the world. And we must never again
find ourselves in a position where we need others more than
they need us.

Furthermore, in the conduct of our diplomacy, we must
once again emphasize substance over symbol. No grand con-
ceptualization is needed to understand the dimensions of
our current difficulties. No moral crusade will ever be
a substitute for a solid foundation of patient diplomacy.

No glittering style can ever successfully replace a cautious prudence. And no amount of bullying -- however aggressive -- can ever disguise genuine weakness.

What Americans must insist upon and must achieve is a renewed economic power and moral authority linked to a reinvigorated partnership with our democratic allies. With it, Western civilization can confront the dangers and the challenges of the world from a position of quiet but unquestioned strength and courage.

Western Europe and the Atlantic Alliance

The strength of our relationship with Western Europe
and the Atlantic Alliance is central to the successful conduct
of our foreign policy. Our ties to Europe touch all facets of
America's interests abroad: relations with the Soviet Union
and China, Middle Eastern and Persian Gulf problems, development in Third World, nuclear and conventional defense capabilities, arms control, energy dependency, human rights, and
many others. These issues are addressed elsewhere in this
program. What follows are the broad principles upon which
an Anderson Administration will build its Western European
policies. Also considered here are Western European issues
not discussed elsewhere in this program.

For more than thirty years, the great and historic partnership between the United States and the nations of Western
Europe succeed in preserving the peace and in providing
a climate within which European skills and energy were
mobilized to produce unprecedented prosperity, stability,
and progress.

There are today significant challenges to the transatlantic relationship. Chief among them are the loss of
control over the supply and price of energy, the relative
decline of the American economy in comparison to the

economies of Europe, and the steady expansion of Soviet military capabilities. These will continue to cause rivalry and tension in transatlantic relations. We reemphasize our belief, however, that close relations between the United States and Western Europe are central to sustaining our freedoms and security.

To pursue and nurture successfully our Atlantic partnership in the next decade, we must have a strong sense of the basic principles that should guide our efforts.

First among these broad principles is the recognition that apart from deterring a physical attack upon the United States itself, there is no more important national interest than the maintenance of our Alliance with Western Europe. We can afford nothing less than a full measure of cooperation and partnership.

Second, we must recognize that the Alliance must be a union of equal partners. Each member must act as a leader in its own right. Each must be prepared to share fairly in the burdens of our joint endeavors, and to justify these sacrifices to its own people. Each must have the steadfastness to persevere in joint initiatives.

Third, we must be prepared to acknowledge that there will be times when European interests are not those embraced by the United States. But we must not use these differences to decry the state of the Alliance. A mature and balanced partnership can accommodate differences of opinion or approach.

Fourth, the United States must cease talking about consultation and actually begin to consult with its allies before embarking on ventures in which it expects them to participate. Reciprocally, our allies must acknowledge that they have a similar responsibility. We must be ever aware of the need to seek counsel, explore proposals, and air ideas in confidence with our allies, before we embark on a course of conduct which we would expect others to follow. We must seek to use those opportunities and organizations that now exist to better advantage. To assist in achieving this goal, we need to broaden the scope of the present summit meetings to cover a wider range of political and security problems as well as economic problems.

An Anderson Administration will also encourage the European Community's evolution toward political union. The first direct election of the European Parliament and the establishment of the European Monetary System are significant indications of a prospering European idea. We believe that the admission of Greece, Spain and Portugal to the European Community will both strengthen the European idea and the future of democracy in Southern Europe.

In the economic sphere, oil and energy policies, monetary problems, and the rise of protectionism continue to crowd
the transatlantic agenda. These issues are of deep concern
to Japan as well, for they affect all the industrial democracies in similar ways. In dealing with these issues, an
Anderson Administration will adhere to two tenets. First,
rebuilt American industries are the mainstay of our international economic relationships. We must rebuild our industrial base and increase the productivity of our workers to
restore our competitiveness in world markets. Second, the
United States and the Western nations must ensure that diver-
gent economic interests do not impair our security relations.
These differences, rather than isolating countries, can
encourage greater efforts towards agreed upon solutions to
our various problems.

Consistent with our strong interest in augmenting
the Atlantic Alliance, we welcome Greece's participation as a
full memeber of the Alliance, and will support efforts at
enhancing stability in the Eastern Mediterranean. We recognize the importance of the Aegean Islands to the security
of Greece, and look forward to a just resolution of Aegean
Island issues.

We believe that the continuing crisis in Cyprus, too
long delayed in its resolution, must be settled through negotiations

between Greece, Turkey, and the Cypriot people.
The principles embodied in United Nations Resolution 3212
and the Ten Point Agreement of 1979 provide the surest
foundation for peace, security, and stability in the region.
An Anderson Administration will be prepared to provide
assistance in the rebuilding of the Cypriot community.

229

THE SOVIET UNION

We have entered a new era in our relationship with the
Soviet Union. The Soviet troops and tanks that poured into
Afghanistan have banished to the history books the business
as usual relations of the 1970's. The problem of how to deal
with the Soviet Union is the greatest task our diplomacy
will face in the years ahead.

Our relationship with the Soviet Union is competitive.
They are our rival, not our partner, in the international arena.
But the elements of our rivalry, while extremely serious, are
neither total nor absolute, largely because our security
interests are not completely separable. We share with the Soviet
Union, and with all nations, a pre-eminent interest in avoiding
a nuclear holocaust.

We must therefore establish a balance of prudent expectations in our relationship with the Soviet Union. An Anderson
Administration will not hesitate to take serious measures to
resist Soviet political and military thrusts, but we will exercise
our power in a responsible manner. We will be energetic in
seeking safeguards to reduce the risks of war, and we will do
our utmost to demonstrate to the Soviets that their interests
are best served by their own restraint.

Toward these ends, the Anderson Administration, as stated elsewhere in this program, will do what is required to maintain the invulnerability of our nuclear forces as the Soviets continue to improve the accuracy of their missiles. We will continue to improve our conventional forces. Without illusions, we will continue the SALT II process, and thereby lay the groundwork for SALT III.

Measured against the resources, skills, and capacities of the West, the Soviet Union is the far weaker force. The successes of the Soviet Union thus depend in great part on the degree of cohesion, firmness, and vigor which the Western world can exhibit. The Anderson Administration's efforts to rebuild the Western Alliance will therefore be a centerpiece of our efforts to conduct diplomacy toward the Soviet Union.

We strongly support the Helsinki process. The broadening of trade, as well as the expansion of scientific, technological, and cultural exchanges, will be dependent upon practices by the Soviet and East European governments which are consistent with basic human rights standards.

231

We respect the desires of the people of Eastern Europe
to determine their own destinies, free of outside interference.
We reaffirm our commitment to respect the territorial integrity
and national sovereignty of Eastern European states and we
expect the Soviet Union to respect that integrity and sovereignty
as well.

Lastly, our relations with the Soviet Union must be
seen in the broader setting of world politics. Activities by
the Soviet Union and East European countries in Third
World areas which endanger our interests must necessarily
impede the broadening of our relationships. But we must
not let our concerns about the Soviet Union distort our
policies toward the nations of Africa, Asia, Latin America,
and elsewhere. With our allies, we will encourage the
forces of nationalism to find expressions not in demagoguery
and military dictatorships, the breeding ground of revolutionary
violence, but in moderate policies of social change.

We will oppose Soviet adventurism wherever necessary,
but we will also seek opportunitites for reducing fear,
uncertainty, and misunderstanding through negotiations.
Above all else, we must be clear, steady, and coherent in
our dealings with the Soviet Union, leaving no doubt about
our determination to maintain and advance our foreign policy
interests.

MIDDLE EAST

The attainment of peace and stability in the Middle East
is a high priority of American foreign policy. In recent years,
the cause of peace has advanced dramatically with the signing
of the Camp David accords by Israel and Egypt. In the Persian
Gulf, however, stability is threatened by the revolution in Iran,
the Soviet invasion of Afghanistan, world dependence on Arab oil,
and religious and ideological disputes among the regional actors.
Our policy throughout the region must be directed towards the
reduction of tensions and, with the support of our allies, the
protection of Western interests.

American policy toward the Arab-Israel dispute must be
conducted with the understanding that a solution to that conflict
will not resolve the energy crisis, the instability of the oil
producers, the turmoil in the Persian Gulf, the plight of the
hostages in Iran or the occupation of Afghanistan. The United
States must remain the guarantor of the Egyptian-Israeli Peace
Treaty.

An Anderson Administration will not exert pressure on the
parties involved nor interfere in the negotiations. The United
States should not attempt to dictate the terms of a peace
settlement with public rebukes of the negotiating parties,
clandestine meetings with those who would abort the

peacemaking process or submission of comprehensive proposals
for peace that are not supported by the countries directly
concerned.

America's political, economic and military commitment to
Israel is fundamental to our strategic interests in the Middle
East.   Israel is committed, as we are, to democratic ideals and
to a free and open way of life that respects human rights.
We should utilize Israel's strategic and technical experience,
its intelligence information and, in an emergency, its
facilities. We will continue to provide military and economic
assistance to Israel at a level sufficient to enable it to
maintain its security as its potential adversaries expand their
military capabilities, and to maintain its economy while
accepting the high costs of withdrawal, relocation and
peace.

The United States must remain committed to a meaningful
peace. A lasting settlement must encompass the principles
affirmed in the Camp David accords, including reconciliation;
the establishment of secure and recognized borders; fully
normalized relations including trade, travel, communications
and the exchange of ambassadors; and an end to military
threats, political attacks and economic warfare.

The courageous efforts of President Sadat to achieve peace
with Israel have encouraged the development of friendly relations
between Egypt and the United States. This relationship with
the Arab world's leading country should be vigorously promoted

with assistance   and diplomatic support, to demonstrate
the value of the Camp David Accords, to promote Western
interests and to help maintain the balance of power in the
region.

An Anderson Administration will continue to support the
recognition of Palestinian rights , embodied in the Camp David
accords, but will oppose the creation of a Palestinian state
between Israel and Jordan. Such a state would be dominated
by the Palestine Liberation Organization, would promote
instability in the Middle East and would threaten other
nations in the area as much as the security of Israel. We
should look to Jordan to help significantly in resolving
the Palestinian questions. The United States must continue
its refusal to recognize or negotiate with the PLO until it
repudiates terrorism, explicitly recognizes Israel's right
to exist in peace, and accepts UN Security Resolutions 242
and 338 unchanged.

An Anderson Administration will weigh its public statements
with care and put greater emphasis on quiet diplomacy through
regular diplomatic channels. We will not, for example, stoop to
the temptation to use UN votes as a means of interfering with
the diplomacy of the peace process. An Anderson Administration
will not label Israeli settlements as "illegal" and as "obstacles
to peace". This prejudges and compromises negotiations from the
outset. The question of the settlements can best be resolved

by Egypt, Israel and the Palestinian residents of the West
Bank and Gaza Strip.

The final status of East Jerusalem must be decided by
negotiation. The United States must support the continuation
of free and unimpeded access to Jerusalem's holy places by people
of all faiths. Jerusalem must remain an open and undivided city.
At the conclusion of the peacemaking process, the Anderson
Administration will recognize Jerusalem as the capital of
Israel and move the U.S. embassy there.

The Anderson Administration will exercise restraint in
approving arms transfers to those nations which oppose the
peace process and do not cooperate with our diplomatic efforts.
The United States should actively use diplomatic channels to
discourage those arms transfers by third parties which might
contribute to regional instability.

The invasion of Afghanistan, the instability in Iran,
and recent events in Saudi Arabia have provided the Soviet
Union with an opportunity to achieve the political encircle-
ment of the Persian Gulf and the states of the Arabian peninsula.
Soviet activity in the Yemens, Syria, Libya, and Ethiopia
increases the danger of this threat and offers immediate
challenges to the United States. Efforts to increase our
presence in the region should proceed with caution, and
be made in close cooperation with our friends in the region and
our European allies.

236

   To give ourselves greater leverage in regional and great
power disputes, we must reduce our costly dependence on foreign
oil. An Anderson Administration will embark on a comprehensive program
of energy independence, outlined elsewhere in this platform.

   Our principal objective in Iran is to secure the prompt
and safe release of our embassy personnel still being held
hostage by the Iranian government. We will use every measure
of quiet diplomacy, bilateral and multilateral, to achieve
this end.

237

EAST ASIA AND THE PACIFIC

Japan

Our relationship with Japan stands at the center of American foreign policy toward East Asia. The bonds of history, though recently forged, are strong. Common interests bind us as well: Japan, next to Canada, is the single largest trading partner of the United States, and our treaty with Japan is the cornerstone of our security interests in East Asia.

We believe that two basic principles should guide our policy toward Japan: that a genuine American-Japanese partnership is fundamental to all else in the Pacific, and that economic and security elements in the partnership cannot be separated.

We recognize that Japanese defense expenditures raise critically difficult problems for both Japan and the nations of East Asia. Japan's role as an economically powerful, but lightly armed, nation significantly contributes to East Asian regional stability. A major shift in Japan's military role in the region could undermine, not enhance, that stability.

An Anderson Administration will not press Japan to expand its military capabilities beyond the level which the Japanese believe their security requires and their constitution permits. Japan should contribute more to collective security, but this need

not be through military measures. We will urge Japan to
increase its economic assistance to other countries, and
to expand its contribution to research and development of
alternative energy resources. We will continue to renegotiate
burden-sharing arrangements on the cost of American bases
in Japan to reflect changes in the value of the yen and the
dollar as well as increases in Japan's economic capabilities.

We will make no military or diplomatic moves in East
Asia, particularly with regard to China and Korea, without
advance consultation with Japan. We will demonstrate
greater sensitivity to Japan's great dependence on imported
energy supplies and to the vital role alternative energy
sources can play in Japan's economy.

Japan's post-war economic ties to the United States have
been fundamental to Japan's own progress and its expansion
into regional and world economies. The ASEAN Nations (the
Association of Southeast Asian Nations comprised of Indonesia,
Malaysia, the Philippines, Singapore, and Thailand), with
its population expected to increase from its present 230
million to 290 million in 1985, is one of the world's fastest-
growing economic regions.

An Anderson Administration will explore ways of
expanding America's role among the ASEAN group which also
enhances our relationship with Japan. One approach to this

end would be to extend current mechanisms for American-
Japanese consultations now dealing with defense issues and
bilateral trade to include funding for ASEAN projects.

Japan is at once our military ally and our economic
rival. Three major issues have troubled American-Japanese
trade relations from our perspective: the large current
trade imbalance; the impact of Japanese exports on the
American automobile industry; and access to Japan's domestic
market.

The principal remedy for these problems is to restore
the dynamism of the American economy to make it more competitive
in the Japanese market. We will press for the removal of
restraints on the import of American goods by Japan, particularly
in telecommunications equipment, computers, and semiconductors,
areas in which the United States has a comparative advantage
over Japan but has not had fair access to Japanese markets.
We will encourage Japan to build additional industrial plants
in the United States to retain jobs now being lost to industry
in Japan.

China

The diplomatic breakthrough with China is a remarkable achievement of twentieth century diplomacy. An Anderson Administration will build on this achievement to develop closer relations with China diplomatically, economically, and culturally.

We have been reduced in recent years to a reliance upon the antagonism between Russia and China to bolster our security position in Asia. We believe that those who talk blithely about playing the fabled "China card" fail to recognize that China is not a card to be played, but a player with cards. China's interests may depart from our own or from those of our Asian allies. We cannot allow China to develop an "America card" for use in her relations with the Soviet Union or with other East Asian countries, who view China with a mixture of awe and fear.

An Anderson Administration will never place the United States in a position where we pressure any of our friends into reaching a dangerous accommodation with their historic antagonists. We must, therefore, never put ourselves in a position where Taiwan is the price for Chinese cooperation against Russia.

We will continue our present informal military and economic relations with Taiwan, at the same time giving quiet

encouragement to the indirect trade relations developing
between Taiwan and China. We strongly oppose restoring our
relationship with Taiwan to governmental status. Such a
course of action would be a disastrous setback for American
foreign policy.

The Anderson Administration will take no steps to increase
antagonism between Russia and China. It is therefore unwise at
this time to become an arms supplier to China.

We will seek to bring China into discussions with the
Soviet Union, Western Europe, and the United States on arms
control. We will search for ways to encourage China's leaders
to take measures to guard against accidental nuclear war, and
to maintain strategic nuclear stability.

The Chinese government has announced plans for a ten-year
economic plan of staggering proportions; the estimated total
investment is some $600 billion, and includes construction
of 120 large industrial projects. China is, however, a great
distance from these goals, and its successful modernization
will require the participation of all industrial nations.

The Anderson Administration will expand scientific,
cultural, and particularly educational exchanges with China.
We will also promote the growth of United States trade with
China through such measures as assisting the American
business community to expand its presence in China. We
will discuss with China ways in which we can assist its efforts

to generate foreign exchange to finance its imports. We
believe that sales of technology to China should encourage
the Chinese to continue to concentrate its efforts on
improving its economic performance.

In broadening trade contacts with China, the Anderson
Administration will adhere to two tenets. First, China
will not provide America with a major market for many years
to come. Second, we must
extend credits to China and accord her full opportunities under
the most favored nation principle at the same time we move
forward in resolving our trade difficulties with Japan. If these
difficulties   are left unresolved, while trade with China
expands, we run the risk of convincing our principal ally in
East Asia that our support is truly feckless.

Southeast Asia

Southeast Asia has once again become an arena of military
conflict and human suffering. The boat people from Vietnam
and the millions of hungry Cambodians assisted through
American-supported international programs are the victims of
these conflicts.

We support swift humanitarian responses to the human
tragedies of Southeast Asia. An Anderson Administration
will place a high priority on American support for Red Cross/
UNICEF humanitarian aid programs for Kampuchea. We will also

support their insistence that no relief goods go to armed
groups in Kampuchea nor those on the Thai border.

But humanitarian responses alone are not enough.
Vietnam's occupation of Kampuchea and Chinese support for
Pol Pot's guerillas, China's threat to invade Vietnam again,
and Soviet access to Vietnamese ports and airfields are parts
of a deepening Southeast Asian crisis. The present trend is
toward the consolidation of Vietnamese control over Kampuchea
and greater involvement by both the Soviet Union and China
in the region.

Our objectives will be the reduction of the Soviet military
presence and political influence in Vietnam, the restoration of
normal life in Kampuchea by an end to the fighting and the
withdrawal of Vietnamese troops, and the assurance of Thailand's
security.

To achieve these objectives we will encourage the ASEAN
nations in their current negotiations with Vietnam. We will,
while forging a new relationship with China, be attentive
to Vietnam's concerns about China, just as we pay heed to
the concerns of Thailand and other ASEAN nations about
Vietnam itself.

We will also announce an end to United States support
for the forces under Pol Pot's command. They represent a mor-
ally reprehensible regime and prolong the suffering of the
Kampuchean people without offering any realistic prospect
of helping to reach a compromise settlement of the conflict.

The United States should not vote for the seating of Pol
Pot's regime at the U.N., but instead support a vacant seat
for Kampuchea until a government emerges with a proper
claim to represent the Kampuchean people.

Korea

Geography and ideology have combined to make the division of Korea a danger to the peace of East Asia and the
world. The United States is responsible for supporting South
Korean security both through the presence of its combat
forces in South Korea and its security treaty with South
Korea. We reaffirm the importance of maintaining our commitment to defend South Korea against attack. We will not
pursue unilateral withdrawal of American combat forces from
South Korea, as was attempted by the Carter Administration in
1977-78. Those unilateral actions increased rather than allayed
tensions throughout the region, raising new questions about
America's seriousness of purpose and capacity for determined
leadership.

The eruptions of anti-government protests demanding
restoration of democratic freedoms and constitutional government in South Korea require far-sighted and coherent United
States policies. Pressures for progress toward these political goals and opposition to physical repression by the
military-dominated government have become far stronger than
in past years. The government's attempt to suppress protest

while failing to establish a timetable for elections and the removal of restrictions on democratic freedoms risks an unprecedented political explosion which might invite intervention by North Korea and trigger a new war.

The problem of security and political stability in South Korea cannot be separated, therefore, from the problem of political freedoms. An Anderson Administration will strengthen American efforts to persuade the military to change its policy. We will make it clear that the United States cannot remain passive in the present situation, given its own heavy responsibility for the defense of South Korea, and that it supports to the fullest extent possible the legitimate aims of those demanding democratic freedoms.

Toward North Korea, we will end the fruitless and dangerous isolation from the United States, moving forward, in consultation with South Korea and Japan, in such areas as cultural and academic exchanges.

The critical issue of stabilizing the Korean situation on a more lasting basis will be a daunting task. We will give active encouragement to North and South Korea to move toward a true accommodation, recognizing that the goal will not be achieved soon and that the issue is of deep concern to Japan and China, and to the Soviet Union.

Australia and New Zealand

Our friendship with Australia and New Zealand, is deep and lasting. The ANZUS Treaty, the continuing symbol of our close ties, will remain a cornerstone of American security in the Pacific.

An Anderson Administration will consult with Australia and New Zealand on security issues of mutual concern. We should pursue a unified approach to strengthening ASEAN and in handling refugee problems in the region. We will consult with Australia and New Zealand before establishing any permanent spent nuclear fuel storage sites in the southern Pacific.

The United States shares with Australia and New Zealand important commercial and economic interests. An Anderson Administration will pay close attention to the issues created by Australian and New Zealand access to American markets.

South Asia

Since the end of World War II, United States foreign policy in South Asia has suffered from misunderstanding concerning the political, economic, and strategic importance of the region, the aims of its principal nations, and the nature of its regional conflicts. As a result, we have repeatedly failed to achieve our foreign policy objectives in the region, and we have helped to create the one condition we sought most to avoid -- namely, the extension of Soviet influence into an area whose leaders and peoples are inclined toward friendship with the United States.

An Anderson Administration's policies toward South Asia will center around three interrelated realities.

First, India lies at the region's center in every sense of the word. None of the major conflicts in the region can be resolved consistent with our interests without considering the interests of India.

Second, there are two principal sources of tension in South Asia: the India-Pakistan conflict and the India-China conflict. Our policy in the 1980's must avoid the past mistake of embracing Pakistan and tilting away from India. We must help each recognize that their common regional security interests should outweigh local differences that have separated them in the past. We must, while developing the new relationship with China, be sensitive to India's concerns about China.

Third, the underlying bases for conflicts among the
South Asian countries are indigenous and regional in character.
They are distorted, not clarified, when viewed solely through
the prism of American-Soviet relations.

The Carter Administration's unsuccessful rush to re-arm
Pakistan following the Soviet invasion of Afghanistan diminished
our prestige, and revived Indian suspicions that the United
States was building an informal alliance which threatened
India's interests.

If the Soviet Union threatens Pakistan's territorial
integrity -- a threat that would also endanger India's
security -- we will consult with Pakistan, India, and
other countries about steps to be taken to meet the Soviet
challenge. An Anderson Administration will be prepared
to consider seriously a request for arms by Pakistan in such
circumstances.

We believe that any economic aid to Pakistan must
genuinely help to maintain the country's integrity and
economy, and should be designed to strengthen Pakistan's
internal stability by improving the standard of living of
its people. It should be concentrated in such areas as
agrarian development and reform, road-building programs,
rural electrification, and improved internal communication.
But if Pakistan is to become truly secure, the government must
be encouraged to broaden its political base, renew its commitment

to constitutional government and fair elections, and move
toward more stable relations with India.

An Anderson Administration will make a major effort
to open a wider window to India, whose size, population,
economic strength, military might, and relative political
stability ensure that it will continue to exercise significant
influence in the region. We will support India's independent
role in world affairs. We will not abandon our commitments to
other countries in the area for the sake of improved relations
with India. But with quiet and patient diplomacy it is both
possible and desirable to establish a more lasting and productive friendship with this enormous land.

To help achieve this goal, the Anderson Administration
will encourage both India and China to continue efforts to
settle their boundary controversies. We will assure the
Indian government that the American naval forces in the
Indian Ocean will not intervene in internal South Asian disputes.

Our interrelated policies toward Pakistan and India
will require diligence and courage. Nowhere will this be
more important than in forging a position on nuclear materials.
First, we must encourage India in the moderate nuclear policies
the country has pursued since its explosion of a nuclear device in 1974. We will link our nuclear materials export programs to the continuation of such policies. Second, we will
help to create a sense of security for Pakistan in order to
reduce its incentives to test a nuclear device.

250

Finally, we cannot accept as permanent any arrangement
which incorporates Afghanistan into the Soviet orbit.   An
autonomous and independent Afghanistan must be our goal.
An Anderson Administration will work with the Government
of India in efforts to influence the Soviet Union to withdraw
its troops from Afghanistan in furtherance of the regional
stability which we and our friends desire.

AFRICA

The United States must recognize that Africa will play
a key role in world affairs in the years ahead. Today many
African states are expressing increased independence   in
world affairs. Africa possesses an abundance of oil and other
raw materials essential to the world economy, and represents
an important potential export market for our manufactured
goods. The success of our global policies will increasingly
depend on our ability to maintain good relations with African
countries.

We must respect the right of Africans to determine their
own destinies. An Anderson Administration's African policies
will promote genuine stability in the continent by helping
the nations of Africa to achieve social justice, political
progress, and economic prosperity for their people.

We believe that the long-term interests of all the people
in Namibia and South Africa will be served best by an orderly
transition to majority rule in each country. The
South African government's continued refusal to permit free
elections in Namibia, or to share power with the black majority
in its own country, threatens the stability of Africa. An
Anderson Administration will look for peaceful means to
increase pressures on South Africa to expedite the resolution
of these conflicts.

South Africa is the only country in the world where all political, economic, and social rights are completely dictated by race. Apartheid, an all-encompassing legal system proclaiming the superiority of the white race, is an affront to human decency.

In an effort to bring a peaceful transition to majority rule in South Africa, an Anderson Administration will:

● continue efforts to bring an end to apartheid in South Africa through negotiations in regional and multilateral forums;

● continue Export-Import Bank restrictions on lending and credit guarantees for investments in South Africa;

● encourage compliance by all countries with the United Nations embargo on the export of military equipment to South Africa; and

● discourage investments in South Africa, whenever possible in cooperation with our allies.

South Africa's refusal to allow for the completion of a negotiated transition to majority rule in Namibia requires a number of immediate steps. An Anderson Administration will:

● work with other members of the Contact Group (Canada, France, West Germany, Britain) to seek a final agreement in Namibia based on U.N. Security Council Resolution 435, which has been accepted by both South West Africa People's Organization and the South African government;

● deny Export-Import credit privileges to corporations making investments in Namibia based on rights secured from South Africa or the present Namibian authorities;

● support all U.N. efforts to speed the transition to majority rule in Namibia; if U.N. efforts prove ineffective, an Anderson Administration will work through other multilateral forums, particularly the Organization for African Unity (OAU), to bring majority rule to Namibia.

Territorial disputes, particularly those in the Western
Sahara and in the Horn of Africa, threaten both the stability
of the countries directly involved, and that of the entire
region. In helping to resolve these disputes, an Anderson
Administration will adhere to two principles. First, all
settlements should be consistent with the principle of territorial integrity endorsed by the Organization of African
Unity. Second, the United States should encourage OAU
peacekeeping and peacemaking initiatives aimed at resolving
these conflicts.

The Cuban and Soviet military presence in Africa is of
deep concern to us. We believe that peace and political
stability in Africa is best assured by African people and
governments resolving their political disputes without the
intervention of outside military forces. We will encourage
the peaceful resolution of African disputes as the surest
means of guaranteeing African regional stability.

American interests in Africa will best be served if our
policies are designed to assist African nations develop their
economies. Thus, an Anderson Administration will increase
the effectiveness of our foreign aid by augmenting our programs
and improving our disbursement practices. (see Foreign Assistance)

We will give priority to assistance programs in those
African countries which have made significant progress toward
responsive, stable governments. Zimbabwe, for example, has
recently undergone a peaceful transition to majority rule,
but the United States has not yet offered assistance adequate
to meet reconstruction needs. An Anderson Administration will
also endeavor to build a close partnership with Nigeria,
which has recently made an encouraging transition from military rule to a system of government whose constitution closely
resembles our own.

Our government should also promote private investment
in Africa which is essential to fostering peaceful progress.

THE WESTERN HEMISPHERE

A fundamental principle of our foreign policy is that
relations with countries that are closest geographically and
in interest and purpose are among the most important. We
must give primacy to maintaining confidence and trust in
these relations. Too often we have assumed, however, that
good relations come naturally and without effort. They do
not. They must be carefully nurtured through positive action
to further and maintain mutual understanding and respect.

Canada

Facts of history, geography, economics, and security
tie the United States closely to Canada. But our ties, no matter
how strong, need constant attention. By failing to resolve
differences when they first appear, we run the risk of having
them turn into more serious problems. There are four initiatives
that the Anderson Administration will take towards Canada.

We will support the conclusion of a treaty on Atlantic
fishing rights. Our countries began negotiations on fishing
rights in August, 1977, culminating in a treaty signed
on March 29, 1979. The Senate has yet to approve this treaty.
But a fishing rights treaty which serves the long-term economic
interests of American fishermen is desperately needed if we
are to avoid the overfishing of the Georges Bank.

We will continue to engage the Canadians in a dialogue
on trade issues of mutual concern, and will work to reach
agreement on a comprehensive tax arrangement on trade between
our two nations.

The United States and Canada must work together to
insure that both our nations have adequate future energy
supplies. Our nations need to increase their cooperation
in energy research and development projects. The Anderson
Administration will work to expedite the construction of
the Alaskan-Canadian natural gas pipeline, a cooperative
effort which offers important benefits to both our nations.
American investment in Canadian energy resource projects
will help Canada achieve energy independence.

Our common border dictates that the United States
and Canada develop a consistent approach to environmental
problems. The United States is presently considering an
increase in its use of coal as an energy source, particularly
in the Northeast. This increase threatens to raise the
level of sulphuric pollution in the atmosphere in Canada
as well as in the United States. The proposed Garrison dam
project would also have serious effects on the Canadian
environment. Canada is thus justifiably concerned with
these and other issues that affect the Canadian environment.
As a responsible ally and neighbor, we must continue to
consult Canada on these matters of mutual interest.

Latin America

For most of the 20th century, our hemispheric neighbors
in Latin America have lived in the military, political, and
economic shadow of the United States. This old, unequal
relationship is now obsolete. Over the past decade, economic
development and social change within the hemisphere have
given our neighbors a new sense of self-confidence and
national pride. Our Latin American relations will thus be
increasingly complex in the years agead. If we accept this
challenge in a spirit of mutual respect and cooperation, our
traditional friendships will be strengthened. If we turn away
from the challenge, ignoring it or seeking to reassert the
paternalism of the past, we will find ourselves increasingly
isolated in our own hemisphere.

Mexico

We have no more important partner in Latin America
than Mexico. Many of the most pressing bilateral issues
between the United States and Mexico have major domestic
implications on both sides of the border. Improving our
relations will require careful, flexible negotiations
which are sensitive to the legitimate interests of both
nations, and that recognize the emerging industrial power
of our southern neighbor.

The Anderson Adminstration will explore more fully the ways in which we can assist Mexico in its program of industrial development. Unless we are able to find fields for mutual cooperation, such as technology transfer, Mexico will naturally seek such assistance elsewhere. Unless we are responsive to the needs of Mexico's industrial development program, it will be difficult to secure Mexico's cooperation on such issues as energy and immigration.

One of the most complex and difficult issues is the immigration of undocumented Mexican workers to the United States. The immigration issue touches the interests of many parties, not only those of our two national governments. It affects local communities on both sides of the border; it affects the American worker as well as the undocumented Mexican worker; and it affects our own Hispanic-American community.

We recognize that there is no easy solution to the immigration problem. Any attempt on our part to close the border would be impractical and enormously expensive. And Mexico would see it as an unfriendly act.

An Anderson Administration will begin to deal with
the issue of immigration within the context of other border
issues. Migration in the border regions has produced local
communities that straddle the border. We have not worked
closely enough with Mexico to fashion policies that address
the unique social problems that these border communities face.
The existing mechanisms for handling specific social problems
in the border region have not been satisfactory.

We propose that a joint American/Mexican
Commission be created to promote cooperative social development
in the border region. This Commission would concern itself
with improving and integrating social services in the border
areas. Among that Commission's tasks would be the strengthening
of organizations like the U.S./Mexico Border Health Association.
The joint Commission would establish a structure responsive to
the basic unmet, human needs in the border region.

Beyond the immediate human problems along our common
border, there are many issues between our two countries that
require and deserve a mechanism for continuing high level
collaboration. The Anderson Administration will expand the
State Department's current modest effort to collaborate with
Mexico by formalizing a permanent consultative mechanism.
An on-going, high-level dialogue on issues such as trade,
agriculture, energy, migration, finance, and industry is
essential to building the kind of partnership that should
characterize our relations with Mexico in the 1980's and
beyond.

Central America

The most dangerous threat to hemispheric peace today
is the acute political crisis in Central America. We must
recognize that the political violence in El Salvador, Guatemala,
and Hondouras is in part the product of real social problems and

human rights violations, and that decades of poverty,
inequality, brutality, and dictatorship have produced the
volatile conditions with which we now must grapple.

The Anderson Administration will take the initiative
in urging the governments of these nations to broaden their
political base, create truly democratic political institutions,
and proceed with the necessary policies of social change without
delay. We will refrain from supporting governments unwilling
to undertake these necessary reforms. We cannot again afford
to wait until a political crisis is full blown, as it is today
in El Salvador, before we begin to seek solutions.

It would be a grave mistake to blame the current political
crises in Central America on Cuban subversion. Cuba will seek
to take advantage of instability in the region, but Cuba is
not the sole cause of such instability. We must not allow our
concerns about Cuba exclusively to shape our policy toward Central
America, or any other part of the hemisphere. No amount of
military aid can make a repressive government popular, and an
unpopular government is never secure for long. The best
antidote to Cuba's promotion of revolution is a region of
sound, popular, democratic governments -- not an armed camp
of military dictators.

Nicaragua

For four decades, the United States supported the corrupt
and unpopular dictatorship of Anastasio Samoza in Nicaragua.
Even though the revolution which drove Somoza from power last

year enjoyed the support of virtually the entire populace,
the United States tried, until the last moment, to prevent
the revolutionary government from coming to power. The
new Nicaraguan government is understandably suspicious
of American intentions.

Nevertheless, Nicaragua and the United States have been
able to maintain cordial relations over the past year. The
new Government of National Reconstruction has committed itself
to political pluralism.   The government's program of reforms
has   created some tensions with the private sector, but
both sides have thus far shown a willingness to compromise in
the interests of national reconstruction.

We believe that providing economic aid to Nicaragua
serves our national interest well. We support the $75 million
aid package recently passed by the Congress. It will speed
economic recovery and will also help sustain the current
atmosphere of compromise and moderation within Nicaragua. To
cut off economic assistance, as proposed in the Reagan platform,
will undermine those political groups which have urged
moderation, push the government towards more radical economic
policies, and drive Nicaragua to seek closer ties with
the Soviet Union.

Cuba

In recent years Cuba has taken new initiatives in both
Central America and the Caribbean. Cuba has provided some
arms to revolutionaries in Central America, and has provided
economic aid to some nations in the Caribbean.

We must not allow our concerns about Cuba to distort
our policies toward the rest of the hemisphere. It would
be a mistake to support repressive governments in Central
America merely because Cuba opposes them; it would be a
mistake to refuse aid to governments in the Caribbean merely
because Cuba aids them.

At the same time, we will not
tolerate direct military intervention by Cuba in Central
America. There must be no Angolas in the Western hemisphere.
We will also oppose any attempt by the Cubans to lead the
nonaligned movement into the Soviet camp.

Others may wish to enter into relations with Cuba, but
we ourselves cannot consider a normalization of relations until
Cuba demonstrates a willingness to compromise on the many issues
that divide us.

Caribbean

The economic situation in most of the Caribbean is particularly difficult today. The small-island economies, which depend on world trade for many critical resources face severe trade imbalances because of the rising price of energy. This has led to a burgeoning foreign debt, inflation, and unemployment, all of which aggravate the already serious problem of poverty in most of the Caribbean.

These conditions have produced both a new potential for political unrest and a new willingness to experiment with different models of economic development. Jamaica, Grenada, and Guyana have adopted democratic socialist models which seek to blend socialist economies with parliamentary democracy.

As Cuba seeks to expand its influence on the region through its own economic assistance programs, the United States should respond not with efforts to contain Cuba, but with efforts to build a strong basis of friendship between ourselves and our Caribbean neighbors. The complex social and economic problems of this region cannot be solved by military responses.

Increased economic assistance is an absolute necessity for some of the Caribbean islands. While the Carter Administration has raised the level of U.S. assistance to the region, even more must be done. The ongoing deterioration in the region's

terms of trade requires balance of payments assistance as well
as development assistance.

To avoid creating an unhealthy bilateral dependency between
the United States and those Caribbean economics that are most
in need of external aid, much of the economic assistance
provided by the United States should be channeled through
multilateral institutions such as the Caribbean Development
Bank.

Increased levels of aid cannot by themselves solve the
economic problems faced by Caribbean countries. Other global
and regional programs will be required if these states are to
experience   sustained growth. Effective commodity agreements,
particularly for sugar, are needed to reduce the vulnerability
of Caribbean economics to the vagaries of the world market.
Initiatives toward regional economic cooperation and integration
should be encouraged. International donors, including the
United States, could support a regional shipping line to
lower transportation costs and stimulate intra-regional trade.
Similar cooperative ventures in such fields as food and energy
should be encouraged as well.

South America

In South America, we must continue to strengthen our diplomatic relations with the continent's democracies. The Andean states of Venezuela, Columbia, Peru, and Ecuador are important allies in our quest for human rights and the restoration of democracy in the region. We must increase the coordination of our policy with theirs in responding to crises such as the recent military coup in Bolivia. Military officers in Bolivia and elsewhere must know that when they destroy a democratic government, they will meet not only the opposition of the United States, but also a solid front of opposition from all the democracies of our hemisphere.

The existing military governments of the southern cone must understand that our commitment to human rights and democracy is firm. Until they demonstrate substantive progress in the field of human rights and towards the restoration of democracy, they can expect no improvement in their relations with the United States. Moreover, we must make clear to them that interference in the internal affairs of their neighbors is incompatible with hemispheric peace and security.

The current U.S. policy of denying foreign assistance to governments that systematically violate human rights is a laudible one and should be continued. But more must be done. In too many cases, American banks and corporations undercut our governmental policy by providing loans and investments to the very countries which are ineligible for governmental aid. Our government must make greater informal

efforts to bring public and private policy into better
coordination.

The case of Chile is a special one. There is strong
reason to believe that the chilean military government was
directly responsible for a brutal act of international
terrorism perpetrated in the United States -- the assassination
of Orlando Letelier and the murder of Ronni Moffitt. The
Chilean government has refused to cooperate with the U.S. in
bringing the responsible parties to justice.

As the scourge of international terrorism spreads, the
United States must take an unequivocal stand that it will not
tolerate acts of terrorism in this country, especially when
those acts are the responsibility of a foreign government.
If Chile continues to refuse to cooperate in the prosecution
of the Letelier-Moffitt case, the U.S. should consider
additional measures to bring diplomatic and economic pressure
on Chile.

Human Rights

To advocate human rights is to insist on respect for and protection of the rights and freedoms of persons -- to be free from political persecution and torture, hunger, and deprivation; to enjoy freedom of thought, conscience, religion or belief.

We must not allow others to come to believe that our commitment to human rights is negotiable, or that it will be sacrificed at the first convenience. Of necessity, we must recognize the limits of our ability to improve the condition of human rights in other nations: the results will be long-term and gradual. But we shall never despair in promoting the full and free development of the individual.

A primary task of the Anderson Administration will be to sustain the framework of international peace and security within which human rights can be discussed, championed, and enlarged. The continuation of stable relations itself is therefore a crucial condition for the improvement of human rights in Eastern Europe and the Soviet Union.

We are angered that the number of Jews permitted to emigrate from the Soviet Union has plummeted, and we deplore the continued harassment of Jews in the Soviet Union. We are also deeply troubled with actions taken by authorities in the Soviet Union and Eastern European countries against individuals monitoring their nation's progress in complying with the Helsinki Accords. We reaffirm the conviction set

forth in the Helsinki Accords of the "right of the individual
to know and act upon his /human7 rights and duties".

We must attend the second Helsinki review conference in
Madrid, and we must insist upon a complete assessment of the
degree to which the Soviet Union and the Eastern European
nations have complied with the Helsinki Accords. We must
make it clear before and during the Madrid conference that
the imprisonment of Helsinki monitors and the punishment of
countless others for their religious or political beliefs is
violative of the Helsinki Accords and repugnant to the common
tenets of civilization.

Under an Anderson Administration, the growth of American
trade with the Soviet Union and Eastern European countries
will require progress toward genuine respect for the right
to emigrate. We see few, if any, justifications for denying
the right of persons to change their citizenship from one
country to another country willing to admit them.

An Anderson Administration will bring to bear on all
countries, through bilateral and multilateral measures,every
possible peaceful influence to prevent, to repair, or to end
gross violations of human rights. Exceptions to our peaceful
intercessions in support of human rights will be narrowly
construed and strictly limited.

An Anderson Administration will:

◆   give strong diplomatic support for democratic
    governments; it will propose new foreign assistance
    legislation that would allow us to furnish these govern-
    ments adequate and timely aid to help secure economic,
    social, and political rights for their people;

◆   limit economic and military assistance to nations
    that overthrow their democratic governments;

◆   deny military and economic assistance to governments
    that systematically violate human rights; and

◆   encourage corporations to conduct their activities
    and policies abroad in ways that are consistent with
    internationally recognized human rights standards.

The plight of refugees seeking haven in America requires

urgent and diligent action. The Refugee Act of 1980 establishes

the first comprehensive statutory basis for our refugee policy,

providing for more equitable refugee admissions and assistance

programs. The Anderson Administration will vigorously implement

this important new legislation.

Equal justice and our commitment to human rights requires

our establishing a sound and humane national immigration policy.

John Anderson has repeatedly urged the Carter Administration

to grant political asylum to the 10,000 Haitian refugees who

have sought refuge in this country since 1971. Our immigration

policies, laws, and practices must safeguard the civil rights

of all Americans and the rights of those visiting our country

for legitimate purposes. The Select Commission on Immigration

and Refugee Policy chaired by Father Theodore Hesburgh will

report to Congress by December on reforming our system of

immigration and our refugee laws. Reform is greatly needed, and the Anderson Administration will move vigorously in this area.

The absence of bold leadership in the past four years has been nowhere more apparent than in the timorous responses of the Carter Administration to the tragedy in Cambodia. An Anderson Administration will press for adequate aid programs and will oppose any reduction in the monthly number of Indochinese refugees who may now be admitted to the United States.

An Anderson Administration will give active support to the private voluntary agencies, the Red Cross, and the various United Nations organizations in their unflagging efforts to provide relief and sustenance to hundreds of thousands of men, women, and children throughout the world who, fleeing war and famine, face disease and starvation. We must, where the need is especially urgent, speed up our timetable for contributing pledged funds. Humanitarian assistance, quickly provided, can mean the difference between life and death for thousands of people.

United Nations

The United Nations, now nearly 35 years old, continues
work that needs to be done, but which the United States
cannot begin to do by itself. The U.N. is helping to eradicate
the ancient scourges of disease and malnutrition through
public health programs. It is organizing help for refugees
and migrants. It is monitoring world-wide environmental dangers.
It is administering safeguards to discourage nuclear proliferation
It is maintaining truce supervisors and peace-keeping forces
in the Middle East and elsewhere.

The Anderson Administration will play a vigorous role in
supporting United States foreign policy objectives in the
United Nations, through the General Assembly, the Security
Council, and the specialized agencies. We will
give strong support in the Congress to those U.N. programs
which further our interests. The agenda is crowded:

- strengthening the peacemaking and peacekeeping
  capacities of the U.N.;

- helping Namibia, through a United Nations presence,
  in its transition from South African control to
  full independence;

- reaching an acceptable conclusion on the Law of the
  Sea negotiations;

- establishing a United Nations High Commissioner for
  Human Rights;

- sustaining the work of the International Labor
  Organization; and

● expanding United Nations efforts in controlling
    international terrorism.

   We must also reassess our role in a number of United

Nations activities.

   Our contribution to the United Nations Development Fund

fell by one-third in real terms during the 1970's. We need

to consider maintaining our financial contribution at his-

torical levels. But more than money is needed. We should

also make significant program contributions. Few economies

have developed and applied technology to their productive

processes so quickly as ours. We should make full use of

our own economic development experiences in launching ini-

tiatives for United Nations development activities.

   We have in recent years given greater attention to

human rights concerns in our foreign policy, but incongruously

we have failed to ratify a number of international human

rights conventions widely accepted in the international

community.

   The Convention on the Prevention and Punishment of the

Crime of Genocide has languished in the Senate for more than

30 years. It has been supported by every administration,

Democrat and Republican. It should be promptly approved by

the Senate. Other human rights agreements are in the Senate,

including the Convention on the Elimination of

All Forms of Racial Discrimination and the International

Covenant on Civil and Political Rights. These covenants

raise important constitutional issues. Our aim should be

their ratification, attaching, where appropriate, reservations

to insure that they are consistent with the United States

Constitution.

The recent decision by the International Court of Justice

calling for the release of our diplomatic personnel held

hostage in Iran underlines the need to strengthen international

legal institutions. If we expect other countries to accept the

jurisdiction of the Court, we must be prepared to do the same by

repealing the Connally Reservation.

We have seen in the Security Council action on Iran and in

the General Assembly condemnation of the Soviet invasion of

Afghanistan how the United Nations can advance the goal of world peace.

We have seen in General Assembly resolutions on Israel and

the Palestine Liberation Organization how our purposes can be

impeded. Neither euphoria, born of success, nor cynicism, born

of frustration, should guide our policies toward the United

Nations.

The United Nations is a political institution. Our

success in it will be in equal measure to the aggressiveness with which we promote our legitimate interests. But we must be unyielding in our efforts to prevent the humanitarian aims of the UN's non-political organizations from being exploited for narrow national, or ideological advantage. An Anderson Administration will strongly oppose efforts to stack committees and to bar nations from participating in regional or organizational activities.

We should not be dismayed at setbacks. Instead, we must move to regain in the United Nations and in its specialized agencies that role which the strength, skills, and democratic practices of this nation suggest should be ours.

Foreign Assistance

The United States should return to its long tradition
of extending assistance to the needy peoples and countries
of the world. Funds channeled through American agencies
and international organizations have been spent in the pursuit
of a wide range of objectives, consistent with our humanitarian
obligations and our political, economic, and security interests.

During the past decade, domestic support for foreign
aid has waned. At present, the United States ranks 13th
among industrialized nations in the percentage of GNP
devoted to foreign assistance. There is a growing belief
among voters that America can no longer afford to spend scarce
resources on foreign assistance programs that seemingly
produce few concrete results.

An Anderson Administration will seek to reverse this
trend by heightening public awareness of the value of foreign
aid programs. American foreign aid:

●   increases world stability by supporting countries
     which are struggling to establish responsive
     political institutions, and prosperous economies;

●   gives us continued access to raw materials by promoting
     steady economic development in Third World countries;

●   provides business and jobs for Americans because roughly
     75 cents of every development aid dollar is used
     to buy American products;

●   promotes a vigorous export sector, which is a key
     element in American economic growth; and

●   adds to the security of our nation by reinforcing
     alliances of strategic value.

These practical reasons for strengthening foreign
aid programs reinforce humanitarian concerns. Foreign
aid enables us to help alleviate the plight of the world's
poor.

Our national interests, humanitarian obligations,
and international responsibility demand that we provide
more funds for foreign assistance. An Anderson Administration
will harbor no illusions about foreign aid programs. The
primary objective of foreign aid, to foster the development and modernization of Third World countries, is an
extremely delicate task that often takes years. We should
do all we can to ensure the success of development programs,
but not lose faith if some development efforts meet with
failure.

Foreign aid funds used to alleviate absolute poverty
should be channeled through multilateral assistance programs
wherever possible. By meeting basic human needs in
nutrition, health, and education, we can provide people with
the means to become self-reliant, and to participate in the
building of their societies.

Long-term economic development will also play a major
role in an Anderson foreign assistance program.

International and regional financial institutions
provide capital essential for the development of Third
World economies. An Anderson Administration will seek
suitable assistance for the World Bank, the United Nations,
and other institutions with similar goals to ensure that
adequate capital is available for multilateral development
programs.

The rising cost of oil has caused the current accounts
deficit of non-oil-exporting developing countries to increase
400 percent in the last seven years. An Anderson Administration
will encourage OPEC states to help Third World countries cope
with an increasing burden of debt.

An Anderson Administration will emphasize economic
assistance over military aid, consistent with our belief
that security is built upon responsive political institutions
and economic prosperity.

Specifically, an Anderson Administration will:

● increase the efficiency of the foreign assistance
  bureaucracy by placing the Agency for International
  Development (AID) once more directly under the
  supervision of the Secretary of State;

● establish a clearer separation of economic aid from
  military aid.

279

●   re-evaluate present assistance allocation policies
     which tend to give small amounts of money to many
     different programs. The result is that some
     projects do not receive enough money to be fully
     successful.

As America moves into the 1980's, we cannot weaken our

commitment to a sound policy of foreign assistance. A

sensible foreign policy requires a strong assistance

program. Misunderstanding, cynicism, and a leadership vacuum

has led to neglect of this vital component of our national

heritage and prosperity.

The Intelligence Agencies

Our intelligence community is passing through the
darkest period of its history. The talents of the intelligence
agencies have been sorely misused in the past and investigations
by congressional committees have raised serious questions about
the integrity and effectiveness of our intelligence effort.

Many claim that a strong intelligence service, with
secrecy necessarily woven into the fabric of its activities,
is basically antagonistic to the exercise of liberty in a free
and open society. We disagree. The work of the intelligence
agencies is a significant and necessary part of America's
efforts to live securely and peacefully in the world. And
we are confident that the intelligence agencies can accomplish
their vital functions without impairing our basic rights and
freedoms.

An Anderson Administration will strongly support
congressional oversight of the intelligence agencies. We
will request Congress to enact charter legislation to
define the nature, breadth, and scope of intelligence
activities. We will also support reduction in the number
of congressional committees to which the intelligence agencies
must report. Through its oversight committees, Congress
should receive prior notification of all significant covert
intelligence operations, and the principle of congressional

access to intelligence agency information and material must
be firmly established.

   We believe that covert operations should be undertaken
only for compelling reasons, and we will support legislation
that prohibits assassination in peacetime and other
practices by our intelligence agencies that are repugnant to
our democratic traditions. We also favor a prohibition on
the paid covert use for intelligence purposes of accredited
American journalists, academicians, those following a full-
time religious vocation, and Peace Corps volunteers. The
Intelligence Oversight Board, too long ineffective, must
meaningfully monitor the propriety of intelligence activities.

   The ability of the intelligence agencies to provide
accurate and timely assessments of actual and emerging
international events requires urgent attention. Two areas
must be immediately addressed. We must strengthen our
ability to make a more discriminating use of intelligence-
collecting resources and to engage in more thoughtful analysis.
We must also vigorously promote better coordination of both
agency information and counter-intelligence activities.

   Finally, we share the widespread concern about the exposure of the identities of our intelligence agents abroad.
An Anderson Administration will consider seeking legislation
to bring criminal charges against individuals who, using sec-
rets learned while employed in an intelligence agency, endanger

lives by revealing an agent's identity. We affirm our conviction, however, that punishing writers who have not worked
for an intelligence agency is inconsistent with First Amendment freedoms. Such measures would be a false promise of
agent safety and national security.

Nuclear Non-Proliferation

For thirty-five years the United States has pursued policies intended to restrict the spread of nuclear weapons. The original objective of the program was to keep weapons design and fabrication techniques secret while promoting the use of nuclear power for peaceful purposes. As other countries developed research expertise, however, the focus shifted toward a framework of multilateral and bilateral agreements to renounce nuclear weapons development and apply internationally administered controls on the technology and supplies required to build atomic weapons.

The unchecked proliferation of nuclear weapons and weapons-grade material directly affects the security of the United States, by altering regional balances, and potentially threatening global stability. The destabilizing effects of nuclear proliferation are compounded by the danger of civil wars, irridentist ambitions, terrorist activities, and the failure of command and control systems.

An Anderson Administration will work in cooperation with other states to safeguard physically all nuclear materials from diversion and to restrain the spread of sensitive nuclear technology. We will devote particular attention to limiting the number of facilities which use or produce plutonium or weapons-grade uranium.

Reprocessing plants are particularly susceptible to the
diversion of nuclear fuels since a commercial plant processes
about 150 tons of plutonium annually and existing accounting
techniques have significant "acceptable" error levels. Even
if new technology was developed which could monitor fuel losses
continuously to an accuracy of one percent, measurement
uncertainties would still greatly exceed the amount needed to
fabricate a bomb. We must therefore, rely increasingly on
physical security measures to deter diversion of nuclear fuels,
while also working to improve the measurement techniques which
provide a crucial technical safeguard. An Anderson Administration
will work to restrict the spread of reprocessing plants to
additional countries since most states with "young" nuclear
industries have no economic need for these facilities.

We believe that the United States must maintain a vigorous
program of nuclear energy research and development if we are to
retain our capacity to contribute technology, managerial skills,
and operational experience to the broad range of nuclear
activities relevant to the prevention or management of nuclear
weapons proliferation. In particular, we must take a lead in
supporting research to develop improved fuel cycle safeguard
technology, including exact and continuous fuel rod assay systems
for use in reprocessing plants. Nuclear weapons can be manufactured from diverted fuel in a matter of days, so exact

and continuous international monitoring of the fuel flow and
stocks in all civilian nuclear facilities should be a long-
range objective of American diplomacy.

Though the detection of "trickle" diversion of fuels from
reprocessing plants may never be possible, technological
improvements and strict internationally supervised safeguards
could make nuclear power and reprocessing systems much more
secure than they are today.

An Anderson Administration will use
every technological and managerial tool at its
disposal to increase still further the distance between
the military and peaceful uses of nuclear energy,
and to secure nuclear

fuel from diversion or misuse. For example, we will support
basic research into alternative designs of the breeder reactor
which do not use plutonium and we will consult closely with
our European allies on all non-proliferation matters.

We must encourage all states to join in improving nuclear
facility safeguards as a means of building confidence between
nations and increasing the genuine security of nuclear fuel
cycles. We will best be able to broaden the appeal of nuclear
safeguards policies by emphasizing their technical aspects and
avoiding public condemnations of our allies. We will promote
internal accounting improvements as a means of boosting quality
control and reducing worker radiation hazards.

An Anderson Administration will support a strengthening of
the safeguards and inspection authority of the International
Atomic Energy Agency (IAEA). We will also encourage efforts
to have the IAEA play a greater role in ensuring the physical
security of nuclear material. Standards for the physical
protection of nuclear materials in transit, whether international
or domestic, should be made as rigorous as current protective
technology will allow.

We believe that the international community will gain
from future efforts along the lines of the International
Nuclear Fuel Cycle Evaluation process and an Anderson
Administration will support such efforts. Technically oriented
meetings presently offer the best procedure for evaluating

elements of civilian nuclear programs and building toward
an international consensus on the issue.

The Non-Proliferation Treaty and the Treaty of Tlatelolco
have helped to build confidence among participating states by
establishing verification procedures as well as a presumption
against nuclear proliferation. Neither treaty has been signed
by every possible signatory, but the agreements have clearly
had a beneficial effect and an Anderson Administration will
search for further opportunities to expand the scope of the
non-proliferation regime.

We believe that exports of nuclear technology should only
be approved by the United States in instances where the
proposed transfer clearly assists American non-proliferation
goals. An Anderson Administration will enforce strict policies
concerning the export of technical data, material, and technology
and we will review the definition of relevant technologies
to ensure that certain non-nuclear technology will be
controlled if that technology, when combined with nuclear
technology, might lead to the further proliferation of
nuclear weapons.

An Anderson Administration will support the provisions of the 1978 Nuclear Non-Proliferation Act. We will seek to strengthen the commitments of all nuclear supplier states to refrain from the transfer of those fuel cycle components which were identified as "least proliferation resistant" at the International Nuclear Fuel Cycle Evaluation conference. We will call on all nuclear supplier states to make known the agreed upon arrangements for disposal of spent fuel from nuclear facilities which they have supported in any way. We will propose negotiations towards an agreement which would involve the IAEA in the approval of design and construction plans for all nuclear facilities worldwide.

An Anderson Administration will take initiatives aimed at satisfying the legitimate research and development needs of countries with small nuclear programs. This approach certainly introduces some minor proliferation risks, but it might prove to be the most effective means of avoiding additional unnecessary programs using weapons-grade fuels. We should initiate joint research programs with scientists from such states, but should simultaneously ask their governments to forego nuclear explosive research and accept all international safeguards.

289

We believe that the United States and other nuclear
supplier nations should join with the IAEA, EURATOM, and
national nuclear authorities to create a fund and technical
advisory service to assist developing nations convert
research facilities using weapons-grade fuel to fuels of
lower nuclear weapons utility. An Anderson Administation
will also increase the amount of foreign aid devoted to
technical and financial assistance for developing countries
which are interested in expanding their "soft path" energy
resource programs.

DEFENSE

Introduction

The fundamental purpose of America's armed forces is to provide for our security and to sustain and advance our national policies. The years ahead will see old and new challenges to our achieving this purpose that will test the patience and wisdom of our people and our leaders.

The greatest of those challenges will continue to be the expansion of Soviet military strength, and the Kremlin's efforts to exploit its military capabilities against the West.

In strategic forces, the Soviets have reached essential equivalence with our own and continue to improve the accuracy of their missiles. In conventional forces, the Soviet Union has greatly augmented its forces in Central Europe. It has sent thousands of ground troops into Afghanistan, and whether directly or through client states, has sought to extend its political and military influence in Southeast Asia, in the Persian Gulf region, and elsewhere.

The United States must therefore contend with the continued growth of Soviet military capabilities.

We must also attend to other challenges to our security, which lie outside the realm of our concerns with the Soviet Union.

In Central and Latin America, Africa, and throughout
the region stretching from the Persian Gulf to the Pacific
Ocean, nations and peoples are undergoing immense political,
economic, and social changes.   Change is inevitable.
It is rapid, often unanticipated, and too frequently causes
human tragedy on a vast scale.   Regions and continents will
not be won or lost by any single power.   But our political,
economic, and military interests in an interdependent world

require consistent attention to the Third World through economic
and political measures, and, where appropriate, through prudent
and effective defense programs.

What must be done to meet these challenges?

Our first priority is to build a defense posture that
demonstrates to the Soviet Union that it cannot gain strategic
advantages over us.

We must take steps to protect the invulnerability of
our nuclear forces.

We must have usable conventional forces to carry out
the tasks dictated by defense needs.

We must proceed with arms control measures that enhance
our security, but at the same time not fall prey to the
illusion that arms control can or should carry the entire
burden of preserving the military balance with the Soviet
Union.

We must do our utmost to modernize our military personnel
policies to retain the skilled men and women whom we need so
much to implement our defense responsibilities.

We must spend what we need for defense, but we must
apply the most exacting standards of efficiency and accountability
to the way we spend defense dollars.

What matters is what we buy with our defense dollars, not
how much we incrementally change our budget. We must discard
simplicities which hold that spending more money will itself
provide a solution to our security problems.

Moreover, we must never forget that arms by themselves
are not sufficient to guarantee our security. As outlined
elsewhere in this program, we must also restore our domestic
economy, which, in the long run, is the true foundation of our
international power. We must encourage further growth of our
technological and scientific capacity. Spending unwisely for
defense while we neglect the steps necessary to increase the
productivity, innovation,   and competitiveness of the
American economy will buy us short-range comfort and long-range
disaster.

Provision for our security also requires that we
invigorate our alliances with Europe and Japan. If these
alliances are preserved on the basis of a full measure of
cooperation and partnership, the West will have more economic,
industrial, and technological resources than any power or
combination of powers that might challenge us. But we must also
recognize that our alliances are unions of partners. Each must
be prepared to share the burden of our joint endeavors fairly
and to justify these sacrifices to its own people.

We cannot enter the international arena of the 1980's either
poorly armed or fearful to do whatever is necessary to meet our
commitments. There is the risk that the world will become a
more hostile environment for the United States, and we must
be prepared for this eventuality .

- We need leadership to develop sound defense programs and
  strategies to implement them.
- We need leadership to work constructively with Congress,
  orchestrating a balanced approach to national security.
- We need leadership to provide steady coherence in the
  conduct of our joint affairs with our allies.

The Anderson Administration will meet the challenges to
our national security as follows:

Strategic Forces

The nuclear weapons relationship with the Soviet Union
is at the center of our military concerns.

Nuclear weapons, because of their enormous destructive
power, their global reach, and the great speed with which they
can reach their targets, have had a revolutionary impact on
the security of nations. Throughout history, the chief purpose
of armed forces has been to win wars. The chief purpose of
nuclear weapons must be to prevent war.

For the past five Administrations, Democrat and Republican,
our nuclear strategy has been based on the principle of
deterrence. Our principal objective is, not to wage nuclear war,
but to prevent it.

An Anderson Administration will unambiguously reaffirm this
traditional strategy. We must hold fast to the conviction that
control of nuclear war is improbable, and that victory in nuclear
war is meaningless. We re-emphasize our belief that the extensive
deployment of weapons which threaten to destroy the other side's
strategic weapons in a first strike undermines the stability of the
strategic balance and can be dangerous in a crisis, for each
side will then have a strong incentive to fire its missiles
before they are destroyed on the ground. We must maintain secure
strategic forces capable of delivering measured, timely, propor-
tionate, and, if necessary, overwhelming responses to any
conceivable attack. We have such forces now. We must protect
their ability to survive in the future.

One component of our strategic arsenal, our fixed,
land-based missiles, is, however, becoming vulnerable to an
all-out surprise attack by Soviet forces. We must recognize
the danger but not be either paralyzed or imprisoned by it. We
should remember that even after absorbing a massive first-strike
against one portion of our nuclear deterrent, our strategic
forces will be able to destroy enough of the Soviet Union's
industries and military facilities to prevent its re-emergence
as a major industrial or military power.

The fundamental question posed by the growing vulnerability
of our land-based missiles is what comprises the most desirable
mix of forces as the American arsenal is modernized in the 1980's.

Should we preserve the three main components of our strategic forces, land-based missiles, bombers, and submarines? Or, as we move into the future, should we place greater reliance on bomber and submarine forces?

A possible solution would be negotiations with the Soviet Union that verifiably reduces the capacity of each party to threaten the other's land-based missiles. Unfortunately, the Soviets have so far rejected such negotiations. We must urgently seek to convince them that their intransigence is forcing us to consider options which may severely impair strategic stability.

The Carter Administration's specific cure for the vulnerability of our land-based missiles -- the proposed mobile land-based MX system -- is unsound. It will be enormously expensive (at least $50 billion, perhaps as much as $100 billion). There is reason to believe that the Soviet Union could destroy the system for less cost than we can build it. The proposed system will consume vast water and energy resources, and will disrupt, perhaps irreparably, the environment in the proposed missile site areas. It would invite Soviet military planners to aim nuclear weapons at thousands of new targets in the United States, and if SALT II is not ratified, the Soviets can develop all the necessary warheads and additional delivery vehicles to overwhelm the system as proposed.

American ingenuity can devise a more flexible and more cost-effective solution to the threat posed to our land-based missiles.

The Anderson Administration will give this matter the fresh and sober consideration it deserves through a comprehensive assessment of strategic doctrines, capabilities, and choices, free from either ideology or illusion.

What specific steps must be taken now to rebuild and modernize our strategic forces?

- Our military command, control and communications systems should be made as survivable as our strategic weapons systems. For much less than it would cost to build the MX system proposed by the Carter Administration, we can insure that our command, control, and communications systems could survive any attack.

- Our intelligence collection and warning systems must be improved, as well as our ability to analyze data and make decisions under war-time conditions.

- We can improve the basing systems for our aircraft and fleet ballistic missiles.

- We must also move ahead with the current Trident submarine program. The technology embodied in the missile and in the submarine will enable us to be more secure and confident in the coming decades.

- We should continue research into other missile-carrying submarines, including a larger number of smaller submarines, as additional means for enhancing our deterrent capabilities, as well protecting our seaborne strategic retaliatory forces against future Soviet anti-submarine warfare capabilities.

- We will continue modernization of the B-52 with air-launched cruise missiles, short-range attack missiles, and with improved navigational and other electronic systems. The B-52 is a formidable weapon of destruction. The Soviet Union obviously does not take it for granted. Neither should we.

● We will continue existing research on new bomber forces,
  including those capable of launching cruise missiles.

Conventional Forces

The brutal invasion of Afghanistan has underscored
that the Soviet Union persists in a foreign policy of opportunistic
expansion. However, in allocating more money for conventional
defense capabilities to help limit Soviet power, we must pause
to assess our situation and to clarify our strategy.

Soviet improvements of their general purpose forces, real
and potential, must be taken seriously. They must also be kept
in perspective. The Soviet Union cannot be assured that with
the outbreak of war in Central Europe,   the East European
countries would be compliant allies. And to the East, there
is a united and hostile China, growing stronger.

In Europe, the size and quality of Western forces continue
to make military aggression appear unattractive to the Soviet
Union. The risk of nuclear escalation imposes even greater
cautions. But to maintain a credible conventional deterrent,
United States forces and those of our European allies will need
to be improved, particularly to address the critical issue of
depth in the alliance's central sector.

An Anderson Administration will:

● Improve personnel effectiveness.

● Increase operations and maintenance funding to improve
  overall force readiness. Too large a proportion of our
  equipment is not ready for action on short notice.

● Pre-position more equipment in Europe. This would allow
  us to send reinforcements to Europe more quickly, and
  would have the added advantage of freeing airlift and
  sealift capabilities to meet threats to stability in
  the Persian Gulf region.

● Reexamine the relation between support to combat roles
in the Army to determine how the "tooth-tail" ratio can
be increased to achieve greater efficiency of fire-power
and use of logistic assets.

● Improve weapons design systems. Advanced technology can
and should be used to strike out in new directions. Too
often, however, we forego simple, reliable, rugged
weapons systems with clear missions in favor of expensive, complex systems which yield only marginal improvements. Multi-purpose weapons systems, while providing
more flexibility, may suffer from four defects: (1) they
are usually very expensive and, hence, fewer can be
bought; (2) because fewer can be bought, additional
resources are often needed to protect them; (3) they may
be less suited to any given mission than simpler single-
purpose systems; (4) this "gold-plating" invariably makes
weapons more difficult to maintain, thereby compounding
our manpower problems. An Anderson Administration will
conduct a thorough assessment of military design and
procurement practices to examine such problems as these
and to establish a sounder basis for making judgements
about the cost-effectiveness of weapons systems.

We welcome our allies' commitment to raise defense spending

by 3 percent a year until 1984. An Anderson Administration

will discuss with our European allies additional measures for

increasing their conventional capabilities in concert with

our efforts. These measures include:

● The role of European reserves as combat-ready forces for
use in the initial phases of combat. Most European
reserves are meant to serve as individual replacements
for casualties in units already in action. These reservists could be organized into actual combat formations to
help cope with a Warsaw Pact armored breakthrough.

● The condition of European war reserve stocks of ammuni-
tion, parts, and replacement equipment. There should be
agreed stockage levels among the allies, as well as
standardization and interoperability to share stockpiled
materials in wartime.

● The level of armaments of European ground forces.

● The role of European civilian airline fleets in airlift
operations, looking towards alterations in wide-bodied
jets to increase the speed at which American reinforcements reach Europe.

Although the defense of Europe remains the central

concern of our overseas conventional force capabilities,

it is necessary to recognize that other areas of the world,

notably the Middle East and the Persian Gulf, may require the

continued deployment of American conventional forces in the

foreseeable future. An Anderson Administration will not

let our primary focus on European force requirements lead us

to neglect our responsibilities in other areas of the world.

The Anderson Administration will develop political and

military measures, wherever possible in cooperation with our

allies and others, to limit Soviet influence in Third World

areas, and to persuade the Soviets that unilateral action on their

part will not be successful. Our conventional capabilities must

also respond effectively to local situations that arise

outside our relationship with the Soviet Union. Economic

and political measures are the principal instruments for

serving our security interests in these areas, but military

forces can provide a necessary ingredient in our overall

posture.

Our military forces in the Persian Gulf area should serve

two purposes: to give confidence to friends and to deter

Soviet action in the Persian Gulf region.

To achieve these goals, an Anderson Administration will improve the Marine Corps' tactical mobility and ground-based fire-power capabilities. We will take measures to deploy a regular naval presence in the Persian Gulf region, without impairing our naval strength elsewhere. We must be able to reinforce this presence rapidly with sufficient military power to contend successfully with Soviet incursions.

An Anderson Administration in its military acquisition practices will recognize that some parts of the world may require equipment that is different from equipment designed for operations in Europe.

An Anderson Administration will also encourage our Western allies and Japan to act in concert with us, whenever possible, in the Persian Gulf Region. The British, Dutch, French, and Australians either maintain bases in the Indian Ocean and/or regularly deploy naval units there. The security of the Persian Gulf area is vitally important to the economies of the West. The United States should not be alone in shouldering the burden of shared concerns.

We will discuss with our friends in the Persian Gulf region ways of pre-positioning equipment in their countries, and use of their air and naval facilities.

In all these measures, we will proceed cautiously, mindful that military capabilities and commitments must not become engines driving our foreign policy.

During the past 20 years, our general purpose naval forces have emphasized capabilities for offensive actions against Soviet sea and land targets. This must remain a significant mission for the Navy. But we believe that the Navy, as a flexible instrument of American statecraft, must give renewed and significant attention to its traditional responsibilities, namely, protecting the sealanes between the United States and our allies and protecting our interests in Third World areas. An Anderson Administration will develop a naval construction program to expand existing capabilities and to meet new challenges to our security interests in the 1980's and beyond.

The Draft and Military Personnel Policies

An Anderson Administration will oppose peacetime draft registration. The freedom to choose individual careers without the threat of government compulsion is a precious one. To protect it, we must make every effort to meet our military manpower needs without conscription.

The all-volunteer forces as currently maintained, however, are not adequate. The armed services are finding it difficult to recruit men and women to their ranks. The average educational competence of new recruits is declining. There is evidence that the military competence of our combat troops has deteriorated.

Career military personnel, whose professional skills are critical to our military effectiveness, are leaving the armed services at disturbing rates. Continued erosion of the size and quality of the armed forces will have serious repercussions for our national security. No more urgent task confronts our armed forces than meeting our military personnel needs.

Fairness to the men and women in the armed services and their families also argues for action. They deserve a quality of life equal to the importance of their responsibilities and the sacrifices we ask of them.

An Anderson Administration will:

- increase basic pay and allowances to compensate for losses since the start of the all-volunteer force;

- support breaking the link between military pay and that of civil service workers;

- provide bonuses for superior job performance by individuals as determined by unit commanders, as well as reenlistment bonuses for those individuals in occupational skills of critical importance to the armed forces;

- eliminate in many instances the "up or out" policy governing military promotions which requires many qualified enlisted personnel and officers to retire from the service even though they could continue to make useful contributions to our national security. We should create a pool of skilled individuals who may remain in the armed services outside the normal promotion path up to age 55 or 60;

- improve base housing, increase housing allowances, and expand social services such as day care facilities for military families;

- increase the cost-of-living allowances for individual service men and women in areas with especially high costs of living;

- grant allowances for all forces stationed overseas in places such as Germany, where, for example, the value of the dollar has declined 66 percent against the mark since 1970;

- adopt independent insurance fee schedules for medical services provided by private physicians to dependents of U.S. military personnel;

- develop a program of lateral entry enlistments for active duty and reserve forces for both enlisted and officer ranks;

- provide enlistment bonuses for those with education or technical training beyond high school;

- provide additional education to enlistees in exchange for an extension of the initial enlistment period;

- provide more extensive training to individual reservists including overseas deployments with active units for two-week periods where appropriate;

- reevaluate the issue of ceilings on the numbers of military dependents overseas.

These measures will cost money. But our nation can make no sounder defense investment. Moreover, these measures will save money in the long run. Reducing the outflow of experienced personnel will mean lower expenditures for recruiting, outfitting, and training. Additional monies can be saved by having the most experienced personnel continue to operate and maintain sophisticated weapons systems.

Arms Control

We face a critical juncture in the pursuit of a sound arms control policy aimed at limiting the levels and types of nuclear weapons as well as conventional forces. SALT II,

the SALT process itself, technological threats to stability,
the continuing proliferation of nuclear weapons, all demand
our closest attention.

What are the fundamental elements of a sound and workable
arms control policy?

● Arms control agreements must enhance our basic security
and must not compromise our ability to protect our
national interests.

● In our major arms control endeavors, we must insure that
present and future agreements will preserve and reinforce the stability of the strategic balance.

● Arms control agreements, particularly our accords with
the Soviet Union, are not agreements between friends.
We cannot rely on the good intentions, or promises on
paper, of our adversaries. Arms control agreements must
be based on adequate, effective verification.

We must develop new ways in which our NATO allies can
participate fully, wherever possible, in the arms control
process. Genuine consultation with our allies is essential
if we are to deal imaginatively with the complex problems
of theater nuclear weapons and the conventional military balance
in Europe.

The Anderson Administration will take steps to complete the
SALT II process, and thereby lay the groundwork for SALT III.
We will propose immediate discussions with Moscow to consider
possible supplementary measures to facilitate ratification

of the pending treaty and to explore an agenda for the next
round of negotiations on strategic weaponry.

The basic security interests of the United States are
well served by ratifying the SALT II treaty. The treaty as
negotiated is adequately verifiable, within the constraints
imposed by national technical means of verification. Critics
of the treaty have not shown how our nation would be more secure
if we rejected it. In the absence of the SALT II constraints,
the Soviets can expand their nuclear armaments to levels well
beyond those provided in the treaty. We would have no choice
but to match arms for arms in a renewed arms
race. Fear and insecurity, the wellsprings of war, would be
the constant lot of both countries.

In Europe, the Soviet Union is deploying nuclear missiles
of sufficient accuracy to threaten land-based nuclear weapons
in Europe. The Western Alliance should proceed with its plans
to modernize its theater nuclear arsenal; at the same time,
we should keep open the possiblity of negotiations with the
Soviet Union to limit theater nuclear forces.

The Anderson Administration will support efforts to
negotiate a ban on the development, testing, and deployment
of anti-satellite warfare systems. Until, however, the Soviet
Union shows a willingness to enter serious negotiations in
this area, we should continue research on an anti-satellite
capability.

We favor conclusion of a short-term comprehensive Nuclear Test Ban Treaty among   the United States, the Soviet Union, and the United Kingdom, with frequent review pending inclusion of all nuclear weapons states.

The United States should continue to seek agreements in such key areas as peaceful nuclear explosions, chemical warfare, and conventional arms transfer restraint.

Conclusion

We cannot help keep the peace, nor retain the confidence of our friends or the respect of our adversaries, if our military strength declines. We must do what is required to sustain the credibility of our nuclear forces, to rebuild our conventional forces, and to retain the services of our most capable military personnel. These actions must be pursued consistently and with common sense.

Our aim must be the wiser use of defense monies to achieve for ourselves and our posterity a peaceful future, confident in America's ability to maintain a defense policy that will insure its security in the years ahead.

VI. HOW AN INDEPENDENT CAN GOVERN

We have set forth a comprehensive program for America.
But this is not enough. The American people want new ideas,
but they also want effective government. The novel possibility
of an Independent administration raises important questions
about governing this nation -- questions to which the American
people deserve answers.

We believe that at this critical juncture, America needs
an Independent President, and we believe that such a President
can work successfully with a Congress organized along party
lines to govern this nation.

We now need an Independent President, for two reasons:

- The major parties have proved unequal to the task of
  formulating a realistic post-New Deal public philosophy.
  The Democratic party is committed to extending the New
  Deal without providing the means to pay for it.
  The Republican party has been captured by forces that
  offer a curious combination of consumption-oriented
  economics and pre-New Deal social policies. The
  Anderson-Lucey National Unity Campaign is based on a
  centrist philosophy that ties its program of social
  policies to those measures needed to rebuild the
  economic base upon which they can rest.

- The traditional parties were reasonably effective
  mechanisms for distributing the dividends of economic
  growth. But during a period in which the central
  task of government is to allocate burdens and
  orchestrate sacrifice, these parties have proved
  incapable of making the necessary hard choices. We
  are prepared to tell the American people what we
  must do, and allocate the burdens in a manner
  sensitive to both economic efficiency and social
  equity.

Most of the key issues confronting the country now cross
traditional party divisions. In the sphere of foreign and
defense policy, the overwhelming majority believes that our
military preparedness must be increased, that our long-standing
alliances with Europe and Japan must be rebuilt, and that our
manufactured goods must be free to compete on a fair basis in
major world markets. In the domestic sphere, we agree that
we must reindustrialize our economy, rebuild our cities,
reduce unemployment, inflation, and energy consumption,
safeguard our environment, and extend the full protection of
civil rights to all who reside within our borders. Conversely,
the issues that most passionately divide us -- the controversy
between capitalism and corporatism, and social issues such as
ERA, abortion, and affirmative action, are debated within
rather than between political parties.

The Anderson National Unity Campaign builds on this
agreement. It transcends the irrelevant quarrels between
an old liberalism and an even older conservatism, and it
offers effective, coordinated means to achieve goals that
enjoy overwhelming public support.

We believe, further, that an Independent President can
be effective. We must, of course, acknowledge that the
context within which presidents must act has become more

complicated and restrictive during the past two decades.
Sober observers have pointed to the decentralization of
Congress, the fragmentation of political parties, the risk
of single-issue constituencies, and the atomization of the
electorate as major elements of this new situation. But
we contend that in 1980 an Independent Anderson Administration
can deal with it more effectively than can a major party
administration.

We have four reasons for this contention.

- An Anderson victory -- in the teeth of the enormous
  institutional bias against independents -- would
  be a dramatic signal to Congress that the nation
  wants and expects action, based on the new consensus
  the campaign has articulated.

- Unlike other post-war independent candidacies, the
  Anderson campaign represents neither a region nor
  a dissident fringe, but rather a coalition of the
  center -- the traditional basis for governing the
  American polity.

- In the absence of Congressional cohesion and party
  discipline, the President's effectiveness rests
  largely on his ability to persuade significant numbers
  of legislators that his proposals are sensible and
  fair. John Anderson and Patrick Lucey are superbly
  equipped to do this. Mr. Anderson has spent two decades
  acquiring a working knowledge of the issues, from a
  national perspective. He is intimately acquainted
  with the intricate process by which ideas are trans-
  lated into proposals, proposals into laws, and laws
  into deeds. And he knows the individuals who make
  the laws -- their concerns, their language, their
  sensibilities. As President, Anderson would have
  the potential to work as effectively with the Congress
  as any post-war chief executive. Mr. Lucey has served
  as an effective Governor of a major state which contains
  virtually all the problems of industry, commerce, and
  agriculture that are found elsewhere in the United
  States.

◖   Congress will work productively with any President who
    enjoyed the trust and confidence of the American people.
    A key determinant of this in modern politics is the
    President's ability to communicate with them, face-
    to-face and through the media. This ability does not
    depend upon the party application of the President,
    but upon the ability of the President to advocate and
    persuade.

We believe with Alexander Hamilton that:

    . . . the true test of a good government is its
    aptitude and tendency to produce a good
    administration.

A good administration, in turn, has two requisites: good

personnel, and prudent use of them.

An Anderson Administration will strive

to appoint talented individuals, without regard to party

affiliation. They will be drawn from a broad range of

backgrounds -- government, business, labor, academia.

Ideally, each will blend general intellectual or theoretical

competence and practical experience -- both in Washington and

elsewhere.

The Administration will attach great weight to judicial

appointments on every level. It will strive to ensure that

only wise and experienced individuals be nominated for these

crucial offices without regard to partisan affiliation. We

believe that the greatest asset of the judiciary is the trust

-- even reverence -- accorded to it by the American people, and

that in the years ahead this high regard can be maintained

only if the judiciary is perceived as broadly representative of the spirit of the nation. Accordingly, we will intensify

the quest for women and members of minority groups from whom

judges and Supreme Court Justices can be appointed.

As to the appropriate use of individuals within the

modern Presidency, two great statesmen and electoral antagonists

have between them succinctly propounded the correct policy.

Adlai Stevenson once stated that there are only three rules

of sound administration: pick good people, tell them not to

cut any corners, and back them to the limit. And Dwight

Eisenhower, whose genius for governance becomes more evident

with every passing year, once reflected on his tenure in office

in the following terms:

> The government of the United States has become
> too big, too complex, and too pervasive in its
> influence on all our lives for one individual
> to pretend to direct the details of its
> important and critical programming. Competent
> assistants are mandatory; without them the Executive
> Branch would bog down. To command the loyalties
> and dedication and best efforts of capable and
> outstanding individuals requires patience, under-
> standing, a readiness to delegate, and an
> acceptance of responsibility for any honest
> errors -- real or apparent -- those subordinates
> might make.

We believe that the greatest administrative failure of

the current administration is its failure to deal successfully

with the Congress. At the heart of its failure lies its

inability to engage in substantive, meaningful consultation.

Such consultation has two components:

● The involvement of relevant Congressional personnel in the drafting of legislative submissions; and

● A constant two-way exchange on the progress of proposed legislation through the Congress.

An Anderson Administration will give relations with Congress the highest priority, assigning to this task experienced senior officials known to and trusted by the Members of Congress.

In general, an Anderson Administration will act on the principle that a strong Presidency rests on a strong Congress. It will respect the traditional prerogatives of the Congress and it will attempt to foster unity rather than foment discord within the Congressional ranks. At the same time, an Anderson Administration will protect and vigorously employ the powers of the Presidency. Our Constitution envisages a perennial mixture of contest and   harmony among the different branches of our government, through which the liberties of the people will be preserved and the general welfare promoted.

Conception of the Presidency

A successful Presidency rests on a clear conception of the Presidency. We believe that:

● The President must be a problem-solver, whose every effort is directed toward the general welfare. The "general welfare" is not a rhetorical fiction, but rather a course of action that promotes individual well-being while complying with the dictates of justice and fair play.

314

● The President must be a policy-coordinator. Government
  fails unless its initiatives are mutually consistent,
  reflecting coherent priorities and a sense of direction.
  Standing at the apex of government, only the President
  is in a position to perform this task.

● The President must give leadership to the Executive
  Branch. He should not recklessly attack federal
  personnel, most of whom are dedicated and hard working,
  but rather ensure that they receive clear signals to
  guide their endeavors.

● A President cannot simply enunciate his preferences but
  must energetically follow through with determined efforts
  to translate them into policy. To this end, the President
  must avoid inflammatory public rhetoric while engaging
  in quiet persuasion and patient, persistent negotiation.

● A President must tell the truth to the American people,
  even when it is unpalatable and unpopular. In current
  circumstances, only an individual prepared to be a
  one-term President, if necessary, can faithfully and
  conscientiously discharge his Constitutional
  responsibilities.

● A President must exhibit constant resolve and
  steadfastness once he has made a decision and embarked
  on a course of action. He should not expect to please
  everyone; nor should he be deterred by criticism. And
  he should not attempt to govern the nation by public
  opinion polls, but should always act to further the
  long-term public good, as he sees that good.

● The President must embody and express an appropriate
  historical perspective. He must strive to link
  significant public acts to the American political
  tradition, to give the American people a sense of
  continuity with their basic values and a feeling of
  participation in a meaningful common enterprise.

It has become fashionable to point to the many constraints

within which modern Presidents must operate. And some political

leaders -- including the present occupant of the Oval Office --

have sought to lower our expectations of presidential
performance and achievement.

We cannot deny the existence of constraints. But for
the most part they are nothing new. They are built into the
structure of the Constitution itself. In the past, great
Presidents have used the many powers of their office to
overcome these obstacles, to promote the common defense
and general welfare.

We believe that it is still possible to do this,
with bold, farsighted, independent leadership. We believe
that the program we have set forth is the basis for such
leadership, and that we can effectively direct the affairs
of this nation in the 1980's.

The essence of presidential responsibility is to assert
the general interest over narrow interests; to make difficult
choices among worthy, but conflicting, objectives; to strike
policy balances that are wise and fair enough to earn the
support of Congress and the nation.

No president can forecast in all respects the precise
course he will follow on all issues. But it is incumbent
upon candidates who seek your vote to state their view of the
country's needs and to identify those initiatives they expect
to undertake.

This we have attempted to do. Many distinguished
Americans have contributed to the studies and position papers

upon which our program is based, but it is our own sketch of the
priorities we believe should guide our country -- not a
mosaic of bargains among special interests or trade-offs
among experts.

We seek a workable synthesis of policy and program, for
the next administration must blend new ideas with old, innovative concepts with traditional values, proven approaches
with tentative ones. In responding to the challenges we
face, government must be frankly experimental in some fields,
conventional in others. It must also be utterly ruthless in
judging its performance and pruning its failures. These convictions will animate our administration.

We speak for a patriotism greater than party. And we
invite patriots of all persuasions to join with us in shaping
a government that can shape the future.

REBUILDING A SOCIETY THAT WORKS:
AN AGENDA FOR AMERICA

JOHN B. ANDERSON
PATRICK J. LUCEY
THE NATIONAL UNITY CAMPAIGN

Washington, D. C.
August 30, 1980

TO THE AMERICAN PEOPLE:

In the past few weeks, the traditional political parties have released their traditional platforms. Now we are releasing ours -- an untraditional program for America that responds to new challenges in new ways.

Our program is presented in two related documents. The first, "Rebuilding a Society that Works; An Agenda for America" highlights many of the major themes and proposals that our National Unity Campaign will offer to the nation. It is relatively short and deliberately selective. It states our goals and sketches in general terms how we intend to promote them. It is intended as a synthesis and an introduction to our program.

The second document, "The Program of the Anderson/Lucey National Unity Campaign," presents the details of our legislative and executive program in every major area of concern to this nation. It is divided into three sections. First, the Introduction sets forth the public philosophy that guides and unifies our program. The second, the body of the document, details our program in the general areas of economic policy, foreign and defense policy, social policy, and civil and human rights. The final section deals with the practical problems of governance. It substantiates our conviction that an Independent administration can effectively govern this nation.

It should be clear that we do not desire to implement every proposal in this program in the first year of an Anderson Administration. The full fiscal impacts of these intiatives are to be spread over the next four years. It would be fiscally irresponsible to do otherwise.

The program does not contain any massive new expenditures on the scale of a $60 billion land-based missile or a $25 billion-a-year comprehensive national health insurance scheme. Nor does the program call for large personal income tax cuts in advance of a balanced budget.

Moreover, we anticipate that the initiatives outlined in this program are small enough in their revenue impacts to be accommodated by the normal real dollar growth in revenues associated with an expanding economy. We will, within the next three weeks, issue a budgetary impact statement for our program.

How does our program differ from traditional party platforms?

First, it is specific. We have not been satisfied to express a vague commitment to abstract goals. We have spelled out our intentions; in many instances we have proposed specific legislation.

Second, it is directed toward problem-solving. We believe that government must be bold and active, but that it should not act for the sake of acting. We firmly believe in the old maxim, "If it isn't broken, don't fix it." In each section of our program, therefore, we begin by stating the real, pressing, unavoidable problems we face. And everything we propose is intended to advance this nation towards solving these problems.

Third, our program is coherent. We believe that government fails when it loses its sense of overall purpose and direction. We believe that the public interest is neglected when government disintegrates into a grab-bag of uncoordinated, contradictory efforts to serve special interests.

Our proposals are consistent with the public philosophy which guides our unity campaign. Its principles are both simple and profound. We believe America is in peril because our tradition of self-government has been eroded. We believe we must prepare for the future; that we must be cognizant of its limits, and aggressively pursue its opportunities. We believe we must rebuild America, and that the government must act as a catalyst to encourage every American to participate in the task of rebuilding. We believe that the rebuilding of America will not have succeeded unless we have persevered in our efforts to establish justice for all Americans.

Fourth, our program is realistic. We know that our resources are limited and that they must be applied to our most basic and pressing needs. We have not promised more than our federal budget and our national economy can bear. And we have not avoided the hard choices. As we constructed this program, we thought in terms of what our responsibilities would be if we were governing this nation. It is a strategy of governance, not a game plan for winning the election.

Fifth, our program is a personal <u>commitment</u>. Harry Truman
was right when he said that a platform ought to be a contract
with the American people. But too often party platforms are
ignored by the candidates, after the election and even during
the campaign. This year, for example, the Democratic National
Convention repudiated much of the economic program of its own
party's nominee, and he, in turn, rejected their decisions.
Alternatively, the Republican Vice Presidential candidate ran
virtually his whole primary campaign <u>against</u> proposals appearing in the platform upon which he is now running. There is no
ambiguity about our commitment to our platform. It's <u>ours</u>, we
mean every word of it, and we'll stand by it, during and after
the national campaign.

Although our program is a personal commitment, it is not
the work of our hands alone. We have consulted with business
executives and assembly-line workers and farmers and with citizens concerned about our nation's future. We have analyzed
and debated every proposal, and we have drafted and redrafted
them until we were fully satisfied. We are proud of this program and we will fight hard for it.

We urge you to read and consider the program, and to compare it with those of the traditional parties. At this time
of national testing, we must move beyond the politics of empty
tactics and superficial images. We must face and debate the
real issues. You may disagree with what we say, but we want
you to know what we believe and what we will do if elected.
You have a right to know what we stand for and what we will

try to get enacted into legislation. The program will also
help you identify the main issues we must debate and the
problems we must solve. Our country needs the energy, the
involvement, the concern of each one of you.

                    Sincerely,

                    John B. Anderson

                    Patrick J. Lucey

As the nineteen eighties begin, where does America stand?

The United States finds itself knee-deep in paradox. Its economy is the most powerful productive system on earth. Its natural resources are still relatively abundant. Its citizens are the most educated and capable work force in history. Its open and mobile society is a magnet for oppressed people throughout the world. Its constitution is a proven design for the governance of a pluralistic community. Yet we are stumbling -- uncertain of our purpose, unsure of our strengths, preoccupied with our differences.

Our weaknesses, some real, some imagined, have begun to sap our confidence in ourselves and our capacities. A lack of foresight and an excess of evasion have compounded problems we should long since have addressed. Things have gotten out of control.

Over a period of years our economy has not kept pace with the rising demands upon it or with mounting competition from abroad.

Our dependence on foreign oil has become a crippling vulnerability, shifting hundreds of billions of dollars abroad, stimulating inflation at home, and hamstringing our foreign policy.

Our national security has eroded in the face of a relentless military buildup by the Soviet Union and the emergence of threats to American interests less susceptible to traditional military responses.

Our standing in the world has declined, among allies whose cooperation we need for an effective international policy, as well as among other nations whose good will and trade we value and whose development we wish to assist.

Our society has suffered shocks to its public and private institutions,

-2-

to its quality of life, and to that sense of community which can flow only from the pursuit of common purposes.

Our federal system is buffeted by conflicting claims and swelling responsibilities of national, state and local authorities, and relations between the legislative and executive branches career periodically toward calamity.

If America is to cope with these challenges, we must marshal our human and material resources far better than we have in recent years. In 1980 the over-riding issues are how we can do so and who is best prepared to lead the effort. No President can solve all the nation's problems, but the nation cannot manage them successfully without effective presidential leadership. Throughout the land there are grave doubts that either President Carter or Governor Reagan can devise a suitable program and provide the leadership to implement it.

Our National Unity Campaign speaks both to Mr. Carter and to Mr. Reagan.

To Mr. Carter, it says that a President must not only declare worthy goals; he must recognize the conflicts among competing goals and set a consistent course to prevent contradictions from rendering us impotent. The sad verdict is that Mr. Carter has failed:

-- failed to rally the nation, the Congress, and our allies to a common standard;

-- failed to fulfill his campaign commitments of 1976;

-- failed to provide coherent and credible leadership.

His own book of promises now stands as an indictment of his tenure. On

-3-

the record no fair observer can conclude that Mr. Carter deserves another term -- or that the nation should have to endure one.

To Mr. Reagan, our campaign says that America will not trade inept management of complexity for doctrinaire assertions of simplicity. However frustrated Americans may be, they are too sensible to believe that relief from present difficulties can come without sacrifice.   They recognize the implausibility of Mr. Reagan's claim that we can

    -- cut taxes massively,

    -- and increase defense spending enormously,

    -- and balance the budget quickly,

    -- and cure inflation permanently.

They question whether the necessity to strengthen our defenses justifies abandoning diplomatic efforts to reduce the threats to our security. On the record, no one can be confident that Mr. Reagan offers the balanced judgement and vision which America has a right to expect of its president.

Our National Unity Campaign responds to these concerns. We espouse a patriotism that is larger than partisanship. We seek to energize the political process by rejecting the Hobson's choice presented by the two major parties in 1980. We plan to tap the best ideas and talents of both parties, and to advance initiatives of our own to deal with the novel problems America faces in the late twentieth century.

Above all, we hope to define the national interest in ways that enlist broad support among Americans. As a nation, we need to rise above the chronic political combat among special interests whose claims, though often worthy, must be subordinated to the common good. To strike such

-4-

balances is the prime   responsibility of the Presidency. To suggest the
priorities that should govern is the central objective of our campaign.

The Anderson-Lucey campaign is based on a public philosophy that
neither repeats nor repeals the past, but builds upon it. Its principles
are clear and simple. America is in peril because her foundations have
been neglected in the past generation. We must plan for the future, we
must save for the future, and we must invest in it. We must rebuild
America. For the most part, government cannot do this directly. Rather,
it must act boldly to create a climate and a framework of incentives that
encourage individuals and businesses to get to work at the task of rebuilding.

Each of us must share these burdens, lest they become unbearable for
all. And we must apportion the sacrifices necessary for national recovery
with fair regard for the ability of individuals and groups to bear them.
The rebuilding of America cannot succeed unless we are united; but we cannot remain united unless we persevere in establishing justice for all
Americans.

More than ever before in peacetime, America must identify the essential tasks before it and focus its energies on them. What are these tasks?
We perceive three of them, around which many important objectives revolve:

(1) To restore economic vitality

(2) To meet human needs and secure social justice

(3) To maintain national security and international cooperation.

-5-

I. ECONOMIC VITALITY

To restore the vitality of the American economy will be neither simple
nor easy; we deceive ourselves to think otherwise.

In launching the effort, the last thing America needs is a political
campaign which exaggerates the differences among us. Republican and Democratic
rhetoric leads in that direction. We should reject it and build upon the
common ground that unites our citizens.

We perceive a latent consensus among the American people.

Americans agree that inflation must be curbed or the United States
will be permanently weakened. In recent years, even when the overall inflation rate (as measured by the Consumer Price Index) has declined, the underlying inflation built into the costs of goods and services has remained high.
For example, when the CPI rate fell below 6% in 1975-76, the underlying rate
remained at nearly 8%. This almost guarantees that each recovery will spawn
a new surge in prices, as producers try to meet demand while recovering
their increased costs of labor and capital. All Americans are fatigued by
a tail-chasing game that has gone on too long.

Americans agree that, to overcome this chronic threat to economic
stability, we must improve productivity through investment in new plant,
equipment and infrastructure. The massive investment required dictates a
high priority to increasing the rate of capital formation through reversing
the drastic drop in savings, increasing the capacity and incentives for
business to invest, and restraining the claims of the public sector.

Americans agree that the principal avenue to solving the grim problem
of unemployment is investment to create and sustain jobs, either by

-6-

launching new industries or by revitalizing old ones. Rising competition
from other countries makes this objective at once more difficult and more
urgent. The only real protection against such foreign competition lies
in strengthening our own ability to compete effectively. Yet there is a
proper demand that government use its influence to promote fair international competition and that, when necessary, transitional arrangements permit
American firms and workers to adjust to changing markets.

Americans agree that expanding jobs in the private sector is preferable
to a bloated government payroll. The virtues of free enterprise still prevail and most Americans do not wish government to collect and allocate an
ever-growing share of the nation's wealth. Yet, while restraining the
growth of government spending, there is a clear public obligation to cushion
the burdens a turbulent economy imposes on those least able to bear them --
the jobless, the elderly, the poor. In steering the nation onto a path of
noninflationary growth, government must improve its performance in helping
to train and place the unemployed.

Americans agree that the global energy crisis threatens to undermine
our best efforts to restore a sound economy. Our country's dependence on
foreign oil, though less than that of our allies, compounds inflationary
pressures and poses an obvious peril to our security. Yet other nations
have shown the way to prosperous and less inflationary economies with much
lower levels of per capita energy consumption. To achieve such growth will
require us to wring energy waste out of the economy and to bring new energy
sources into service.

-7-

In order to meet these objectives, we need three kinds of measures.

A.   First, the Anderson-Lucey Administration will take immediate action on inflation and unemployment to counteract the economic dislocation and human distress produced by the Carter economic policies of the past four years.

Inflation

Although inflation, as measured by the consumer price index, has receded from the 18 percent rate recorded in the first quarter of 1980, the underlying inflation rate remains at historically high levels. A central focus of national economic policy must be a progressive, year-by-year reduction in the inflation rate until reasonable price stability is achieved.

While fiscal and monetary restraint is essential to the achievement of price stability, we must also endeavor to reach a broader national accord on appropriate wage and price increases. We will construct a Wage-Price Incentives Program. Our administration will invite labor and management leaders to agree upon fair and realistic guidelines and to determine appropriate tax-based incentives to encourage compliance with those standards. By discouraging inflationary expectations, this wage-price incentives policy will be a key weapon in the campaign for stable economic growth.

In the absence of sharp and prolonged increases in the rate of inflation, we will oppose mandatory wage and price standards. Experience has domonstrated that such controls are difficult to administer and result in misallocation of economic resources.

Full Employment

A sound economic policy must incorporate a commitment to full employment.

-8-

We reaffirm the goals of the Humphrey-Hawkins Act, and regret the President's failure to consult with Congress before altering the timetables set forth in that Act. The establishment and attainment of national economic objectives are the joint responsibility of the President and Congress.

While America's full employment policy must focus on the creation and preservation of productive, private-sector jobs, there will be a continuing role for complementary federal programs to deal with chronic employment problems.

(1) We propose pilot projects to integrate state unemployment benefits with retraining benefits for those with long records of unemployment.

(2) To increase the effectiveness of the employment tax credit for small businesses, we will study the advisability of making the tax credit refundable.

(3) To deal with the critical problem of youth unemployment, particularly among minorities, we propose:

-- enactment of the proposed Youth Act of 1980 to provide over $2 billion a year for job-training and state and local educational programs designed to improve the employability of disadvantaged and out-of-school youth;

-- increased funding for youth career intern programs;

-- a youth opportunity wage incentive that would exempt eligible youths and employers from social security taxes during the first months of employment; and

-- a Youth Energy Projects Act that would provide up to $1 billion a year for multi-year energy and conservation projects, including

-9-

mass transit, offering career opportunities for economically

disadvantaged youth.

We will work with educators and employers to smooth the transition from

school to job.

B.   Second, the Anderson-Lucey Administration will undertake basic

structural initiatives to create conditions for long-term economic growth

with lower inflation and higher purchasing power.

(1) We will set a new balance between fiscal and monetary policy to

dampen inflation, lower interest rates, and foster a predictable environ-

ment for long-range planning by investors and government alike.

While declining tax revenues and increasing transfer payments can be

expected to unbalance the budget during times of economic difficulty, the

budget should move toward balance or surplus during expansionary periods.

Once balance in the federal budget has been achieved, the Anderson-

Lucey Administration will propose to index personal income tax brackets to

prevent inflation from pushing taxpayers into higher tax brackets. As

further economies are made in federal spending, we will propose tax cuts

that go beyond the tax relief afforded by indexing.

We will oppose any new Constitutional limitation on the spending

and taxing powers of Congress. Reforms limiting government spending to

an appropriate percentage of GNP should be enacted as amendments to the

Congressional Budget Act.

In the interest of more effective fiscal management, we will propose

administrative procedures, subject to legislative veto, to meet changing

economic conditions by (a) adjusting tax rates upward or downward by 10%

-10-

or less and (b) accelerating or slowing certain federal expenditures.
Timely and orderly action on these fronts can diminish the wasteful scramble
of federal agencies to spend remaining funds in the closing days of each
fiscal year. Such flexibility can also relieve the strain on monetary policy
by permitting prompt fiscal intervention to counter adverse trends.

(2) We will use the tax code to encourage greater personal savings
and capital formation.

We must make it both possible and desirable for the average American
to save again. Lowering the inflation rate will be a powerful stimulus to
savings. Phasing out interest rate restrictions on savings accounts,
recently approved by Congress, will also be an important stimulant. We should
remove other disincentives to savings and investment from the tax code. We
propose:

-- expanding gradually the interest and dividend income exclusion to $750
    individuals, $1500 for married couples filing jointly;

-- liberalizing eligibility requirements and income limitations for
    Individual Retirement Accounts, particularly for homemakers; and

-- instituting a further review of capital gains taxes.

The current state of the economy and of our most basic industries, including automobiles and steel, requires adoption of added capital cost
recovery measures to ensure that troubled companies and industries will not
suffer a competitive tax disadvantage in undertaking capital expansion and
improvements.

To enable less profitable companies to modernize their plants and
equipment, we will propose to make the investment tax credit refundable.

To ensure adequate congressional review of this measure, we propose a three-
year limit on the refundability provision, subject to extension.

(3) We will use tax incentives and direct federal assistance to stimulate research and development and to spur productivity.

To revive our flagging R & D effort, we propose a number of initiatives
and improvements. An Anderson-Lucey Administration will seek to:

-- reverse the decline in the real level of federal funding for
   research and development;

-- provide a 10 percent investment tax credit for qualifying research
   and development expenditures;

-- establish a federal program to re-equip the laboratories of
   universities, non-profit research centers, and government facilities;

-- redefine the working relationship between government and universities so as to avoid substituting paperwork for creativity;

-- provide fixed objectives and more predictable project funding
   for scientists and engineers on the cutting edge of technology;

-- establish regional technology centers under the aegis of the
   National Science Foundation and NASA to lower the costs of selling
   and licensing new technologies to private business;

-- establish a more uniform patent policy for all federal agencies;

-- require federal agencies to determine expeditiously whether they
   will retain patents on inventions developed by private contractors
   with federal monies;

-12-

--   reorganize and increase the funding of the Patent and Trademark
Office to improve its operations;

--   explore the possibility of a separate patent court to reduce the
time needed to establish a valid patent.

(4) We will prune regulations that waste capital and do not serve valid
regulatory objectives.

We will seek legislation that would:

--   set an eight-year timetable for thorough congressional review of
regulatory agencies;

--   require the President to submit in the first session of each new
Congress a regulatory reform plan for each of the regulatory
agencies scheduled for review;

--   require Congress to act on the regulatory reform plan by August 1st
of the second session;

--   assure congressional action by denying the affected agency power
to promulgate new rules and regulations until Congress has acted.

An Anderson-Lucey Administration will be firmly committed to the growth
and maintenance of competition in our modern economy. We support recent
efforts towards deregulation of the transportation industry, and we will
support thorough review of antitrust and other federal laws affecting competition.

(5) We will use a tough, conservation-oriented energy program to curtail the rapid outflow of American capital to pay for imported oil.

We will expand production of energy and induce conservation of energy
through policies that are equitable, economical, environmentally and

-13-

technologically sound. We would couple decontrol of oil and gas prices
with an excise tax of 50 cents per gallon on gasoline, the full revenues of
that tax being returned to individuals through reductions in payroll taxes
and increased Social Security benefits. Gasoline prices will still remain
well below those of other industrial nations. We will employ tax credits
and other incentives to promote substitution of non-petroleum energy for oil,
adoption of energy-efficient systems in industry and elsewhere, improvements
in transportation and energy production technologies, and development of
less wasteful structures for home and commerce.

We will explore a wide range of energy supply options -- from mini-
hydropower to renewable resources to fusion -- to determine which are
appropriate medium-term investments and which should be deferred or abandoned. We will emphasize environmental and safety controls as we explore
wider use of coal through such techniques as liquefaction, gasification and
fluidized bed combustion. We will propose financial concessions to construct rail, port and slurry pipeline facilities for expanded domestic and
foreign trade in coal.

In considering policy for nuclear power, we will act on the recommendations of the Rogovin and Kemeny Commissions to make certain that installation of any future plants is preceded by demonstration of satisfactory standards
and action on the nuclear waste question. We will assess nuclear power in light
of its dependence on public subsidy and of the possibility that slower
growth in demand may enable us to phase in other energy supplies in preference to nuclear systems.

We will accelerate the use of solar energy, particularly by using

-14-

federal procurement to encourage uniform performance standards and economies of scale. We will devise suitable loan and credit mechanisms to stimulate residential and other applications. We will actively investigate the potential for renewable energy sources.

C.   Third, the Anderson-Lucey Administration will adopt a new industrial policy, specifically targeted to encourage the re-industrialization of the U.S. economy.

(1) We propose an industrial policy sensitive to the special needs of our basic industries:

    --   an Industrial Development Administration authorized to speed development of new technologies and cost-saving techniques by providing loan guarantees to industry;

    --   an Industrial Development Council, chaired by the President, will engage government, labor and management in a continuing review of government policies affecting industrial matters, in fostering closer relations between management and labor, and in encouraging American industry to adapt to the rapid changes in international economics, technology, and consumer preferences;

    --   liberalized depreciation allowances, refundable investment tax credit, and 10 percent R & D tax credits for the auto and steel industries.

(2) We propose policies designed to restore small business to its traditional role as a generator of new ideas and new jobs:

    --   allow small businesses to elect to write-off the first $50,000 in investments in equipment and machinery each year;

-15-

-- provide simplified and liberalized depreciation allowances for
   capital equipment and structures;

-- provide an investment tax credit for qualifying research and
   development expenditures;

-- defer capital gains tax on the sale of a small business if the
   proceeds are reinvested in another qualified small business within six months; and

-- reduce corporate tax rates by two percentage points across-the-
   board by 1986.

Small businesses are often less suited or equipped to deal with federal
regulatory requirements. Legislation should require federal agencies to
consider the feasibility of less burdensome regulations for small businesses,
providing they satisfy important safety and health standards.

(3) We propose policies designed to ensure that our transportation
system can meet the demands of a changing economy. We must repair our
nation's railbeds, maintain our highways, upgrade our port facilities, and
update our air traffic control systems.

(4) We propose to revitalize our space program, an important source
of technological innovation and economic progress.

(5) We propose measures to remove barriers to exports and to work
aggressively to increase them:

-- expanded, competitive U.S. Export-Import Bank financing of a
   broader range of exports;

-- reduced taxation of American nationals living abroad and
   engaging in export activities;

-16-

-- duty-free entry of machinery and materials for use in export
manufacture in foreign trade zones;

-- anti-trust immunity for certified export activities by business
associations;

-- measures to encourage formation of export trading companies to
assist small and medium-sized firms;

-- an Agricultural Export Credit Revolving Fund;

-- renewed efforts to obtain international agreement on foreign
business practices.

(6) We will strengthen our trade and our currency through increased
international economic cooperation. To this end, we pledge:

-- continued cooperation with our allies to achieve energy conservation and production targets set forth in the recent Venice
Summit Agreement;

-- closer cooperation among our trading partners to reduce frictions
which, left unattended, could lead to arbitrary trade restrictions;

-- more effective coordination of economic and financial policy
among the leading industrialized nations through the International Monetary Fund (IMF) and the Organization for Economic
Cooperation and Development (OECD);

-- continued efforts to enhance the effectiveness of IMF exchange
rate surveillance;

-- expanded financial and technical assistance to non-OPEC developing
countries in their efforts to explore and market new energy sources; a

-17-

--   support for a stable monetary order through refinement and
      extension of the Special Drawing Rights.
We will not pursue the fantasy of a return to the gold standard, as contem-
plated by the Reagan platform.

(7) Finally, we must preserve and extend the gains working men and
women have achieved in nearly a century of organization and struggle.

--   We support a fair and equitable minimum wage that bears a consis-
      tent relation to the average manufacturing wage.

--   We support the full and effective enforcement of the Occupational
      Safety and Health Act of 1970, and we oppose legislation now
      before the Congress that would drastically weaken OSHA.

--   We support worker participation in determining the structure of
      the workplace.

--   We support extension of job-retraining and relocation assistance
      for displaced workers, Economic Development Administration assis-
      tance to distressed communities, and adoption of work-sharing
      programs on a pilot-project basis.

--   We oppose repeal of the Davis-Bacon Act of 1931.

--   We support selective improvements in the National Labor Relations
      Act to guard further against unfair labor practices.

-18-

II. HUMAN NEEDS AND SOCIAL JUSTICE

A dynamic and growing economy is the necessary condition of social progress, of domestic harmony, and of national security. And only such an economy can allow all its citizens the basic freedom to choose and to pursue their own occupations. But economic health is not an end in itself. The worth of every society is determined by what its members do -- as individuals and as citizens -- with the wealth they create.

We believe that a modern society must accept its responsibility to provide for basic human needs by furnishing those public goods citizens cannot attain through individual effort

--   to care for its cities, its transportation, and its environment;

--   to assist those who cannot support themselves;

--   to create a climate within which human beings can strive to fulfill their own needs.

To fulfill this responsibility, we will shape
an adaptable government, responsive to its
citizens and effective in its functions. The potential for institutional deadlock has grown acute and with it a dispiriting sense that little can be done to achieve our public goals. This we must overcome.

A.   We will launch an evolutionary effort to energize our political institutions and to adapt them to contemporary responsibilities. We will seek to establish a new and healthier equilibrium in the federal system. To examine the current condition of federal-state relations, we will assemble the constitutional partners in a Convocation on Federalism. This will not be a convention to act on constitutional amendments, as

-19-

proposed by some state governments, but the Convocation will present recommendations to the President and Congress for statutory or constitutional
change through normal legislative procedures.

Among issues to be addressed will be ways to reverse the incessant
trend toward centralization of government, to establish balance between
public sector and private sector claims on national wealth, and to improve
the conduct of programs which must be handled on an intergovernmental basis.
In short, without running the risks associated with a plenary convention,
the Convocation will permit a thorough assessment of the federal system and
of the Constitution, as it completes its second century. Our goal will be
an allocation of responsibility among federal, state and local government
that is clear and efficient.

Respecting the dual needs of executive initiative and legislative
prerogative, the National Unity Administration will work closely with legislative leaders. To avoid the recurrent paralysis of legislative-executive
relations, we will be prepared to consider far-reaching innovations, compat-
ible with the separation of powers, to coordinate decision-making between
the branches more effectively. We will discuss with the majority and
minority leaders of both Houses whether they wish to take part in specified
deliberations of the Cabinet and National Security Council, particularly
those relating to international crises. Without abridging the President's
right to privileged counsel, we will facilitate access of designated
legislators to studies and analyses prepared for executive policy-making.

-20-

B.   Together with state and local authorities, we will mount a systematic campaign to rebuild America's cities.

(1) Urban foundations.

The deterioration of our massive investment in urban capital stock -- housing, roads, bridges, public transportation, sewers, water systems -- is the most serious problem now confronting the cities. Squeezed between declining tax bases and escalating costs, many cities have been forced to defer essential maintenance to meet immediate operating needs.

To address this problem, an Anderson-Lucey Administration will propose an Urban Reinvestment Trust Fund (URTF). Funded through dedicated revenues from the federal alcohol and tobacco excise taxes and phased in over three years, it will disburse approximately $3.9 billion annually. It will be used for upgrading, repair and replacement of capital plant and equipment.

Because the revenues from the federal excise taxes on alcohol and tobacco have been rising more slowly than the rate of inflation, at the end of the phase-in period we will consider raising current excise tax rates to meet the urgent national needs to which our Trust Fund is addressed.

-21-

(2) Housing.

We face a looming crisis in housing. Construction has dropped below the level at which new families are being formed and economic and regulatory constraints have virtually shut down the multifamily housing industry. We propose:

--   to reduce interest rates by stabilizing the economy

--   to dampen the erratic housing cycle through a countercyclical mortgage subsidy program

--   to work for simplification and standardization of federal, state, and local building regulations

--   to stimulate private construction of multifamily housing, through increased interest rate subsidies and tax incentives, including accelerated depreciation

--   to accelerate renovation of existing housing stock

--   to encourage conversion of abandoned buildings from other uses to housing

--   to encourage low-income families to buy their own dwellings through federal mortgage guarantees

--   to increase the supply of mortgage funds by policies to expand personal savings.

-22-

(3) Neighborhoods.

A healthy city requires vigorous and thriving neighborhoods, secure
in their differences, linked by common interests and purposes. For too long,
federal policy has damaged neighborhood interests while neglecting programs
that directly benefit neighborhoods.

We will review and, where appropriate, implement the recommendations
of the largely ignored report of the National Commission on Neighborhoods.
We will support neighborhood associations through tax credits, federal matching money, and increased funding for federal programs that work directly with
local groups. We will use the Small Business Administration and the Urban
Development Action Grants to promote economic development in neighborhoods.
We will make federal policy more responsive to the plight of displaced urban
dwellers.

(4) Enterprise zones.

Within our distressed older cities, there are zones of devastation,
blighted by crime, arson, and population flight. The traditional tools of
federal policy do not work, and cannot be expected to work, in these areas.

We favor legislation that would create "enterprise zones" in these
areas, by lowering corporate, capital gains, payroll, and property taxes
and by furnishing new tax incentives to small businesses.

C.   We will work to transform America's surface transportation network.

Through years of neglect, profligate energy consumption,
and   lack of federal leadership, the United States has slid into a dependence
on imported oil that threatens our economic viability and our national
security. Transportation consumes half the petroleum used in this country.

-23-

It is in this sector that we must effect the greatest economies.

To promote a balanced, cost-effective, energy-efficient transportation system:

--   We should establish a new Community Transportation Trust Fund
        to finance capital and maintenance costs of metropolitan and
        local transit systems, while general revenues would finance
        operating costs. Funded with dedicated revenues from the federal
        alcohol and tobacco excise taxes, it would disburse $15 billion
        over the next five years, $2.5. billion in the first year.

--   After suitable consultation with states and communities, the
        federal government should establish a twenty-year community trans-
        portation plan that lays out goals and funding priorities.

--   We should use tax incentives and selective subsidies to encourage
        the participation of the private sector in public transportation
        and to encourage the development of transportation alternatives
        for rural Americans.

We will implement a national railroad policy to catalyse the development of versatile, competitive and attractive freight and passenger services.
This policy will give due weight to related policies on energy, agriculture
and industry. While affording reasonable protection to shippers captive to
rail transportation, we will move to end ananchronistic regulations and place
increased reliance on market forces to determine railroad pricing and operating practices. Our administration will participate actively in efforts to
upgrade the nation's dilapidated roadbeds and antiquated transfer facilities.
We will consider equitable user charges for transportation modes benefiting

-24-

from public subsidies in order to assure a less distorted and more competitive market for freight services.

D.   We will construct an environmental policy that seasons idealism with
realism and mobilizes Americans to combine restrained development with constant vigilance for the preservation of our natural assets -- land, air and
water. The fragility of our environment must evoke frugality in our steward-
ship of America.

We embrace the spirit of idealism and farsightedness that has enabled
the environmental movement to flourish over several decades. We will guard
and consolidate the achievements in every field of environmental protection
and preservation. While mindful of the need to assess the economic impact
of proposed environmental safeguards, we reaffirm our long-standing
commitment to protecting our resources against pollution and depletion.

In addition to aggressive implementation of existing programs to protect air and water resources, we will launch new efforts to deal with safe
disposal of toxic substances, with problems of acid rain and air-borne carbon dioxide, and with the detection and control of likely cancer-causing
substances. We will undertake a broad range of policies to protect our
wildlife, our public lands, our coastal zones and international environments like the ocean. We will ensure that federal water projects respect
environmental concerns.

The complex and delicate relationship between energy and environmental
policy necessitates constant surveillance. Conservation is the essential
link between them. While all energy options require environmental safeguards,
the distinctive aspects of nuclear power give urgency to the establishment

-25-

of a Nuclear Regulatory Authority under a single administrator to assure
the operational and environmental safety of reactors, fuel handling and
waste disposal.

E. We will strive to improve the health of Americans by closing the gaps
in our health care system and by promoting more effective delivery of services
without inducing exorbitant inflation in their cost. These are familiar
goals and the nation's failures to achieve them are equally well-known. We
must prevent public policy from impeding a more competitive and cost-conscious market for health services. We would phase out retroactive cost-plus
reimbursement under federal programs and replace it with prospective rate
or fixed-premium financing, in order to give incentives to contain costs.
Such a change should reduce the expensive cost-accounting and reporting
practices now borne by hospitals, nursing homes and other agencies. We
will take steps to allow Health Maintenance Organizations and other prepaid
insurance options to compete for the federal health care dollar. We will
analyze cost-sharing procedures to deter over-utilization and wasteful
treatment under Medicare and Medicaid. To spur competition in the private
sector we will recommend making health insurance payments by employers tax
                                (including catastrophic coverage)
deductible only if they offer multiple options/which permit employees to
choose the most cost-efficient plan for their individual circumstances.

We will ground health policy in the existing private structure, gradually
augmenting present coverage to reach the twenty-two million Americans who
are now unprotected. An important mechanism to bring professional care to
areas which are inadequately served is the National Health Service Corps,

-26-

which we will enlarge.

We will act to correct the under-emphasis on preventive medicine and health research -- which now accounts for only 2% of total health care expenditures. We will give close attention to disseminating the results of research on the health implications of lifestyle, diet and environmental factors. Programs to prevent and treat problems of drug abuse, alcoholism and mental health are increasingly important in contemporary society; we will sustain them.

F.   We propose to rationalize the welfare system and to meet the changing requirements of families and individuals in need. We will improve administration of the principal welfare programs -- Aid for Dependent Children (AFDC), Supplemental Security Income   (SSI), Medicaid and Food Stamps -- and will consider the possibility of uniform application procedures for them. We support a national minimum benefit standard and uniform eligibility requirements for AFDC. To avoid further weakening of families in dire need, we advocate mandatory AFDC coverage of two-parent families in the 24 states now lacking it. There should be standard procedures for periodic determination of income and eligibility, as well as expansion of the National Recipient System (NRS) to eliminate erroneous payments.

Even with administrative improvements, the income transfers made by these programs are near their practical limits. We must place greater stress on earned income for the disadvantaged by reducing the marginal tax on entry of poor workers into the labor force. We propose a standardized benefit reduction formula to assure higher real income for welfare recipients who obtain work.

-27-

We would expand the Earned Income Tax Credit to
increase incentives for the working poor and to increase their ability to
accumulate savings. We favor expansion of day care facilities for the
children of these families.

The welfare of our people depends on far more than the welfare system.
It also requires sturdy families able to cope with the stress of modern life.
We would bolster the family's economic base by ending the so-called "marriage
tax" on two-earner families and inheritance or gift taxes on transfers
between spouses. We support authority for homemakers to establish Individual
Retirement Accounts and programs to assist displaced homemakers. We favor
added tax relief for families providing home care for relatives who would
otherwise be institutionalized.

With a growing population of older Americans -- of whom nine million
live in poverty -- we must also focus policy on their needs. While working
to reduce inflation as the key to durable economic relief for all citizens,
we will retain adequate indexation for Social Security benefits and resist
their taxation. We will also encourage the ablebodied elderly to enjoy the
financial and emotional benefits of work by phasing out limits on earnings
for Social Security recipients and strengthening the Age Discrimination in
Employment Act.

A major objective will be to curtail unnecessary institutionalization
by supporting arrangements which enable the elderly to remain in the community.
Among other measures, we recommend

   --   broader   health care coverage to aid persons or families who
          incur huge medical expenses while caring for the elderly at home

-28-

or outside hospitals

--   adult day care centers to aid those for whom overnight and weekend
     care is available at home

--   "respite services" to assure families that elderly members will
        be cared for competently during vacations and other absences.

Making it possible for the elderly to remain in the home and neighborhood
can produce substantial savings to provide increased funding for those truly
in need of long-term institutional care.

Another group of Americans, young and old, deserves more help from
government. They are the 30 million veterans of our armed forces. The shortcomings of the Veterans Administration demand correction. The physical and
psychological traumas inflicted by the war in Southeast Asia require the
succour of a caring nation. Our programs will focus on the disproportionate
unemployment and readjustment problems suffered by Vietnam veterans. We
would extend educational benefits for these veterans, and permit such entitle-
ments to be used as reimbursements to employers for wages and other training
expenses related to jobs for eligible veterans. We will step up personal
counselling services for Vietnam veterans and will conduct a major outreach
program to contact and assist victims of Agent Orange or other contaminants
used in the war.

G.   We will dedicate ample resources to the manifold missions of education.
To break down communications barriers among federal, state and local educational officials, and to provide supplemental aid to hard pressed local school

-29-

districts, we will provide substantial funding to the Department of Education -- a worthwhile innovation which will require active and sensitive direction. The virtues of diversity in education warrant federal deference for wide latitude in local school policies, and we will press the Department to cut back the thicket of regulations, subject only to monitoring federally mandated programs and accountability for federal funding. We will frame executive orders to govern future regulations.

We will defer to self-regulation by states or school districts except when it proves demonstrably unsuccessful or incompatible with overriding federal interests. At the same time we will uphold by all means at the government's disposal the right of every child to an equal educational opportunity.

A continuing goal will be to advance the education of handicapped children, including opportunities to learn vocations conducive to productive and self-directed lives. We will place emphasis on linking special education programs for the handicapped to affirmative action efforts by private employers. The Department of Education will intensify its activities in behalf of disabled children in poorer districts, and work to overcome the present shortage of special education teachers generally.

Taking account of the changing demography of education at all levels, we will encourage diversification of schools and colleges into adult and continuing education programs for people of all ages who are eager to enlarge their knowledge and skills. We will strive to bring coherence and adequate resources to the varied programs of federal financial aid to students in higher education.

"Learn awhile to serve" reads an English school motto. That is but

-30-

one worthy goal of learning. Knowledge and skill are economic tools but
they are also instruments for personal fulfillment. We will strive to make
them accessible to all with the capacity and determination to learn.

H.   We will marshal increased support for the arts and humanities.

A difficult mission for government lies in the support of the arts
and humanities -- creative endeavors whose justification rests on artistic
and scholarly grounds rather than on the pragmatic reasons associated with
science and technology. Fostering an environment in which art and the
humanities can flourish with significant public funding but without unwarranted public control is a challenge we have begun to meet. We will support
the principal federal institutions for these purposes, the National Endowments for the Arts and the Humanities, and will try to protect these valuable
programs against the ravages of inflation and budget cuts. We favor the
creation of a National Arts Bank to purchase and lease for exhibition works
of American art. We will encourage wider use of tax credits available to
individuals and corporations contributing to the arts. We will investigate

additional improvements in copyright and patent laws to guarantee fair compensation to artists. We will also lend our endorsement to the proposed
Artists Tax Equity Act to facilitate donations of works of art to public
institutions and to eliminate unfair taxation of artists and their heirs.
These material measures can help the artistic spirit thrive in communities
throughout America.

I.   We will erect a government devoted to ending discrimination and
advancing justice for every person in our society.

An important goal on the social agenda will be to bring women into
full partnership in all our institutions. We are committed to ratification
of the Equal Rights Amendment. We oppose government intrusion in the most
intimate of family decisions -- the right to bear or not to bear children --
and will fight against any constitutional amendment prohibiting abortion.
We support public funding of family planning services and other efforts to
enable women to find acceptable alternatives to abortion. Women will hold
responsible positions in every department of our administration.

We will be diligent in enforcement of affirmative action programs
and other measures to assure equal protection of the laws for minorities
and other victims of discrimination. Vigorous administration and stronger
enforcement provisions for federal Fair Housing legislation will be crucial
as the nation strives to surmount its serious housing shortage. The
ability to read is indispensable to meaningful opportunity in America; we
will direct the Department of Education to attack the massive problem
of functional illiteracy, from which an estimated 20 million adults suffer.
We will strengthen our commitment to bilingual education and provide

-32-

appropriate assistance to local authorities for development of responsive and effective bilingual education programs. We advocate reaffirmation of the nation's democratic principles by fair and equal representation in Congress for the citizens of the District of Columbia.

Fundamental questions of justice hinge on the reform of the U.S. Criminal Code. Our first objective will be to prevent crime and to protect its victims. We also favor a cautious and deliberate approach to the sensitive issues of civil liberty involved in such reform. Intricate issues arise, for example, in attempting to frame systematic principles for sentencing convicted offenders and for plea bargaining. Out of respect both for the constitutional ban on double jeopardy and for the need to avoid coercion in plea bargaining, we oppose giving prosecutors the right to appeal a sentence. Reform should correct disparities in sentencing and promote guidelines for the use of fines, community service orders and restitution in preference to incarceration in appropriate cases.

Law enforcement is principally a state and local function, but we will act firmly to fulfill federal responsibilities, including protection of individuals against policy brutality. We will reinforce the capacity of the Community Relations Service to deal with local tensions. Prison reform looms large among the challenges of the coming decade and we will take steps to relieve overcrowding and abuses in the prisons, as well as to increase the range of opportunities for inmate work release programs, and other rehabilitative efforts.

Concern over the treatment and status of immigrants joins our domestic and international policy. We will seek humane solutions to the dilemmas

-33-

arising in this field, by extending civil rights protection to aliens and by negotiating actively with Mexico and other nations to devise satisfactory international arrangements regarding illegal aliens.

In appointments to executive and judicial offices, we will steadfastly oppose the application of ideological "litmus tests" and adhere strictly to standards of qualification, competence, and equal opportunity for women and minorities. To diminish the recurrent conflicts of loyalty to which recent Attorneys General have been subject, we will underscore the Attorney General's obligations to the courts by consulting with the Judicial Confer- ence of the United States prior to submitting any nomination for that office.

-34-

III. NATION SECURITY AND INTERNATIONAL COOPERATION

On issues of foreign policy and national security, as on the economy, we must find areas of consensus on which the United States can build sound policy.

The first priority for American foreign policy must be to rebuild our domestic strength -- the bedrock of our international posture.

The next priority for American foreign policy is to restore and nurture our historic alliances.

Most Americans agree that the continuing growth of both Soviet strategic and conventional forces requires the United States to strengthen its defenses.

We agree that it is essential to recruit and retain capable men and women to serve in our armed forces -- and that to do so without resorting to conscription will demand substantially greater pay and benefits for volunteers.

We agree that beyond the Soviet-American rivalry lie new threats to our vital interests -- threats arising from technological change and the possible spread of nuclear weapons, from the potentially explosive competition for resources in an age of global interdpendence, from unchecked racism and over-zealous nationalism, from famine and widespread disease.

And we agree that mutual, verifiable and realistic arms limitations can contribute to our security.

Meeting these challenges   successfully will tax America's wisdom even more than its material wealth. What do we propose?

Defense and National Security:

A.   In strategic forces, we will maintain a stable balance by preserving
essential equivalence with the Soviet Union. To meet an evolving threat to
our deterrent we will modernize and diversify our strategic arsenal.

Specifically, we will take the following steps:

--   Our military command, control and communications systems should
be made as survivable as our strategic weapons systems.

--   Our warning systems must be improved, as well as our ability to
analyze data and make decisions under war-time conditions.

--   We will improve the basing systems for our aircraft and fleet
ballistic missiles.

--   We will move ahead with the current Trident submarine program.

--   We should continue research into other missile-carrying submarines, as additional means for enhancing our deterrent capabilities in the face of changing Soviet anti-submarine warfare
capabilities.

--   We will continue modernization of the B-52 with air-launched
cruise missiles, short-range attack missiles, and with improved
navigational and other electronic systems.

--   We will continue research on new bomber forces, including those
capable of launching cruise missiles.

The growing concern over the threat to fixed, land-based missiles
poses an urgent problem to both the United States and the Soviet Union.
Economically, environmentally, and strategically, the specific cure proposed
by the Carter administration -- the MX system -- is unsound.

-36-

The fundamental question posed by the growing vulnerability of our land-based missiles is what comprises the most desirable mix of forces as the American arsenal is modernized in the 1980's. Should we preserve the three main components of our strategic forces, land-based missiles, bombers, and submarines? Or, as we move into the future, should we place greater reliance on bomber and submarine forces?

A possible solution would be negotiations with the Soviet Union that verifiably reduced the capacity of each party to threaten the other's land-based missiles. Unfortunately, the Soviets have so far rejected such nego-tiations. We must make clear to them that their intransigence is forcing us to consider options which may severely impair strategic stability.

The Anderson-Lucey Administration will give this matter the fresh and sober consideration it deserves through a comprehensive assessment of strategic doctrines, capabilities, and choices, free from either ideology or illusion.

American ingenuity can devise a more flexible and more cost-effective solution to the threat posed to our land-based missiles.

For the past five administrations, Democrat and Republican, our nuclear strategy has been based on the principle of deterrence. Our principal objective is not to wage nuclear war, but to prevent it.

The Anderson-Lucey Administration will unambiguously reaffirm this traditional strategy. We hold fast to the conviction that control of nuclear war is improbable, and that victory in nuclear war is meaningless. For, as Douglas MacArthur said, "If you lose, you are annihilated. If you win, you stand only to lose."

B.   The National Unity Administration will <u>emphasize versatile and usable</u>
<u>forces to counter any conventional attack on our vital interests</u>. Our first
priority here will be to redress the grave personnel problems of the armed
forces. We oppose peacetime conscription, but to make the volunteer army
work will require additional funds for military pay and benefits. We will
support both performance and reenlistment bonuses, as well as other measures
to ensure retention of those with critical skills. We will take steps to
rectify the serious shortcomings in military housing and social services.
We will offer new educational incentives to aid recruitment.

To attract more qualified personnel, we will encourage lateral entry
in selected categories for both enlisted and officer ranks; to retain them
we will eliminate the "up or out" policy on promotions and permit skilled
individuals to remain on active duty outside the normal promotion path.
Improved retention should make possible substantial savings in training
budgets to help offset the costs of these personnel policies.

Beyond strengthening our military manpower base, we will stress improved force readiness through increased operations and maintenance funding. We will press for further improvements in the "tooth-to-tail" ratio.
To facilitate more rapid action in Europe and other critical areas we will
expand programs to pre-position equipment overseas and to increase U.S. air
and sealift capabilities.

In guiding weapons design and procurement, our policy will be to demand a better balance between advancing technology and producing in quantity;
we need more weapons with adequate capability and high reliability, rather
than fewer weapons with excess capability and low reliability. To guarantee
our ability to operate on a global scale, we will allocate more resources
to naval forces, including those needed for operations in the Persian Gulf

-38-

and Indian Ocean.

C.   We will <u>invigorate the international quest for arms control</u>. Our policy
will be based on the fundamental principles:

--   Arms control agreements must enhance our basic security and must
      not compromise our ability to protect our national interests.

--   Agreements must preserve and reinforce the stability of the stra-
      tegic balance.

--   Arms control agreements, particularly with the Soviet Union, are
      not agreements between friends. We cannot rely on the good
      intentions or paper promises of our adversaries. Arms control
      must be based on adequate, effective verification.

The Anderson-Lucey Administration will take steps to complete the
SALT II process, and thereby lay the groundwork for SALT III.

The Western Alliance should proceed with its plans to modernize its
theater nuclear arsenal; at the same time, we should keep open the possibility
of negotiations with the Soviet Union to limit theater nuclear forces.

Our administration will support efforts to negotiate a ban on the
development, testing, and deployment of anti-satellite warfare systems.
Until, however, the Soviet Union shows a willingness to enter serious
negotiations in this area, we should continue research on an anti-satellite
capability.

We favor conclusion of a short-term comprehensive Nuclear Test Ban
Treaty between the United States, the Soviet Union, and the United Kingdom,
with frequent review pending inclusion of all nuclear weapons states. This
will be a valuable element in the firm policy we will conduct to discourage

proliferation of nuclear weapons.

Our anti-proliferation policy will devote particular attention to limiting the number of facilities which use or produce plutonium or weapons-grade uranium.

The United States must maintain a basic   program of nuclear energy research and development if we are to retain our command of the broad range of nuclear activities relevant to the problems of nuclear weapons proliferation.

We will use every technological and managerial tool at our disposal to increase still further the distance between the military and peaceful uses of nuclear energy. In addition, we believe that exports of nuclear technology should only be approved by the United States in instances where the proposed transfer comports with non-proliferation goals.

D.   For a more effective defense, we will rely heavily on collective security arrangements with our principal allies in NATO and Japan. Unlike the Soviet Union, the United States enjoys the support of willing allies, not reluctant satellites. To strengthen deterrence of war in Europe, we will consider ways to reinforce NATO against potential Warsaw Pact attacks, including the organization of reserve forces for combat use in the early stages of conflict. We will work to upgrade the quality, standardization and inter-operability of alliance weapons and equipment, and to provide ample war reserve stocks in Europe. We will refine joint arrangements to expand air-lift capacity by suitable alterations and command arrangements for wide-bodied aircraft in allied civil fleets.

We will also look to our allies to share the burden of defending

-40-

Western interests in such regions as the Persian Gulf, either directly
or through flexible arrangements for employment of American forces assigned
to NATO and the Far East. We believe Japan should assume a security role
appropriate to its situation and commensurate with its capacity. Given
Japan's substantial shipbuilding assets, this role could well include contributions to sealift and anti-submarine warfare capabilities. An alliance
of equal partners, proceeding with mutual concern and genuine consultation,
can make "division of labor" more than just a slogan.

Foreign Policy and International Cooperation

We are dedicated to a reinvigorated partnership with our democratic
allies. With it, Western civilization can confront the dangers and the
challenges of the world from a position of calm but unquestioned strength
and courage. Our diplomacy is a key to our security. We must be prepared
to confront challenges to our basic interests around the globe with an
active and forward diplomatic effort.

A.   We will work to reinforce and enhance our historic partnership with
our Western European allies. To many, the ills of the Alliance are beyond
cure. But we have a uniqueopportunity to extend the fundamental partnership
which has been such a source of strength for the free world for the past
thirty years. If the Alliance was important to our world position in 1949,
when America's power was at its zenith, it is even more so today as we face
even greater challenges around the world.

To bolster our Atlantic partnership in the next decade, we need a clear
sense of the basic principles which should guide our efforts.

First among these broad principles is the recognition that apart

-41-

from deterring a physical attack upon the United States itself, there is no
more important national interest than the maintenance of our Alliance with
Western Europe.

Second, we must recognize that the Alliance must be a union of equal
partners.

Third, we must be prepared to acknowledge that there will be times
when European interests are not those embraced by the United States. A mature
and balanced partnership can accommodate differences of opinion or approach.

Fourth, the United States must cease talking about consultation and
actually consult with its allies before embarking on ventures in which it
expects them to participate. Reciprocally, our allies must acknowledge a
similar responsibility.

B.   The National Unity Administration will give priority to stabilizing
the critical relationship with the Soviet Union. We will maintain and
reinforce the military balance. We will support international efforts to
end Soviet aggression in Afghanistan. We will adopt measures to deter or
counter Soviet intervention, whether direct or through proxies, in areas
vital to our interests, including specifically the Persian Gulf.

The superpower relationship is central to world peace and neither side
can allow it to degenerate further. Recent developments -- the SALT deadlock, Afghanistan, rising military competition -- have rendered the limited
working relationship between Washington and Moscow more limited than working. Particularly when tensions are high, it is incumbent on the United
States and the Soviet Union to maintain active communications. That will
be our policy.

-42-

A realistic relationship will demand that both sides act on their vested interest in mutual restraint. The Strategic Arms Limitations process is a valuable means of testing and defining mutual acceptance of that fact and we will take steps to revive that process. Specifically, we will propose to Moscow supplementary measures that could make possible the ratification of the SALT II Treaty and the start of SALT III negotiations. These proposals will respond to concerns expressed in the U.S. Senate regarding such issues as verification and future force reductions. They could take the form of joint declarations and treaty interpretations not requiring renegotiation of the existing treaty language.

We strongly support the Helsinki process. The broadening of trade, as well as the expansion of scientific, technological, and cultural exchanges, is dependent upon practices by the Soviet and East European governments which are consistent with basic human rights standards.

C.   The establishment and maintenance of peace in the Middle East will be an urgent objective.

A lasting settlement must encompass the principles affirmed in the Camp David accords.

Our administration will support the recognition of Palestinian rights as embodied in the Camp David accords, but will oppose the creation of a Palestinian state between Israel and Jordan.

The United States will not recognize or negotiate with the Palestine Liberation Organization unless that organization repudiates terrorism, explicitly recognizes Israel's right to exist in peace, and accepts UN Security Council Resolutions 242 and 338 unchanged.

-43-

The questions of Israeli settlements on the West Bank and the final
status of East Jerusalem must be decided by negotiations. The United
States will support free and unimpeded access to Jerusalem's holy places by
people of all faiths. Jerusalem should remain an open and undivided city.
At the conclusion of the peace making process and as a final act of settlement, we will recognize Jerusalem as the capital of Israel and
to move the U.S. Embassy there.

D.   In strengthening our diplomatic alliances, we will continue to build
on our strong ties to Japan to enhance our security in the Pacific region.
We will carefully nurture our new relationship with China.

We believe that two basic principles should guide our policy toward
Japan: a genuine American-Japanese partnership is fundamental to all else
in the Pacific, and economic and security elements in the partnership cannot
be separated.

Japan is at once our military ally and our economic competitor.
American-Japanese trade relations have been troubled by the large current
trade imbalance, the impact of Japanese exports on the American automobile
industry, and American difficulty in gaining access to Japan's domestic
market.

In resolving these issues, the Anderson-Lucey Administration would be
guided by three propositions. First, decisions reached without full consultation and indifferent to Japanese concerns will be worse than no decision
at all. Second, our bilateral economic relations are related to basic and
far-reaching movements in the global economy. Third, both the United States
and Japan must ensure that trade problems do not impair our security
relations.

-44-

Concerning China, we believe that those who blithely talk of playing the fabled "China card" do not understand the nature of the relationship. It is not in our interest to give China an "American card" for use in her relations with other East Asian countries or with the Soviet Union.

From a renewed position of domestic and international strength, the Anderson-Lucey Administration would work to discourage antagonism between Russia and China. We should not become an arms supplier to China. We should work for better understanding by China's leaders of the consequences of nuclear war, of measures that should be taken to guard against accidental war, and of ways to make the nuclear balance more stable.

Finally, our administration would abide by both the letter and spirit of the Taiwan Relations Act. We would maintain our contacts with Taiwan but would not establish official relations with its government.

Elsewhere in the region, we would continue to support the security of Thailand. We would not normalize relations with Vietnam without real progress on outstanding issues.   We reaffirm our commitment to defend South Korea against attack.

E.   In Latin America our diplomacy would promote U.S. ideals and interests, while respecting the sovereignty and independence of every nation in the hemisphere.

There is no more important partner than Mexico.

One of the most complex and difficult issues is the immigration of undocumented Mexican workers to the United States. We recognize that there is no easy solution to this problem. We would work with Mexico to improve the economic conditions of that country in order to diminish the basic

causes of the migration. We will also propose a joint American/Mexican
Commission to promote cooperative social development in the border region.
An on-going dialogue on issues such as trade, agriculture, energy, migration,
finance, and industry is essential to forging the kind of partnership that
should characterize our relations with Mexico in the 1980's and beyond.

We will make clear that the United States will not tolerate direct
military intervention by Cuba in Central America. There must be no Angolas
in the Western Hemisphere. We will also oppose any attempt by the Cubans
to lead the nonaligned movement into the Soviet camp.

However, we must not allow our concerns about Cuba to distort our policy
toward other parts of the hemisphere. No amount of military aid can make a
repressive government popular, and an unpopular government is never secure
for long. The best antidote to Cuba's promotion of revolution is a region
of sound, popular, democratic governments -- not an armed camp of military
dictators.

Providing economic aid to Nicaragua serves that goal. It will ease
the suffering of Nicaragua's poor and should promote an atmosphere of
moderation within that country.

F.   In South Asia, the Anderson-Lucey Administration will make a major
effort to open a wider window to India. We will support India's independent
role in world affairs. We will maintain our commitments to other countries
in the area. We will encourage both India and China to continue efforts to
settle their boundary controversies. We will press for Soviet withdrawal
from Afghanistan, where the gravest threat to regional stability now lies.

G.   We will promote stability in Africa by helping the nations of that

-46-

continent achieve their social, political, and economic goals.

We will:

-- work toward majority rule in South Africa through negotiations
   in bilateral and multilateral forums.

-- continue restrictions on Export-Import Bank restrictions on credit
   for investments in South Africa.

-- encourage compliance with the United Nations embargo on the export
   of military equipment to South Africa.

-- as circumstances warrant, and in cooperation with our allies,
   discourage investments in South Africa.

Our administration will aggressively pursue a final agreement in Namibia
based on UN Security Council Resolution 435 which has been accepted by both
SWAPO and the South African government.

H.   We will cooperate with the developing nations in ways which respect
their individuality and independence and which serve our mutual interests
in trade and development. We will follow a carefully differentiated policy
toward these countries working through both multilateral and bilateral
arrangements. The fact that the North-South dialogue has deteriorated into
a harangue by the so-called Group of 77 should not blind us to the necessity
to work toward a more equitable international economic order.

Our objective will be not one global bargain, but a workable global
structure in which individuals, firms and nations can strike the countless
bargains necessary to a productive international economy. And we will urge
oil-exporting nations to take the lead in relieving the hardship drastic oil
price increases inflict on less-developed countries.

-47-

CONCLUSION: HOW AN INDEPENDENT CAN GOVERN

We have set forth a program for America. But that is not enough.
Those who would form an Independent Administration should also explain how
they could accomplish these tasks.

We believe that, at this critical juncture, an Independent Administration with ties to both parties can work successfully with a two-party Congress to govern the United States.

The two parties have not yet formulated a realistic post-New Deal
public philosophy.

They have found it exceedingly difficult to make the hard choices
needed when government is obliged not to distribute the dividends of economic
growth, but to allocate burdens and orchestrate sacrifices.

And many of the key issues confronting this country now cross traditional party divisions.

We believe that an Independent President can be effective. We acknowledge
that the context within which Presidents must act has become more complicated
and restrictive during the past two decades. Sober observers have pointed
to the decentralization of Congress, the fragmentation of political parties,
the rise of single-issue constituencies, and the atomization of the electorate as major elements of this new situation. But we contend that in 1980

-48-

an Anderson-Lucey Administration can deal with it more effectively
than a party administration can.

Victory by our ticket -- in the teeth of enormous institutional biases
against independents -- would be a dramatic signal that the nation wants and
expects action based on the consensus the campaign has articulated. Our campaign represents a coalition of the center -- the traditional basis for
governing the country.

We are confident that Congress -- which includes men and women of high
civic dedication -- will work productively with any President who enjoys the
trust of the American people. We hope to earn and hold that trust.

The essence of presidential responsibility is to assert the general
interest over narrow interests, to make difficult choices among worthy, but
conflicting, objectives, to strike policy balances that are wise and fair
enough to gain the support of Congress and the nation.

No President can forecast in all respects the precise course he will
follow on all issues. But it is incumbent on candidates who seek your vote
to state their view of the country's needs and to identify those initiatives
they expect to undertake -- to point a direction even when they cannot provide a full map.

That we have attempted to do. Many distinguished Americans have contributed to the studies and position papers on which this program is based,
but it is our own sketch of the priorities we believe should guide our
country -- not a mosaic of bargains among special interests or trade-offs
among experts.

We seek a workable synthesis of policy and program, for the next

administration must blend new ideas with old, innovative concepts with traditional values, proven approaches with tentative ones. In responding to
the challenges we face, government must be frankly experimental in some
fields, conventional in others. It must also be utterly ruthless in judging
its performance and pruning its failures. These convictions will animate
our administration.

We speak for a patriotism greater than party. And we invite patriots
of all persuasions to join with us in shaping a government that can shape
the future.

It won't be easy -- but it will be worth it.

APPENDIX TO THE ANDERSON/LUCEY PROGRAM

BUDGET IMPACT STATEMENT

JOHN B. ANDERSON

PATRICK J. LUCEY

THE NATIONAL UNITY CAMPAIGN

October 13, 1980

TO THE AMERICAN PEOPLE:

It is an election year and the fall air is filled with campaign promises. Seldom are those promises subjected to close scrutiny, either by the candidates or the public. In recent years this failure has resulted in higher federal budget deficits, higher inflation, and a disillusioned electorate.

In 1976, the voters elected a candidate for President who promised lower defense spending, a balanced budget, four percent unemployment, four percent inflation, labor law reform, comprehensive national health insurance, comprehensive welfare reform, and a host of other initiatives that remain unrealized 48 months later.

In 1980, a new candidate is in the running. He promises to cut personal income tax rates by one-third, substantially hike military spending, and still balance the federal budget...despite a near-record $63 billion federal budget deficit for the fiscal year that ended less than two weeks ago.

And this year, despite their commitment to immediate income tax relief and major new spending initiatives, both major party candidates make claims to fiscal restraint.

We believe that fiscal restraint begins with fiscal accountability. We believe that candidates for national office have an obligation to give a full accounting of the budgetary and inflationary impacts of their proposals.

In observance of that obligation, we pledged a few weeks ago to give a full accounting of our proposed program and its fiscal policy implications. The attached document fulfills that pledge. It is intended to be a full and fair exposition of the Anderson/Lucey program released five weeks ago.

Using the recent recommendations of the Senate Budget Committee as a base line for comparison, we have sought to show how our proposals would impact on estimated expenditures and receipts in fiscal years 1981-85.

We do not embrace the underlying economic assumptions contained in the Senate Budget Committee's report; we hope to do better in terms of both inflation and unemployment. Our purposes in using their estimates is simply to provide a fair basis for comparison and understanding.

Budget estimates are no better than the underlying economic assumptions. It serves no useful public purpose to make promises on the basis of economic assumptions that may prove to be wholly unrealistic. Thus, while the program analysis that follows projects a balanced budget for fiscal year 1983 under the Anderson/Lucey program, we make no such pledge. Nor do we promise a specified level of tax relief, even though the accompanying projections show considerable room for tax relief, beginning in fiscal year 1983.

We believe, however, that the accompanying budget analysis reveals the realistic nature of the Anderson/Lucey program. It does not rely upon "mirrors." No attempt has been made to put forth spurious, self-serving claims regarding the ability of the next administration to root out fraud and abuse in federal programs as a means of reducing federal expenditures. Nor does it make claims of large "revenue feedbacks" from proposed tax reductions.* It is a simple, straight forward attempt to show the budget impact of the proposed Anderson/Lucey program.

An Anderson Administration will endeavor to make economies in government spending to eliminate waste, and to curb fraud and abuse in federal programs. Every reasonable effort must be made to control the burgeoning cost of publicly (and privately) financed health care. Every effort must also be made to curb the waste in categorical grant-in-aid programs to state and local governments. It would be imprudent, however, for any administration to formulate a federal budget around projected cost-savings that may never materialize.

Candidates for public office should never promise more than they can deliver, and they should deliver all that they promise.

We believe that our program is an achievable one. It can be done. It is a prudent, restrained program that marshalls our limited resources in an intelligent and consistent fashion. It recognizes areas of critical need and responds accordingly.

It makes no attempt to win votes with the promise of immediate tax relief—relief that would soon be negated by the rising inflation that would result from a large tax cut at this time.

It does not promise comprehensive national health insurance or even comprehensive welfare reform. It does promise, however, selective and necessary reforms in each of those areas.

It does not promise large increases in defense spending that cannot be justified in light of our economic, as well as, defense posture. It offers instead, a program of very necessary improvements in our conventional force capability.

---

*The Reagan/Bush campaign recently released a one-page five year budget projection that assumes a $39 billion revenue feedback from its tax cuts and a $64-93 billion cut in annual expenditures to be realized through the reduction of fraud and abuse in federal programs.

In all these areas, we have sought to establish national priorities. Some may argue with our choice of priorities, but few can argue with the need for a realistic portrayal of the choices before us.

We can no longer afford to delude ourselves with vain hopes and false promises. Our problems are too serious to be made the object of election-year fantasies.

We think the American people are prepared for the truth, that they are prepared to make an informed judgment, if they are presented with the facts.

It is our hope that the two major party candidates will present a full and fair cost accounting of their respective party platforms. We are confident that any such objective analysis would reveal internal inconsistencies of a very fundamental nature in both major party platforms.

An analysis of the Democratic platform by Senator Orrin Hatch alleges that its various programs, including comprehensive national health insurance, would cost an additional $431 billion in outlays over the next five years.

A similar analysis of the Republican platform by anonymous Office of Management and Budget (OMB) sources alleges that "the Republican's would have to cut about 40 percent from the non-defense budget to achieve balance" in 1985 and still accommodate the Republican tax cuts.

In both instances, it is evident that neither the Republican nor the Democratic platform presents a true and honest picture to the American people of the difficult choices in the decade ahead.

It is time to level with the American people. It is time for politicians to stop promising the American people more than they can deliver. It is time for "truth in campaigning."

JOHN B. ANDERSON

PATRICK J. LUCEY

TABLE OF CONTENTS

Cover letter -- To the American People

401

I. BACKGROUND

1

Budget Impact Statement
for
The Anderson/Lucey Program

Background

On August 27, 1980, the Senate Budget Committee filed its report on the Second Concurrent Resolution on the Budget for fiscal year 1981. The report contained budget projections for fiscal years 1981-85 based on various spending and economic assumptions.

The Anderson/Lucey program utilizes the Senate Budget Committee recommendations as a basis of comparison only. No attempt has been made to adjust the economic assumptions used by the Committee. This does not mean, however, that the Anderson/Lucey campaign in anyway embraces the underlying economic assumptions; the Anderson/Lucey administration hopes to do better in terms of both inflation and unemployment.

The enclosed budget impact statement accommodates the revenue and expenditure suggestions contained in the Anderson/Lucey program. While the Anderson/Lucey administration intends to eliminate ineffective, duplicative, or wasteful government spending, for purposes of this budget analysis, no such assumption has been made. Thus, spending under an Anderson/Lucey administration may in fact be lower than the totals presented here.

The accompanying analysis does not contain references to either the proposed gasoline tax/payroll tax rebate plan or the proposed Wage-Price Incentives Program. Both proposals are intended to be largely neutral in their impact on federal revenues and the deficit, and therfore were not included in this anaylsis.

Spending totals are broken down into the 18 functional categories set forth in the Congressional Budget Act and further subdivided into "missions" to provide a detailed analysis.

A separate analysis of the revenue section is provided. Revenue estimates are broken down into fiscal years. Fiscal year totals may differ substantially from a calendar year breakdown for the first year of any tax change (the first fiscal year covers only eight months of a calendar year, if the tax cut becomes effective on January 1st, of that fiscal year.)

A summary sheet is provided for each fiscal year containing spending totals for each function, an aggregate spending total, a current law revenue estimate, proposed revenue changes, and an estimated surplus or deficit.

All dollar figures are "current dollars", meaning that all 1985 estimates reflect 1985 dollars. Thus, while expenditures under the Senate Budget Committee' assumptions rise from $633 billion in fiscal year 1981 to $920 billion in fiscal year 1985, the bulk of that increase is accounted for by inflation, not real dolla increases in government spending.

The Senate Budget Committee's estimate relied upon the following economic assumptions:

	FY1980	FY1981	FY1982	FY1983	FY1984	FY1985
Inflation Rate—CPI	13.7	10.9	9.8	8.7	8.0	7.5
Inflation Rate—GNP deflator	9.1	9.8	9.3	8.7	8.0	7.6
Unemployment rate average	6.9	8.5	8.3	7.6	6.9	6.1
Real GNP growth, %	−0.2	1.0	3.3	3.8	3.8	3.8
Nominal GNP (billions of dollars)	2518	2793	3152	3555	3983	4446

II. BUDGET IMPACT HIGHLIGHTS

3

Budget Impact Highlights

The Anderson/Lucey Program, under this budget analysis:

—reduces federal outlays as a percent of the gross national product from 22.7 percent in fiscal year 1981 to 21.3 percent in fiscal year 1985;

—balances the federal budget by fiscal year 1983;

—reduces defense spending below the Senate Budget Committee projection by $8 billion in fiscal year 1985;

—increases defense spending by over 3 percent a year in real dollar terms to accommodate pay comparability hikes for military personnel and improvements in the combat readiness of America's conventional military forces;

—eliminates funding for the land-based mobile MX missile system, but provides funding for less-costly alternative improvements in the sea-based nuclear deterrent;

—allows for substantially higher international development assistance;

—provides real dollar funding increases for the basic sciences;

—reinstates portions of the NASA five-year budget proposal;

—increases funding for energy supply research and development above the Senate Budget Committee's recommendation;

—allows for a larger energy conservation program;

—allows for the filling of the Strategic Petroleum Reserve;

—reduces funding for water projects below the Senate Budget Committee's recommendation;

—provides funding for the hazardous substance and oil spill cleanup funds;

—provides more adequate and predictable funding for community transportation through a Community Transportation Trust Fund;

—allows for the creation of an Urban Reinvestment Trust Fund to help cities rebuild decaying bridges, streets and sewers;

III. FISCAL YEAR SUMMARIES

5

Summary Sheet

The Senate Budget Committee Recommendation	FY1981	FY1982	FY1983	FY1984	FY1985
Outlays (in billions)	633.0	709.9	777.7	844.6	920.1
Revenues (in billions)	615.1	698.7	792.1	898.7	1101.4
Deficit (−) or Surplus (+) (in billions)	−17.9	−11.2	+14.4	+54.1	+81.3
Tax Change from Current Law	+5.2	−13.3	−35.6	−52.5	−100.4

*   *   *   *   *   *   *   *   *   *   *   *   *   *

Anderson/Lucey Recommendation	FY1981	FY1982	FY1983	FY1984	FY1985
Outlays (in billions)	635.4	715.6	785.6	862.3	946.2
Revenues (in billions)	608.7	697.2	789.6	878.4	972.9
Deficit (−) or Surplus (+) (in billions)	−26.7	−18.5	+4.0	+16.4	+26.7
Tax Change from Current Law	−1.2	−14.8	−38.1	−72.8	−128.9

6

FISCAL YEAR 1981

FUNCTION		SENATE BUDGET COMMITTEE RECOMMENDATION	THE ANDERSON/LUCEY RECOMMENDATION
050:	National Defense	159.4	158.9
150:	International Affairs	10.6	10.8
250:	General Science Space, and Technology	6.2	6.2
270:	Energy	7.4	7.4
300:	Natural Resources and Environment	13.1	13.1
350:	Agriculture	2.2	2.2
370:	Commerce and Housing Credit	0.5	0.5
400:	Transportation	19.3	19.5
450:	Community and Regional Development	9.7	9.7
500:	Education, Training, Employment, and Social Services	29.4	29.9
550:	Health	63.6	63.6
600:	Income Security	228.4	229.9
700:	Veterans	22.0	22.0
750:	Administration of Justice	4.6	4.6
800:	General Government	4.5	4.5
850:	General Purpose Fiscal Assistance	6.7	7.2

FISCAl YEAR 1981, Cont'd.

	SENATE BUDGET COMMITTEE RECOMMENDATION	THE ANDERSON/LUCEY RECOMMENDATION
FUNCTION		
900: Interest	70.1	70.1
950: Undistributed Offsetting Receipts	−24.7	−24.7
TOTALS—	633.0	635.4
Current Law Revenues	609.9	609.9
Proposed Tax Revenue Changes	+5.2	−1.2
Net Tax Revenues	615.1	608.7
Surplus (Deficit)	−17.9	−26.7

FISCAL YEAR 1982   8

	SENATE BUDGET COMMITTEE RECOMMENDATION	THE ANDERSON/LUCE RECOMMENDATION
FUNCTION		
050: National Defense	186.8	183.5
150: International Affairs	10.2	11.6
250: General Science Space, and Technology	6.8	7.1
270: Energy	10.2	10.6
300: Natural Resources and Environment	13.4	13.4
350: Agriculture	4.2	4.2
370: Commerce and Housing Credit	2.7	2.9
400: Transportation	20.0	20.9
450: Community and Regional Development	8.8	9.8
500: Education, Training, Employment, and Social Services	31.1	32.2
550: Health	75.0	75.4
600: Income Security	255.2	256.8
700: Veterans	23.3	24.0
750: Administration of Justice	4.6	4.8
800: General Government	4.8	4.8
850: General Purpose Fiscal Assistance	6.4	7.4

FISCA1 YEAR 1982, Cont'd.   9

	SENATE BUDGET COMMITTEE RECOMMENDATION	THE ANDERSON/LUCEY RECOMMENDATION
FUNCTION		
900: Interest	73.8	73.8
950: Undistributed Offsetting Receipts	-27.4	-27.4
TOTALS--	709.9	715.6
Current Law Revenues	712.0	712.0
Proposed Tax Revenue Changes	-13.3	-14.8
Net Tax Revenues	698.7	697.2
Surplus (Deficit)	-11.2	-18.4

FISCAL YEAR 1983   10

		SENATE BUDGET COMMITTEE RECOMMENDATION	THE ANDERSON/LUCEY RECOMMENDATION
FUNCTION			
050:	National Defense	212.2	205.1
150:	International Affairs	9.9	12.0
250:	General Science Space, and Technology	7.0	7.5
270:	Energy	11.3	11.9
300:	Natural Resources and Environment	13.4	13.3
350:	Agriculture	4.5	4.5
370:	Commerce and Housing Credit	2.8	2.9
400:	Transportation	21.0	22.2
450:	Community and Regional Development	8.6	10.2
500:	Education, Training, Employment, and Social Services	32.1	34.3
550:	Health	84.7	87.1
600:	Income Security	281.7	284.5
700:	Veterans	25.6	26.1
750:	Administration of Justice	4.7	4.8
800:	General Government	5.0	5.0
850:	General Purpose Fiscal Assistance	6.5	6.5

FISCAl YEAR 1983, Cont'd.   11

	SENATE BUDGET COMMITEE RECOMMENDATION	THE ANDERSON/LUCEY RECOMMENDATION
FUNCTION		
900: Interest	76.4	77.5
950: Undistributed Offsetting Receipts	−29.7	−29.7
TOTALS—	777.7	785.6
Current Law Revenues	827.7	827.7
Proposed Tax Revenue Changes	−35.6	−38.1
Net Tax Revenues	792.1	789.6
Surplus (Deficit)	+14.4	+4.0

		FISCAL YEAR 1984	12
		SENATE BUDGET COMMITTEE RECOMMENDATION	THE ANDERSON/LUC RECOMMENDATION
FUNCTION			
050:	National Defense	239.4	232.2
150:	International Affairs	11.0	13.3
250:	General Science Space, and Technology	6.8	8.0
270:	Energy	10.1	11.4
300:	Natural Resources and Environment	13.5	13.4
350:	Agriculture	5.2	5.2
370:	Commerce and Housing Credit	2.6	2.8
400:	Transportation	21.5	23.1
450:	Community and Regional Development	8.8	11.9
500:	Education, Training, Employment, and Social Services	33.7	36.7
550:	Health	95.6	100.6
600:	Income Security	305.8	311.1
700:	Veterans	27.6	27.8
750:	Administration of Justice	5.0	5.1
800:	General Government	5.3	5.3
850:	General Purpose Fiscal Assistance	6.6	6.6

FISCAl YEAR 1984, Cont'd.   13

	SENATE BUDGET COMMITTEE RECOMMENDATION	THE ANDERSON/LUCEY RECOMMENDATION
FUNCTION		
900: Interest	79.9	81.6
950: Undistributed Offsetting Receipts	-33.9	-33.9
TOTALS—	844.6	862.3
Current Law Revenues	951.2	951.2
Proposed Tax Revenue Changes	-52.5	-72.8
Net Tax Revenues	898.7	878.4
Surplus (Deficit)	+54.1	+16.4

FISCAL YEAR 1985   14

		SENATE BUDGET COMMITTEE RECOMMENDATION	THE ANDERSON/LUC RECOMMENDATION
FUNCTION			
050:	National Defense	270.4	262.3
150:	International Affairs	11.2	15.1
250:	General Science Space, and Technology	6.7	8.2
270:	Energy	9.3	10.4
300:	Natural Resources and Environment	13.6	13.5
350:	Agriculture	5.2	5.2
370:	Commerce and Housing Credit	2.3	2.5
400:	Transportation	21.8	24.0
450:	Community and Regional Development	8.8	12.2
500:	Education, Training, Employment, and Social Services	34.8	40.0
550:	Health	107.9	114.4
600:	Income Security	332.7	340.0
700:	Veterans	29.7	29.8
750:	Administration of Justice	5.2	5.3
800:	General Government	5.6	5.6
850:	General Purpose Fiscal Assistance	6.8	6.8

FISCAL YEAR 1985, Cont'd.   15

FUNCTION		SENATE BUDGET COMMITTEE RECOMMENDATION	THE ANDERSON/LUCEY RECOMMENDATION
900:	Interest	84.7	87.7
950:	Undistributed Offsetting Receipts	−36.5	−36.5
TOTALS—		920.1	946.2
Current Law Revenues		1101.8	1101.8
Proposed Tax Revenue Changes		−101.4	−128.9
Net Tax Revenues		1001.4	972.9
Surplus (Deficit)		+81.3	+26.7

IV. FUNCTION OUTLAYS AND EXPLANATIONS

Function 50:   NATIONAL DEFENSE

Outlays
(in billions of dollars)

Senate Budget Committee Recommendation		FY1981	FY1982	FY1983	FY1984	FY1985
Mission 1:	Strategic Warfare Forces	17.3	20.1	23.1	27.1	30.6
Mission 2:	Tactical Warfare Forces	98.1	116.7	133.4	150.4	170.5
Mission 3:	Defense-Wide Forces and Support	26.8	29.8	33.2	37.4	42.6
Mission 4:	Other National Defense	17.2	20.3	22.4	24.6	26.7
TOTAL—		159.4	186.8	212.2	239.4	270.4

*   *   *   *   *   *   *   *   *   *   *   *   *

Anderson/Lucey Recommentation		FY1981	FY1982	FY1983	FY1984	FY1985
Mission 1:	Strategic Warfare Forces	17.2	19.1	21.5	25.3	28.5
Mission 2:	Tactical Warfare Forces	97.7	114.6	128.0	145.0	164.5
Mission 3:	Defense-Wide Forces and Support	26.8	29.8	33.2	37.4	42.6
Mission 4:	Other National Defense	17.2	20.3	22.4	24.6	26.7
TOTAL—		158.9	183.5	205.1	232.2	262.3

Function 50, Cont'd

EXPLANATION

Strategic Warfare Forces   The Senate Budget Committee's recommendation assumes funding of the proposed land-based mobile MX missile system, as well as, significant improvements in other strategic forces, including cruise missiles and the sea-based nuclear deterrent. The Anderson/Lucey program rejects the proposed land-based mobile MX missile system and proposes consideration of alternative improvement in our sea-based nuclear deterrent.

Tactical Warfare Forces   The Senate Budget Committee's recommendation assumes an 11.7 percent pay raise and Nunn-Warner benefit package for military personnel, along with major increases in funding to improve the readiness of U.S. military forces. The Anderson/Lucey program accepts the pay raise and benefits provisions, but anticipates a slower growth in military procurement spending for new weapons systems through emphasis on less-expensive systems.

Defense-Wide Forces and Support   The Senate Budget Committee's recommendation provides for the President's level for Defense-Wide Forces and Support plus additional requirements for fuel and other inflation needs.   The Committee's recommendation also provides for the full amount of pay comparability for military—11.7 percent versus the administration's proposed 7.4 percent—and allows for only 20 percent absorption of the pay raise, instead of the 40 percent required by the administration's budget.   The Anderson/Lucey program accepts these recommendations.

Other National Defense   The Committee's recommendation provides funding for the expansion of the military activities of the Department of Energy and allows for an annual, instead of a semi-annual cost-of-living increase for military retired pay. The Anderson/Lucey program accepts these recommendations.

18

Function 150:   INTERNATIONAL AFFAIRS

	Outlays (in billions of dollars)				
Senate Budget Committee Recommendation	FY1981	FY1982	FY1983	FY1984	FY1985
Mission 1: International Development Programs	3.7	4.0	4.3	4.6	4.5
Mission 2: International Security Programs	3.1	2.9	2.6	2.6	2.7
Mission 3: Diplomatic Operations and International Financial Programs	3.8	3.3	3.1	3.7	4.0
TOTAL—	10.6	10.2	9.9	11.0	11.2

*   *   *   *   *   *   *   *   *   *   *   *   *   *

Anderson/Lucey Recommentation	FY1981	FY1982	FY1983	FY1984	FY1985
Mission 1: International Development Programs	3.9	5.4	6.3	7.0	8.4
Mission 2: International Security Programs	3.1	2.9	2.6	2.6	2.7
Mission 3: Diplomatic Operations and International Financial Programs	3.8	3.3	3.1	3.7	4.0
TOTAL—	10.8	11.6	12.0	13.3	15.1

19

Function 150, Cont'd.

EXPLANATION

International Development Programs   The Senate Budget Committee recommends a decline in real dollar funding for international development programs. The Anderson/Lucey program anticipates significantly higher real dollar outlays for both bilateral and multilateral assistance.

International Security Programs   The Senate Budget Committee anticipates continued military assistance to U.S. allies, including Israel, Egypt and Turkey. The Anderson/Lucey program accepts the recommended funding level.

Diplomatic Operations and International Financial Programs   The Senate Budget Committee provides for $5.4 billion in Eximbank direct credits to finance American exports and U.S. participation in the 50 percent increase in the resources of the International Monetary Fund. The Anderson/Lucey program accepts this recommendation.

20

Function 250:   GENERAL SCIENCE, SPACE AND TECHNOLOGY

Outlays
(in billions of dollars)

Senate Budget Committee Recommendation	FY1981	FY1982	FY1983	FY1984	FY1985
Mission 1: Science	1.5	1.6	1.7	1.8	1.9
Mission 2: Civilian Space Program	4.7	5.1	5.2	5.0	4.8
TOTAL—	6.2	6.8	7.0	6.8	6.7

*   *   *   *   *   *   *   *   *   *   *   *   *   *

Anderson/Lucey Recommentation	FY1981	FY1982	FY1983	FY1984	FY1985
Mission 1: Science	1.5	1.7	1.9	2.2	2.4
Mission 2: Civilian Space Program	4.7	5.3	5.6	5.8	5.8
TOTAL—	6.2	7.1	7.5	8.0	8.2

EXPLANATION

        Science   The Senate Budget Committee recommends increases in program funding slightly below the pace of inflation. The Anderson/Lucey program anticipates a reverse in the decline in the real dollar level of funding for basic science.

        Civilian Space Program   The Senate Budget Committee's recommendation assumes continuation of space shuttle development and production on current schedule and funding for two new program starts: The Gamma Ray Observatory and the National Oceanic Satellite System. The Anderson/Lucey program assumes the reinstatement of other program initiatives, including an intensified effort to achieve routine operational use of the Space Shuttle, establishment of an operational Landsat-type system, and proper support for long-term programs to explore the solar system.

21

Function 270:   ENERGY

		Outlays (in billions of dollars)				
Senate Budget Committee Recommendation		FY1981	FY1982	FY1983	FY1984	FY1985
Mission 1:	Energy Supply	4.9	5.6	5.2	4.3	3.8
Mission 2:	Energy Conservation	0.7	0.8	0.8	0.8	0.8
Mission 3:	Emergency Energy Preparedness	1.0	3.0	4.4	4.1	3.8
Mission 4:	Other Energy Programs	0.8	0.9	0.9	0.9	1.0
TOTAL—		7.4	10.2	11.3	10.1	9.3

*   *   *   *   *   *   *   *   *   *   *   *   *   *

Anderson/Lucey Recommentation		FY1981	FY1982	FY1983	FY1984	FY1985
Mission 1:	Energy Supply	4.9	5.9	5.6	5.3	4.6
Mission 2:	Energy Conservation	0.7	0.9	1.0	1.0	1.1
Mission 3:	Emergency Energy Preparedness	1.0	3.0	4.4	4.1	3.8
Mission 4:	Other Energy Programs	0.8	0.9	0.9	0.9	1.0
TOTAL—		7.4	10.6	11.9	11.4	10.4

EXPLANATION

Energy Supply   The Senate Budget Committee recommendation assumes fundi
of an away-from-reactor nuclear spent fuel storage program and continued support of
energy supply activities including construction of demonstration plants and ongoing
research activities. The Anderson/Lucey program anticipates a higher level of outla
to accomodate expanded R&D in the areas of new coal-based technologies and alternati
fuels including both fusion and renewable energy sources. Also included in the
Anderson/Lucey program is a commitment for a larger federal procurement program in t.
area of photovoltaics.

Function 270, Cont'd.

Energy Conservation   The Senate Budget Committee recommendation
anticipates continued support of energy conservation initiatives and funding of the
solar/conservation bank. The Anderson/Lucey program assumes a higher funding level
to accomodate increased funding for federally funded insulation and weatherization,
and federal demonstration projects.

Emergency Energy Preparedness   The Senate Budget Committee
recommendation provides funding to recommence the acquisition of a minimum of
100,000 barrels of oil per day for the stategic petroleum reserve. The
Anderson/Lucey programs supports this recommendation.

Other Energy Programs   The Senate Budget Committee recommends current
law funding levels for the activities of the various energy regulatory agencies.
The Anderson/Lucey program accepts this recommendation.

Function 300:   NATURAL RESOURCES AND ENVIRONMENT

			Outlays (in billions of dollars)			
Senate Budget Committee Recommendation		FY1981	FY1982	FY1983	FY1984	FY1985
Mission 1:	Water Resources	3.9	4.1	4.0	4.2	4.3
Mission 2:	Conservation and Land Management	2.2	2.2	2.2	2.3	2.4
Mission 3:	Recreational Resources	1.4	1.6	1.6	1.7	1.8
Mission 4:	Pollution Control and Abatement	5.6	6.0	6.1	6.2	6.2
Mission 5:	Other Natural Resources and Environment Programs	−0.1	−0.4	−0.6	−0.8	−1.0
TOTAL—		13.1	13.4	13.4	13.5	13.6

*   *   *   *   *   *   *   *   *   *   *   *   *   *

Anderson/Lucey Recommentation		FY1981	FY1982	FY1983	FY1984	FY1985
Mission 1:	Water Resources	3.9	4.0	3.8	4.0	4.1
Mission 2:	Conservation and Land Management	2.2	2.3	2.3	2.4	2.5
Mission 3:	Recreational Resources	1.4	1.6	1.6	1.7	1.8
Mission 4:	Pollution Control and Abatement	5.6	6.1	6.2	6.2	6.2
Mission 5:	Other Natural Resources and Environment Programs	−0.1	−0.4	−0.6	−0.8	−1.0
TOTAL—		13.1	13.4	13.3	13.4	13.5

24

Function 300, Cont'd.

EXPLANATION

Water Resources   The Senate Budget Committee's recommendation for
water projects is substantially greater than its recommendation for the First
Concurrent Budget Resolution. The Anderson/Lucey program anticipates spending
levels closer to the first concurrent Budget Resolution recommendation.

Conservation and Land Management   The Senate Budget Committee's
recommendation could force cutbacks in land and forest management activities that
in turn could lead to declines in productivity. The Anderson/Lucey program
projects a more adequate level of outlays.

Recreational Resources   The Senate Budget Committee's recommendation
recommends modest reductions from current law funding levels.   The Anderson/Lucey
program accepts this recommendation.

Pollution Control and Abatement   The Senate Budget Committee
recommends funding of a hazardous substances cleanup fund. The Anderson/Lucey
program endorses this recommendation and provides additional monies for an oil
spill cleanup fund not contained in the Senate's recommendation.

25

Function 350:   AGRICULTURE

	Outlays (in billions of dollars)				
Senate Budget Committee Recommendation	FY1981	FY1982	FY1983	FY1984	FY1985
Mission 1: Farm Income Stabilization	0.8	2.6	2.7	3.3	3.2
Mission 2: Agricultural Research/Services	1.5	1.6	1.7	1.9	2.0
TOTAL—	2.2	4.2	4.5	5.2	5.2

*   *   *   *   *   *   *   *   *   *   *   *   *   *

Anderson/Lucey Recommentation	FY1981	FY1982	FY1983	FY1984	FY1985
Mission 1: Farm Income Stabilization	0.8	2.6	2.7	3.3	3.2
Mission 2: Agricultural Research/Services	1.5	1.6	1.7.	1.9	2.0
TOTAL—	2.2	4.2	4.5	5.2	5.2

EXPLANATION

Farm Income Stabilization   The Senate Budget Committee's recommendation includes funding for increased loan rates for grain in the farmer owned reserved program and a food security reserve for humanitarian aid using the wheat acquired by the CCC as a result of the Soviet grain embargo. The Anderson/Lucey program makes no changes in these budget recommendations, other than a commitment to re-examine the parity formula and other proposals for measuring the equitability of farm commodity prices.

Function 350, Cont'd.

        Agricultural Research and Services The Senate Budget Committee's recommendation includes funding for an expansion of the federal crop insurance program, as proposed in the Anderson/Lucey program. The Anderson/Lucey program also calls for a shifting of research efforts on food processing to a review of non-farm related costs and additional funding for the FmHA real estate loan program for young farm families.

Function 370   COMMERCE AND HOUSING CREDIT

		Outlays (in billions of dollars)				
Senate Budget Committee Recommendation		FY1981	FY1982	FY1983	FY1984	FY1985
Mission 1:	Mortgage Credit and Thrift Insurance	-2.2	-0.3	-0.3	-0.4	-0.7
Mission 2:	Postal Service	1.1	1.1	1.0	0.9	0.8
Mission 3:	Other Commerce and Housing Credit	1.6	2.0	2.1	2.2	2.3
TOTAL—		0.5	2.7	2.8	2.6	2.3

*   *   *   *   *   *   *   *   *   *   *   *   *   *

Anderson/Lucey Recommentation		FY1981	FY1982	FY1983	FY1984	FY1985
Mission 1:	Mortgage Credit and Thrift Insurance	-2.2	-0.1	-0.2	-0.3	.-0.7
Mission 2:	Postal Service	1.1	1.1	1.0	0.9	0.8
Mission 3:	Other Commerce and Housing Credit	1.6	2.0	2.2	. 2.5	2.5
TOTAL—		0.5	2.9	2.9	2.8	2.5

Function 370, Cont'd

Mortgage Credit and Thrift Insurance   The Senate Budget Committee's recommendation would accomodate funding at the level of current law and inflation adjusted support for the Section 202 housing program. The Committee also recommends greater use of shallower subsidies to accomodate more housing units. The Anderson/Lucey program assumes a somewhat higher outlay will be required to meet housing needs in later years, particularly for the elderly and the handicapped.

Postal Service   The Senate Budget Committee projects funding for the Postal Service at a level which will allow continuation of 6-day mail delivery. The Anderson/Lucey program accepts this recommendation.

Other Commerce and Housing Credit Programs   The Senate Budget Committee provides current law funding levels. The Anderson/Lucey program accepts this recommendation, but also anticipates funding for the proposed Industrial Development Administration and additional monies for the Patent and Tradmark Office.

29

Function 400:   TRANSPORTATION

	Outlays (in billions of dollars)				
Senate Budget Committee Recommendation	FY1981	FY1982	FY1983	FY1984	FY1985
Mission 1: Highways	9.2	8.2	8.7	8.7	8.7
Mission 2: Railroads	1.6	1.6	1.6	1.7	1.6
Mission 3: Mass Transit	2.9	3.1	3.3	3.3	3.0
Mission 4: Air Transportation	3.9	4.1	4.3	4.6	4.8
Mission 5: Other Transportation	2.5	2.6	2.7	2.9	3.1
TOTAL—	19.3	20.0	21.0	21.5	21.8

*   *   *   *   *   *   *   *   *   *   *   *   *   *

Anderson/Lucey Recommentation	FY1981	FY1982	FY1983	FY1984	FY1985
Mission 1: Highways	9.2	8.2	8.7	8.7	8.7
Mission 2: Railroads	1.6	1.6	1.6	1.7	1.6
Mission 3: Mass Transit	3.1	3.9	4.4	4.8	5.1
Mission 4: Air Transportation	3.9	4.1	4.3	4.6	4.8
Mission 5: Other Transportation	2.5	2.7	2.8	3.0	3.2
TOTAL—	19.5	20.9	22.2	23.1	24.0

Function 400, Cont'd.

EXPLANATION

Highways   The Senate Budget Committee's recommendation assumes funding for highway spending priorities in the Federal-aid highway program, especially for safety-related construction and roads damaged by disasters such as Mt. St. Helens. The Anderson/Lucey program accepts this recommendation.

Railroads   The Senate Budget Committee's recommendation assumes completion of the Northeast Corridor Improvement Project, continuation of the Amtrak system, and an expanded program of assistance to the rail industry for restructuring, rehabilitation and improvement. The Anderson/Lucey program accepts this recommendation.

Mass Transit   The Senate Budget Committee assumes funding for mass transit at a level that will permit the completion of construction and extension projects currently underway. The Anderson/Lucey program anticipates a higher level of outlays, with existing capital and maintenance support being funded out of a proposed Community Transportation Trust Fund (CTTF), while operating cost subsidies will continue to be funded out of general revenues. The CTTF will be funded by existing federal alcohol and tobbacco excise taxes, rather than general revenues. While the CTTF will receive an estimated $3.8 billion a year, when fully funded, initial outlay projections are somewhat smaller, due to the lead-times associated with community transportation projections.

Air Transportation   The Senate Budget Committee recommends increases requested by the President for airport development, facilities and equipment, and research, engineering and development programs. The Anderson/Lucey program supports this recommendation.

Other Transportation   The Senate Budget Committee recommends increases beyond current law funding for the Coast Guard and Maritime Administration. The Anderson/Lucey program accepts this recommendation, but also provides funding for the proposed Coal Export Authority.

31

Function 450:   COMMUNITY AND
                                  REGIONAL DEVELOPMENT

		Outlays (in billions of dollars)				
Senate Budget Committee Recommendation		FY1981	FY1982	FY1983	FY1984	FY1985
Mission 1:	Community Development	5.5	5.1	4.9	4.9	4.9
Mission 2:	Area and Regional Development	2.7	2.9	2.9	3.1	3.2
Mission 3:	Disaster Relief and Insurance	1.5	0.8	0.7	0.8	0.7
TOTAL—		9.7	8.8	8.6	8.8	8.8

*   *   *   *   *   *   *   *   *   *   *   *   *   *

Anderson/Lucey Recommentation		FY1981	FY1982	FY1983	FY1984	FY1985
Mission 1:	Community Development	5.5	6.1	6.5	8.0	8.3
Mission 2:	Area and Regional Development	2.7	2.9	2.9	3.1	3.2
Mission 3:	Disaster Relief and Insurance	1.5	0.8	0.7	0.8	0.7
TOTAL—		9.7	9.8	10.2	11.9	12.2

32

Function 450, Cont'd.

EXPLANATION

Community Development The Senate Budget Committee assumes current law funding levels for the community development block grant program and a phase out of the urban renewal program. The Anderson/Lucey program accepts this recommendation, but anticipates higher outlays resulting from the proposed Urban Reinvestment Trust Fund.

Area and Regional Development The Senate Budget Committee recommends reductions in the real dollar funding of the regional development commissions and increases in the economic development programs, including the Economic Development Administration. The Anderson/Lucey program accepts this recommendation.

Disaster Relief and Insurance The Senate Budget Committee recommends full funding for disaster assistance programs at funding levels required during years with a typical incidence of disasters. The Anderson/Lucey program supports this recommendation.

Function 500:   EDUCATION, TRAINING
                            EMPLOYMENT AND SOCIAL SERVICES

		Outlays (in billions of dollars)				
Senate Budget Committee Recommendation		FY1981	FY1982	FY1983	FY1984	FY1985
Mission 1:	Elementary, Secondary, and Vocational	7.5	8.4	9.0	9.9	9.8
Mission 2:	Higher Education	5.5	5.2	5.3	5.3	5.8
Mission 3:	Research and General Education Aid	1.4	1.5	1.6	1.6	1.7
Mission 4:	Training and Employment	8.8	9.3	9.5	9.6	10.0
Mission 5:	Other Labor	0.6	0.6	0.7	0.7	0.7
Mission 6:	Social Services	5.5	6.1	6.0	6.5	6.8
TOTAL—		29.4	31.1	32.1	33.7	34.8

*   *   *   *   *   *   *   *   *   *   *   *   *   *

		FY1981	FY1982	FY1983	FY1984	FY1985
Anderson/Lucey Recommentation						
Mission 1:	Elementary, Secondary, and Vocational	7.6	8.9	9.4	10.5	10.5
Mission 2:	Higher Education	5.5	5.3	5.7	5.8	6.3
Mission 3:	Research and General Education Aid	1.4	1.5	1.6	1.7	1.8
Mission 4:	Training and Employment	9.1	9.8	10.5	10.7	11.2
Mission 5:	Other Labor	0.6	0.6	0.7	0.7	0.7
Mission 6:	Social Services	5.6	6.1	6.4	7.0	7.3
TOTAL—		29.9	32.2	34.3	36.5	37.9

Function 500, Cont'd.

      Elementary, Secondary, and Vocational The Senate Budget
Commitittee's recommendation assumes funding of the education portion of the
proposed youth employment initiative and a 9 percent increase in funding for the
hanicapped and disadvantaged. The Anderson/Lucey program anticipates a somewhat
higher level of funding, including increased federal funding of federally-imposed
education costs.

      Higher Education The Senate Budget Committee assumes a real dollar
reduction in the basis educational opportunity grant (BEOG) funding, due in part
to declining enrollments. The Anderson/Lucey program anticipates changes in the
BEOG grant level to reflect changes in the cost of education. The Anderson/Lucey
program also calls for improvements in the half-cost rule, the TRIO programs
(including Talent Search, Upward Bound, and special Services for Disadvantaged
Students), and the establishment a merit scholarship program. The Anderson/Lucey
program also provides higher funding for language and international study
programs, as well as, other improvements in higher education.

      Research and General Education Aid The Senate Budget Committee
proposes reductions in funding for the libraries and learning resources programs
and for the programs of the National Endowments for the Arts and Humanities. The
Anderson/Lucey program anticipates the maintenance of real dollar funding levels
for the National Endowments and continued support of libraries.

      Training and Employment The Senate Budget Committee's recommendation
includes funding for the youth employment initiative and the Job Corps. The
Senate Budget Committee's recommendation, however, proposes cutbacks in CETA
funding beyond the targets set forth in the First Concurrent Budget Resolution
for Fiscal Year 1981. The Anderson/Lucey program anticipates higher levels of
funding for the Title VII (Private Sector Jobs Initiative), a special Youth
Energy Projects Act to be funded by up to $1 billion by FY1983, and other
targeted programs including the work incentive (WIN) program.

      Other Labor The Senate Budget Committee recommends current law
funding of the National Labor Relations Board and the Department of Labor. The
Anderson/Lucey program accepts this recommendation.

      Social Services The Senate Budget Committee assumes full funding of
the Title XX program, which provides social services to the poor, and an increase
in funding for child welfare services, as well as, increased funding to fully
compensate social services and nutrition programs for the elderly against
inflation. The Anderson/Lucey program projects a higher level of outlays to
support more extensive child care funding, homemaker services, and other social
services.

Function 550:   HEALTH

	Outlays (in billions of dollars)				
Senate Budget Committee Recommendation	FY1981	FY1982	FY1983	FY1984	FY1985
Mission 1: Health Care Services	58.6	69.5	79.1	90.0	102.2
Mission 2: Health Research	3.4	3.6	3.7	3.7	3.7
Mission 3: Education and Training of the Health Care Workforce	0.6	0.8	0.8	0.8	0.8
Mission 4: Consumer and Occupational Health and Safety	0.9	1.0	1.1	1.1	1.2
TOTAL--	63.6	75.0	84.7	95.6	107.9

*   *   *   *   *   *   *   *   *   *   *   *   *   *

	FY1981	FY1982	FY1983	FY1984	FY1985
Anderson/Lucey Recommentation	FY1981	FY1982	FY1983	FY1984	FY1985
Mission 1: Health Care Services	58.6	69.9	81.4	94.8	108.4
Mission 2: Health Research	3.4	3.6.	3.7	3.8	3.8
Mission 3: Education and Training of the Health Care Workforce	0.6	0.8	0.9	0.9	0.9
Mission 4: Consumer and Occupational Health and Safety	0.9	1.0	1.1	1.2	1.3
TOTAL--	63.6	75.3	87.1	100.6	114.4

Function 550, Cont'd.

EXPLANATION

Health Care Services   The Senate Budget Committee's recommendation
assumes enactment of the Child Health Assurance Program (CHAP), as provided for in
the Anderson/Lucey program. The committee estimate also assumes funding to expand
medicaid and medicare benefits and services beginning in FY1982, along with
cost-savings through proposed medicare and medicaid reimbursement reforms. The
Anderson/Lucey program accepts these recommendations, but assumes larger medicaid
and medicare benefit liberalizations will be phased in beginning in FY1982,
including expanded medicaid elegibility and medicare benefits (including home
health care services).

Health Research   The Senate Budget Committee's recommends real dollar
reductions in current law outlays for FY1982 and future years. While the
Anderson/Lucey program concurs with the Committee's judgment that existing
research should be more closely focussed on prevention, the Anderson/Lucey program
would expand current law outlay projections to insure adequate funding of
biomedical and health care research in the area of prevention. The Anderson/Lucey
recommendation also includes expanded funding for the Institute on Aging.

Education and Training of the Health Care Workforce   Between 1981 and
1985, current law funding recommended by the Senate Budget Committee would reduce
real funding by 33 percent. To insure adequate funding of the National Health
Service Corps, the Anderson/Lucey program recommends a higher funding level in
FY1983 and beyond.

Consumer and Occupational Health and Safety   The Senate Budget
Committee recommends current law funding levels that would result in a 14 percent
reduction in real dollar funding by 1985. Consistent with its emphasis on
preventive medicine and health care, the Anderson/Lucey program recommends
increases beyond current law funding levels.

Function 600   INCOME SECURITY   37

		Outlays (in billions of dollars)				
Senate Budget Committee Recommendation		FY1981	FY1982	FY1983	FY1984	FY1985
Mission 1:	General Retirement and Disability Insurance	145.8	166.8	187.1	207.5	228.5
Mission 2:	Federal Employee Retirement and Disability	16.6	19.9	22.4	25.0	27.5
Mission 3:	Unemployment Compensation	24.5	21.9	21.3	18.8	19.1
Mission 4:	Public Assistance	26.9	30.3	32.6	34.3	35.7
Mission 5:	Nutrition Programs	4.8	5.3	5.9	6.3	6.6
Mission 6:	Housing Assistance	6.5	7.9	9.3	10.9	12.5
Mission 7:	Other Income Security Programs	3.0	3.0	3.1	3.0	2.9
TOTAL—		228.4	255.2	281.7	305.8	332.7

*   *   *   *   *   *   *   *   *   *   *   *   *   *

Anderson/Lucey Recommendation		FY1981	FY1982	FY1983	FY1984	FY1985
Mission 1:	General Retirement and Disability Insurance	145.8	166.8	187.4	209.6	232.0
Mission 2:	Federal Employee Retirement and Disability	16.8	19.9	22.4	25.0	27.5
Mission 3:	Unemployment Compensation	26.0	22.2	21.3	18.8	19.1
Mission 4:	Public Assistance	26.9	31.4	35.4	37.5	39.5
Mission 5:	Nutrition Programs	4.8	5.3	5.9	6.3	6.6
Mission 6:	Housing Assistance	6.5	7.9	9.3	10.9	12.5
Mission 7:	Other Income Security Programs	3.0	3.0	3.1	3.0	2.9
TOTAL—		229.9	256.8	284.5	311.1	340.0

Function 600, Cont'd.

General Retirement and Disability Insurance   The Senate Budget
Committee's recommends a full annual cost-of-living adjustment for social
security beneficiaries and assumes enactment of reforms to make the railroad
retirement program solvent. The Anderson/Lucey program accepts these
recommendations, but also makes provision for liberalization of the Social
Security retirement test and revision of Social Security laws to provide equity
for homemakers beginning in 1984.

Federal Employee Retirement and Disability   The Senate Budget
Committee assumes the adoption of an annual, rather than the current semi-annual,
cost-of-living adjustment for Federal civil service retirees, and other proposed
reforms of the civil service retirement system. The Anderson/Lucey program
accepts these recommendations.

Unemployment Compensation   The Senate Budget Committee recommends
full funding of the current trade adjustment assistance and unemployment
compensation programs. The Anderson/Lucey program accepts this recommendation,
along with an extension of unemployment benefits in states of high unemployment
through January 1, 1982.

Public Assistance   The Senate Budget Committee does not contain any
funding for the welfare reform bill approved by the House of Representatives in
1979. The Anderson/Lucey program assumes enactment of welfare reform
legislation.

Nutrition Programs   The Senate Budget Committee's recommendation
assumes Congressional action to achieve savings in the school lunch and special
milk programs and increased funding for nutrition assistance to women, infant and
children (WIC) in order to maintain existing real dollar funding. The
Anderson/Lucey program accepts this recommendation.

Housing Assistance   The Senate Budget Committee's recommendation
assumes funding at the level of current law, which could accomodate as many as
236,000 additional public housing and Section 8 subsidized private rental housing
units in FY1981. The Anderson/Lucey program accepts this recommendation.

Other Income Security Programs   The Senate Budget Committee
recommends annual funding of $2.0 billion for low-income energy assistance and
full funding of the Refugee Act of 1979. The Anderson/Lucey program supports
this recommendation.

Function 700:   VETERANS BENEFITS AND SERVICES

Outlays
(in billions of dollars)

Senate Budget Committee Recommendation		FY1981	FY1982	FY1983	FY1984	FY1985
Mission 1:	Income Security for Veterans	13.2	14.7	16.4	18.2	20.0
Mission 2:	Veterans Education, Training and Rehabilitation	1.8	1.4	1.6	1.5	1.5
Mission 3:	Hospital and Medical Care	6.7	6.5	6.9	7.1	7.3
Mission 4:	Other Benefits and Services	0.3	0.7	0.8	0.8	0.9
TOTAL—		22.0	23.3	25.6	27.6	29.7

*   *   *   *   *   *   *   *   *   *   *   *   *   *

Anderson/Lucey Recommentation		FY1981	FY1982	FY1983	FY1984	FY1985
Mission 1:	Income Security for Veterans	13.2	14.7	16.4	18.2	20.0
Mission 2:	Veterans Education, Training and Rehabilitation	1.8	2.0	2.0	1.7	1.6
Mission 3:	Hospital and Medical Care	6.7	6.6	7.0	7.1	7.3
Mission 4:	Other Benefits and Services	0.3	0.7	0.8	0.8	0.9
TOTAL—		22.0	24.0	26.1	27.8	29.8

Function 700, Cont'd.

Income Security for Veterans   The Senate Budget Committee recommends a disability compensation cost-of-living increase of 14.3 percent, effective October 1, 1980.   The Anderson/Lucey program accepts this recommendation.

Veterans Education, Training and Rehabilitation   The Senate Budget Committee assumes a new and improved GI bill which would attract more enlistees of higher quality to the armed forces.   The Anderson/Lucey program accepts this recommendation, but also make provisions for increased education and training benefits for Vietnam-era veterans.

Hospital and Medical Care   The Senate Budget Committee's recommendation assumes increased efficiencies in VA hospital and medical costs.   The Anderson/Lucey program accepts these recommendations, but provides additional monies to undertake an expanded outreach program to contact possible victims of Agent Orange poison.

Other Benefits and Services   The Senate Budget Committee's recommendation assumes improvements in the administrative efficiency of non-medical VA operations. The Anderson/Lucey program accepts this recommendation.

41

Function 750:   ADMINISTRATION OF JUSTICE

                                              Outlays
                                        (in billions of dollars)

Senate Budget
Committee Recommendation   FY1981   FY1982   FY1983   FY1984   FY1985

Mission 1: Federal Law Enforcement   2.4   2.5   2.6   2.8   2.9

Mission 2: Criminal Justice   0.5   0.3   0.2   0.2   0.2
            Assistance

Mission 3: Other Justice Programs   1.8   1.8   1.9   2.0   2.1

TOTAL—   4.6   4.6   4.7   5.0   5.2

*   *   *   *   *   *   *   *   *   *   *   *   *   *

Anderson/Lucey
Recommentation   FY1981   FY1982   FY1983   FY1984   FY1985

Mission 1: Federal Law Enforcement   2.4   2.6   2.7   2.8   2.9

Mission 2: Criminal Justice   0.5   0.3   0.2   0.2   0.2
            Assistance

Mission 3: Other Justice Programs   1.8   1.9   1.9   2.1   2.2

TOTAL—   4.6   4.8   4.8   5.1   5.3

EXPLANATION

        Federal Law Enforcement   The Senate Budget Committee recommends
current law funding which allows for annual pay increases. The Anderson/Lucey
programs support an increase in staffing for the Justice Department's criminal
division, with special emphasis on minority recruitment. The Anderson/Lucey
program also endorses "adequate staffing" of the civil rights division and
expansion of the Community Relations Service.

Function 750: Cont'd.

Criminal Justice Assistance   The Senate Budget Committee recommends
a significant reduction in the level of law enforcement assistance grants, but
allows for the continuation of federal research and statistical activities and
the Juvenile Justice Delinquency Prevention Program. The Anderson/Lucey program
accepts this recommendation.

Other Justice Programs   The Senate Budget Committee's recommends
cuts in current law funding that would allow continuation of only limited
construction in the Federal Prison System and no growth over FY1980 funding for
the Legal Services Corporation. The Anderson/Lucey program does not call for
cuts in these areas.

43

Function 800   GENERAL GOVERNMENT

		Outlays (in billions of dollars)				
Senate Budget Committee Recommendation		FY1981	FY1982	FY1983	FY1984	FY1985
Mission 1:	Legislative Functions	1.0	0.9	0.9	0.9	0.9
Mission 2:	Other General Government Functions	3.5	3.8	4.1	4.4	4.6
TOTAL—		4.5	4.8	5.0	5.3	5.6

*   *   *   *   *   *   *   *   *   *   *   *   *   *

Anderson/Lucey Recommentation		FY1981	FY1982	FY1983	FY1984	FY1985
Mission 1:	Legislative Functions	1.0	0.9	0.9	0.9	0.9
Mission 2:	Other General Government Functions	3.5	3.8	4.1	4.4	4.6
TOTAL—		4.5	4.8	5.0	5.3	5.6

EXPLANATION

Legislative Functions The Senate Budget Committee recommends current law funding. The Anderson/Lucey program accepts this recommendation.

Other General Government Functions The Senate Budget Committee recommends current law funding. The Anderson/Lucey program accepts this recommendation.

44

Function 850:   GENERAL PURPOSE
                                 FISCAL ASSISTANCE

Outlays
(in billions of dollars)

Senate Budget Committee Recommendation	FY1981	FY1982	FY1983	FY1984	FY1985
Mission 1: General Revenue Sharing	5.1	4.6	4.6	4.6	4.6
Mission 2: Other General Purpose Fiscal Assistance	1.6	1.8	1.9	2.0	2.2
TOTAL—	6.7	6.4	6.5	6.6	6.8

*   *   *   *   *   *   *   *   *   *   *   *   *   *   *

Anderson/Lucey Recommentation	FY1981	FY1982	FY1983	FY1984	FY1985
Mission 1: General Revenue Sharing	5.1	4.6	4.6	4.6	4.6
Mission 2: Other General Purpose Fiscal Assistance	2.1	2.8	1.9	2.0	2.2
TOTAL—	7.2	7.4	6.5	6.6	6.8

EXPLANATION

General Revenue Sharing The Senate Budget Committee recommends full funding of local revenue sharing. The Anderson/Lucey program accepts this recommendation.

Other General Purpose Fiscal Assistance The Senate Budget Committee does not recommend any countercyclical revenue sharing. The Anderson/Lucey program recommends a two-year countercyclical revenue sharing program.

Function 900:   INTEREST

		Outlays (in billions of dollars)			
Senate Budget Committee Recommendation	FY1981	FY1982	FY1983	FY1984	FY1985
Mission 1: Interest on the Public Debt	82.1	87.9	92.1	96.7	102.2
Mission 2: Other Interest	−12.0	−14.1	−15.7	−16.8	−17.5
TOTAL—	70.1	73.8	76.4	79.9	84.7

*   *   *   *   *   *   *   *   *   *   *   *   *   *

	FY1981	FY1982	FY1983	FY1984	FY1985
Anderson/Lucey Recommentation					
Mission 1: Interest on the Public Debt	82.1	87.9	93.2	98.4	105.2
Mission 2: Other Interest	−12.0	−14.1	−15.7	−16.8	−17.5
TOTAL—	70.1	73.8	77.5	81.6	87.7

EXPLANATION

Interest on the Public Debt The Senate Budget Committee recommendation is consistent with its economic assumptions and fiscal policy recommendation. The Anderson/Lucey program anticipates higher interest payments due to changes in the projected deficit or surplus.

Other Interest The Senate Budget Committee recommendation is consistent with its economic assumptions and Congressional Budget Office assumptions concerning the activities of Federal agencies. The Anderson/Lucey program, for purposes of this analysis, does not anticipate any changes.

Function 950:   UNDISTRIBUTED   46
                              OFFSETTING RECEIPTS

                                              Outlays
                                       (in billions of dollars)

Senate Budget
Committee Recommendation   FY1981   FY1982   FY1983   FY1984   FY1985

Mission 1: Rents and Royalties/OCS -5.2   -6.1   -6.4   -6.4   -6.4

Mission 2: Employer Share,
            Employee Retirement   -6.2   -6.9   -7.4   -8.0   -8.6

Mission 3: Interest/Trust Fund   -13.3   -14.4   -15.9   -17.5   -19.4

TOTAL---   -24.7   -27.4   -29.7   -33.9   -36.5

*   *   *   *   *   *   *   *   *   *   *   *   *   *

Anderson/Lucey
Recommentation   FY1981   FY1982   FY1983   FY1984   FY1985

Mission 1: Rents and Royalties/OCS -5.2   -6.1   -6.4   -6.4   -6.4

Mission 2: Employer Share,
            Employee Retirement   -6.2   -6.9   -7.4   -8.0   -8.6

Mission 3: Interest/Trust Fund   -13.3   -14.4   -15.9   -17.5   -19.4

TOTAL---   -24.7   -27.4   -29.7   -33.9   -36.5

                                    EXPLANATION

        Undistribute Offsetting Receipts   The Anderson/Lucey program, for
purposes of this analysis, makes no changes in The Senate Budget Committee
Recommendation.

47

REVENUES

(current year dollars)
(in billions)

	FY1981	FY1982	FY1983	FY1984	FY1985
Current Law	609.9	712.0	827.7	951.2	1101.8
Anderson/Lucey Recommendation					
Liberalized Depreciation Allowances	−4.3	−13.4	−18.2	−18.9	−19.9
Refundable Investment Tax Credit	−2.1@	−4.1@	−3.9@	+nea	+nea
Youth Payroll Tax Reduction		−*	−*	−0.1	−0.1
Energy Conservation Tax Credits for Industrial Users		−*	−*	−*	−*
Oil Conversion Tax Credits for Industrial Users		−*	−*	−*	−*
Investment Tax Credit, R&D			−1.2@	−3.2@	−3.6@
Targeted Jobs Credit, Extension			−0.3	−0.3	−0.4
Reduced Taxation of American Nationals Living Abroad			−0.2	−0.4	−0.5
Small Business Captial Gains Tax Rollover			−0.4	−0.8	−0.7
Increase in Earned Income Tax Credit			−0.2	−0.5	−0.5
Interest and Dividend Income Exclusion, Expansion			−1.7	−3.9	−5.4

Revenues, Cont'd.

(current year dollars)
(in billions)

	FY1981	FY1982	FY1983	FY1984	FY1985
Individual Retirement Accounts, Expansion			−0.5	−1.1	−1.2
Capital Gains Tax, Liberalization			−1.1	−3.2	−3.6
Subchapter S Elegibility			−*	−*	−*
Enterprise Zones			−0.5@	−1.5@	−1.8@
Neighborhood Improvement Tax Credit			−*	−*	−*
Care of Elderly Tax Credit			−*	−*	−0.1
Estate and Gift Tax Liberalization			−0.2	−0.5	−0.6
Removal of Architectural Barriers for the Handicapped			−*	−*	−0.1
Duty Free Entry Provision			−*	−*	−*
Artist Equity Tax Reform			−*	−*	−*
Corporate Tax Rate Reduction				−1.6	−3.2
Marriage Tax Reduction			−4.0	−9.2	−10.0
Other Personal Income Tax Relief			− 8.0	−30.0	−80.0
Senate Approved Tax Reconciliation/Tariff Changes	+5.2	+2.8	+2.7	+2.8	+3.0
Net Revenue Change	−1.2	−14.8	−38.1	−72.8	−128.9
TOTALS—	608.7	697.2	789.6	878.4	972.9

NOTES:

@	=	preliminary estimate
nea	=	no estimate available
*	=	less than $50 million

APPENDICES

APPENDIX I:
THE ANDERSON SCHEDULE

The Anderson Schedule

Tables 1 through 3 present a synopsis of the events on the campaign schedule for John Anderson from his "Independent Course" announcement of April 24, 1980 through the election on November 4, 1980. We have divided the schedule into six periods by months, with the days in April added to those in May and the days in November added to those of October.

These statistics were compiled from a complete set of the publically released schedules of the National Unity Campaign.

Table 1 presents the number of campaign days that occurred in each of the six periods, together with the actual number of scheduled campaign events which took place during that time period. Tables 1 through 3 present the number of events which took place in each of thirteen categories of events for the respective time period. For purposes of comparison, a statistic is provided which gives the average number of such events per event day for each category in each period. A "campaign day" is a day on which at least one scheduled event occurred. Some of these were partially "down" days with only a single event, but most are full campaign days. The tables also present the percentage of total events represented by each category of events.

The following list defines the categories of events and offers a few observations about the significance of the numbers:

Substantive speeches (Table 1). Substantive speeches are defined as major speeches that introduced new policy proposals or defined new political directions. These also included the announcement and concession speeches. The overwhelming percentage of the speeches dealt with policy areas. A complete listing of the sixty-six substantive speeches appears in Table 4, by date, location, and topic. Table 1 shows that a large proportion of these speeches were delivered after the first of September as a major part of the fall campaign. During September and October Anderson was delivering, on average, nearly two major policy statements every three days. Although this was consistent with his "campaign of ideas" commitment, many critics have suggested that it was a form of overkill that ultimately was not as effective as Reagan's "single speech" approach. Nevertheless, Anderson, between the platform and this large volume of substantive speeches ranging over a wide field of domestic and foreign issues, established a public policy record probably unmatched in modern campaign history. The degree to which this material actually reached the national public through the intermediation of the press, however, is another story.

Short addresses and rally speeches (Table 1). These were less formal speeches which did not contain major new policy pronouncements. A large percentage of them were rallies on college campuses. Others were addresses to smaller gatherings. All, however, were formal presentations to assembled groups. Anderson's own campaign style required that these speeches vary in approach and text. He did not like to give the same speech twice. Many of them, however, were "modular" speeches with interchangeable parts upon which he then built during the address. As with the substantive speeches, the volume increases dramatically after Labor Day.

Briefing sessions (Table 1).   These are described in the Introduction.   For the most part they were not designed to be publicity spectaculars but were actual working sessions.   Most of the briefing sessions were platform-related and took place before the issuance of the platform.   To give a measure of the issue commitment of the campaign, it should be noticed that about 5 percent of the total campaign events consisted of these briefing sessions.   During June and July, however, the percentages rose to 12 percent and 8 percent respectively, a large commitment of scarce campaign time to this purpose.   A list of scheduled briefing sessions, with date and topic, appears in Table 5.

Press conferences (Table 2).   This table lists the *scheduled* press conferences.   The number of these is staggering, compared to number of press conferences held by Reagan and Carter.   Anderson averaged nearly one per day in September and more than one per day in October/November.   The latter statistic reflects the fact that during the last few weeks of the campaign separate press conferences were held for the local and for the national media.

Editorial board meetings (Table 2).   These were exclusively newspaper editorial board meetings as stated on the schedule.

Wire and print interviews (Table 2).   These are *scheduled* interviews with wires service reporters, columnists, and private interviews with representatives of the print media: chiefly major newspapers and newsmagazines. The statistics, however, greatly understate the actual number of such interviews because there were many unschedlued interviews, especially on the plane.

Radio interviews (Table 2).   These are scheduled radio interviews.   The same caveat about numbers applies here although to a somewhat lesser degree than to the print interviews.

Television interviews (Table 2). The chart lists the scheduled TV interviews, both national and local. Again, unscheduled interviews took place on the plane or in hotel rooms and the numbers here understate the actual number of interviews granted. The importance of T.V. in the campaign process is demonstrated by the very large number of T.V. interviews granted. They represent more than 12 percent of the scheduled events in the campaign. They outnumber both the substantive speeches and the rally speeches (although not the two combined). It should be remembered that many of the press conferences and most of the speeches were also taped by television crews.

Visuals (Table 2). These were campaign events staged primarily for television footage, such as market walk-throughs, appearances with fishermen, and appearances in front of the proverbial dying steel mill. As the table shows, the number of these increased dramatically after Labor Day. This may in part have been the result of new scheduling people being brought into the campaign at the end of August.

Fundraisers (Table 3). These included formal scheduled fundraisers and scheduled blocks of candidate time set aside for fundraising telephone appeals. Unless the schedule specifically stated that the event was a fundraiser or a "reception" with no other designation, the event was not counted as a fundraiser. When the candidate was scheduled to meet prominent people but there was no mention of fundraising on the schedule, the event was cataloged as either a meeting with a community leader or as a meeting with a campaign supporter. In some cases, however, the meetings were clearly multipurpose, and thereore the time allotments to fundraisers understates reality. Eleven percent of the campaign

events were in this category.   Candidates of the major
parties, of course, had full federal funding and did not
need to schedule such events.   It will be noticed that the
number of these dropped substantially during the fall
when the campaign began to rely almost exclusively on
direct mail fundraising.

Meetings with supporters (Table 3).   These included individual meetings with supporters, headquarters
openings, volunteer receptions, and similar events.   A
large number of these took place during the "ballot access" phase of the campaign to encourage the formation
of campaign organizations.

Meetings with community leaders (Table 3). These
included meetings with important individuals and community leaders, often from an organized group such as
women, blacks, clergymen, or environmentalists.   Although
many of these meetings were, in effect, briefing sessions
and the distinction between the two was blurred in some
cases, an attempt was made in categorizing to separate
the more politically relevant from the more issues relevant meetings.

Meetings with foreign community leaders (Table
3).   Most of these took place on the overseas trip.   They
included people such as Prime Minister Menachem Begin,
President Anwar Sadat, Chancellor Helmut Schmidt, and
Prime Minister Margaret Thatcher, together with other
members of foreign governments.

These tables show the issue orientation of the campaign.   We do not present estimates of the amount of
time devoted in press conferences and interviews to presenting "ideas."   Nor do we convey the degree to which
the "visuals" were used to make a point about an issue.
Even without these statistics it should be clear from

these tables that the campaign was issue oriented. Valuable campaign time was taken to ensure that the candidate (and staff) were briefed in depth on a wide range of issues, and a considerable amount of time was devoted to presenting issue positions to the voter. The statistics suggest that the "campaign of ideas" designation was not fiction. It is our hope that others with access to the equivalent Reagan and Carter schedules will present comparable data to make valid comparisons possible.

Table 1

Speeches and Briefing Sessions

Date	Days	Events	I		II		III	
April/May	29	138	5	(.17)	21	(.72)	8	(.27)
June	26	159	8	(.30)	14	(.53)	19	(.73)
July	28	128	9	(.32)	4	(.14)	10	(.35)
August	25	124	8	(.32)	8	(.32)	8	(.32)
September	26	137	16	(.61)	16	(.61)	1	(.03)
Oct./Nov.	32	189	20	(.62)	29	(.90)	1	(.03)
TOTALS	166	875	66	(.39)	93	(.56)	47	(.28)
% Total Events				8%		11%		5%

Days = Campaign days, which are defined as days (during the time period) on which at least one campaign event was scheduled.

Events = Scheduled events, as described in the text on the pages immediately above.

I = Substantive speech.

II = Short addresses and Rally speeches

III = Briefing session.

The figures in parenthesis give the average number of such events per campaign day. For example, (.50) means that on average such an event occurred every two campaign days; (.33), every three campaign days; (.10), every ten campaign days, etc. For a full explanation of the categories, please see pages immediately preceding.

Table 2

Scheduled Media Contacts

Date	I		II		III		IV		V		VI	
Ap./May	19	(.65)	7	(.24)	8	(.27)	4	(.13)	7	(.24)	6	(.20)
June	18	(.69)	8	(.30)	4	(.15)	3	(.11)	20	(.77)	7	(.26)
July	19	(.67)	0	(.00)	5	(.17)	1	(.03)	14	(.50)	8	(.28)
August	17	(.68)	3	(.12)	4	(.16)	2	(.08)	18	(.72)	8	(.32)
Septem.	21	(.80)	8	(.30)	12	(.46)	6	(.23)	23	(.88)	13	(.50)
Oct./Nov.	43	(1.34)	6	(.18)	10	(.31)	4	(.12)	35	(1.09)	16	(.50)
TOTALS	137	(.82)	32	(.19)	43	(.25)	20	(.12)	117	(.70)	58	(.34)
% Total events	16%		4%		5%		2%		13%		7%	

I = Press Conferences

II = Editorial Board Meetings

III = Wire services and print media interviews

IV = Radio interviews

V = T.V. interviews (Note this includes 2 foreign T.V. interviews for June and 4 for July.)

VI = visuals.

The figures in parenthesis represent the average number of such events per campaign day. For the total number of campaign days and events, please see Table 1 above. For a full explanation of the categories, please see pages immediately preceding Table 1.

Table 3

Scheduled Fundraisers and Meetings

Date	I		II		III		IV	
Apr./May	24	(.82)	19	(.65)	10	(.34)	0	(.00)
June	25	(.96)	22	(.84)	11	(.42)	0	(.00)
July	15	(.53)	5	(.17)	4	(.14)	34	(1.21)
August	19	(.76)	14	(.56)	14	(.56)	0	(0.00)
September	10	(.38)	7	(.26)	4	(.15)	0	(0.00)
Oct./Nov.	5	(.15)	13	(.40)	7	(.21)	0	(0.00)
TOTALS	98	(.59)	80	(.48)	50	(.30)	34	(0.20)
% Total events	11%		9%		6%		4%	

I = Fundraising events

II = Meetings with supporters

III = Meetings with community leaders

IV = Meetings with foreign community leaders

The figures in parenthesis represent the average number of such events per campaign day. For the total number of campaign days and events, please see Table 1 above. For a full explanation of the categories, please see pages immediately preceding Table 1.

Table 4

Substantive Speeches

Date	Location	Topic
April 24	Washington	Taking an independent course
May 1	Detroit	Economic policy
May 7	New York	Mid East Policy
May 26	Colleyville, TX	Vietnam Veterans
May 30	New York	Arms control
June 2	Washington	Environment
June 6	Baltimore	Women in crisis
June 9	Seattle	Urban policy
June 9	Los Angeles	Middle East
June 18	Cleveland	A new economy
June 23	Washington	Industrial policy
June 24	St. Louis	Neighborhood policy
June 28	Washington	Justice/Hispanic Citizens
July 1	Washington	Formal Announcement
July 1	Miami	Jobs and Justice
July 8	Jerusalem	Policy towards Israel
July 11	Cairo	Policy towards Egypt
July 14	Bonn	America and World Industry
July 17	London	Global Responsibilities
July 23	San Francisco	Western Alliance
July 24	Burbank, CA	Energy
July 25	San Diego	US./Latin American Relations
August 4	New York	Program for Black Americans
August 5	Denver	An Independent Candidacy
August 7	Pittsburgh	Transportation
August 8	Cleveland	Economic justice
August 19	Waltham, MA	Entrepreneurship/Technology
August 19	Boston	Defense: Strategic balance
August 20	Chicago	Defense: Conventional arms
August 21	Des Moines	Farm policy
September 4	Washington	Israeli Security
September 5	Washington	Justice for American Indians
September 6	New York	General Policy Speech
September 11	Redono Beach, CA	Technology Policy
September 12	San Francisco	The Economy/Budget restraint
September 14	San Francisco	Civil Rights
September 15	Portland, OR	Women's rights
September 16	Denver	Resources
September 23	Philadelphia	Interest rates
September 23	Harrisburg	Nuclear energy in crisis
September 24	New York	U.S. - Soviet Relations
September 24	New York	Senior Citizens
September 26	Cleveland	The Carter/Reagan Choice
September 27	Bangor	Environment
September 29	Washington	Freedom for Black Americans
September 29	Washington	Religious toleration

Substantive Speeches (Continued)

Date	Location	Topic
October 1	Denver	Third World Development
October 3	Compton, CA	Minority Business
October 3	Annaheim, CA	The Economy
October 4	San Diego	Savings and interest rates
October 7	Boston	Don't Count Me Out
October 8	New Haven	Morality and the Right Wing
October 8	Columbus	Health Insurance
October 9	New York	The Independent Candidacy
October 14	Chicago	Fiscal Accountability
October 15	Seattle	What a Campaign Means
October 17	Santa Barbara	Crisis in the Persian Gulf
October 17	San Francisco	East Asia Policy
October 18	Minneapolis	Health Care
October 19	Chicago	Anti-Semitism
October 20	Schenectady, NY	Cleaning up politics
October 22	Washington	Political Realism
October 22	Toledo	Education
October 23	Detroit	Industrial Policy
October 23	Buffalo	Commonsense and jobs
November 4	Washington	Concession Speech

Table 5

Scheduled Briefing Sessions*

Date	Location	Topic
May 2	Boston	Health policy
	Boston	Energy policy
	Boston	Defense policy
May 5	Washington	Middle East
May 9	Durham, N.C.	Deregulation
May 14	El Reno, Okla.	Railroads
May 17	Washington	Foreign Policy
May 30	New York	Soviet Union
June 2	Washington	Middle East
	Washington	Security policy
	Washington	Security policy
	Washington	China policy
June 7	Washington	Urban, Transportation
	Washington	Security policy
June 10	San Francisco	Gay Rights
	San Francisco	Environment
	San Francisco	Third World
June 13	Washington	Foreign policy
	Washington	Egypt
	Washington	Israel
June 16	New York	Middle East
	New York	Industrial policy
	New York	Labor policy
June 21	Washington	Naval policy
June 28	Washington	Hispanic Americans
June 30	New York	France
	New York	Germany
July 2	Washington	Intelligence policy
	Washington	International trade
	Washington	France
July 3	Washington	Iran
	Washington	Security policy
July 5	Washington	Britain
July 6	Washington	Germany
July 7	Washington	Mideast, Iran
August 6	Detroit	Auto industry
	Detroit	Auto industry
August 7	Pittsburgh	Steel industry
August 18	Boston	Education
August 20	Des Moines	Farm policy
August 22	San Francisco	Environment
August 26	Washington	Labor
September 12	Washington	Handicapped
October 5	Washington	Iran

*Please note that these do not include staff briefings, of which there were many, on such topics as the economy, civil right, women's rights, etc.

APPENDIX II:
STAFF OF THE RESEARCH DEPARTMENT

Clifford W. Brown, Jr., Director of Research
Robert J. Walker, Chief Domestic Policy Advisor
Alton K. Frye, Director of Policy Planning
William McKenzie, Deputy Director of Research
William Galston, Chief Speechwriter, issue coordinator for Urban Policy
George Lehner, Senior Research Associate and liason to the road.
Mary MacArthur, Director of Political Research
Melissa Norton, Director of State and Local Research
Peter Berry, Director of Opposition Research
Jonathan Knight, Chief Issue Coordinator, Foreign Policy
Richard Thau, speechwriter
Tony Kerpel, speechwriter
Susan Rethy, speechwriter
Charles Bullock, speechwriter
Steven McGonegal, article drafter
Jo Ellen McDonald, issue coordinator, health policy
Katherine Kiggins, issue coordinator, health policy
Catherine East, issue coordinator, womens rights
Alex Levin, issue coordinator, civil rights
Michael Fulda, issue coordinator, science, space, technology
Rosamond Katz, issue coordinator, energy
Brian DeBoinville, issue coordinator, energy*
Michael Hoon, issue coordinator, welfare
Keith Brady, issue coordinator, transportation
Douglas Lister, issue coordinator, selected economic issues
Patricia Loudis, issue coordinator, education
June Blender, issue coordinator, labor
Grace Pierce, issue coordinator, the environment
Sarah Gaston, issue coordinator, agriculture

Nicole Schloss, issue coordinator, international
  economics
Robin Laird, issue coordinator, Western Europe,
  defense
Chris Reich, issue coordinator, Africa, third world
Robert Feron, issue coordinator, Middle East
William Leogrande, issue coordinator, Latin America*
Gareth Porter, issue coordinator, Asia*
Steven Mandell, assistant researcher
Margery Gilbert, logistics

*Part time

INDEX

Small Business Administration, 131, 207, 366
Social Security, 152-56, 357, 371, 449
Social Welfare Reform Amendments of 1979, 149
Solar energy. *See* Energy, solar
Solar system exploration, 431
South Africa, 269-70, 390
South America. *See* Latin America
South Asia, 265-68. *See also* India; Pakistan
Southeast Asia, 260-62
Space program, U.S., 21, 77, 103-5, 359. *See also* Science, Space, Technology, outlays
Space shuttle, 104, 431
Space station, 105
Space telescope, 105
Spain, 244
Special Drawing Rights, 109, 361
Special interests, 17
Speed limit, 60
Spending increases, 34
Spending and taxing limits, 44-45
State Student Incentive Grants, 175
Steel industry, 79-80, 84-85
Stevenson, Adlai III, xxii
"Stop and go" economic policies, 42
Strategic Arms Limitation Talks, (SALT), 23, 313, 321-23, 382, 385
Strategic forces, 314-15, 379
Strategic Petroleum Reserve, 63, 409, 433
Strip mining, 66-67
Students, college, 175
Subchapter S (Tax code), 87, 459
Subsidies, 39
Supplemental Educational Opportunity Grants, 175
Supplemental Security Income Program, 149, 370
Supreme Court, U.S. xviii

Taft, Robert, xvii
Taiwan, 258-59, 388
Targeted Jobs Credit, 458
Tax credits, 21, 60, 66, 206. *See Also* Investment tax credit
Tax laws, 20, 30-31, 41, 60
Taxation, equitable system of, 24
Taxes: alcohol and tobacco, 124; corporate, 87, 359, 459; cuts in, 24, 34, 43-44; deductions for caring for elderly, 158; gasoline, 21, 59, 357; income, 18, 24, 459; inheritance, 158; on nationals living abroad, 359, 458; rate adjustments in, 353-54. *See also* Investment tax credits, Tax credits; Tax laws

Technology Assessment, Office of (OTA), 84
Technology, improvements in, 21, 50. *See also* Science, Space, Technology, outlays for
Third World, 238-39, 309, 319
Three Mile Island, 70-71
Tlatelolco, Treaty of, 305
Topping, John, xxxvi
Tower, John, xv
Toxic substances, 145, 199-201, 368. *See also* Hazardous substances
Toxic Substances Control Act, 199-200
Toxic Waste Superfund, 200-1
Trade, 83, 108-9, 360
Training. *See* Education
Transportation, 22, 66-67, 77, 88-94, 134-38, 359, 366-67; air, outlays for, 440-41; outlays for, 414, 416, 418, 420, 422, 440-41
Transportation, Department of, 186
Trident program, 379
Truman, Harry, xii
Truth-in-lending, 160
Tuition tax credits, 166
Turkey, 246, 430

Udall, Morris, xx
Udall-Anderson Alaska Lands Bill, 189
Undistributed Offsetting Receipts, projections for, 415, 417, 419, 421, 423, 457
Unemployment, 22, 24-25, 33, 349-350, 406; minority, 37; youth, 37. *See also* Employment
Unemployment compensation, 37, 113, 449
U.S.S.R., 237-39, 247-49, 253, 259, 263, 268, 271, 286-87, 385-6
U.S. Commission on Civil Rights, 24
U.S. Steel, xliii
United Nations, 226, 252, 262, 289-91
United Nations Convention on the Elimination of All Forms of Discrimination Against Women, 226
United Nations Resolutions 242 and 338, 252
Universities: relationship to government, 51, 355. *See also* Education, higher
Upward Bound, 175, 445
Urban Development Action Grant (UDAG), 131, 366
Urban parks, 192
Urban Reconstruction Trust Fund (URTF), 22, 123-25, 206, 364, 409, 443
Utility pricing reform, 58

About the Compilers

CLIFFORD W. BROWN, JR., presently Associate Professor of Political Science at Union College in Schenectady, New York, was Research Coordinator and later Research Director of the Anderson for President and the Anderson/Lucey National Unity campaigns. He is the co-editor of and a contributor to *Struggles in the State* and the co-author of *Jaws of Victory* and articles appearing in *Financing the 1972 Election, Polity, Western Political Quarterly,* and the *American Journal of Political Science.*

ROBERT J. WALKER, currently Legislative Director for Representative Morris K. Udall, was Chief Domestic Policy Advisor for the Anderson/Lucey Campaign and also served as Anderson's Legislative Director. He has contributed articles to the *Texas International Law Journal, Cahiers de Droit Européen*, and the *Virginia Journal of International Law.*